THINKING ABOUT THINKING

THINKING ABOUT THINKING

A Fifth Generation Approach to Deliberate Thought

Clark McKowen

Crisp Thinking   Critical Thinking
Whole-Brained Thinking

William Kaufmann, Inc.
Los Altos, California

Library of Congress Cataloging-in-Publication Data

McKowen, Clark.
    Thinking about thinking.

    Includes index.
    1. Thought and thinking—Text-books.   I. Title.
B105.T54M35   1985   153.4   85-23947
ISBN 0-86576-097-7

ISBN 0-86576-097-7

William Kaufmann, Inc.
95 First Street
Los Altos, California 94022

*Thou has made me endless, such is thy
pleasure. This frail vessel thou emptiest again
and again, and fillest it ever with fresh life. . . .*

*Thy infinite gifts come to me only on these
very small hands of mine. Ages pass, and still
thou pourest, and still there is room to fill.*
                    —Rabindranath Tagore, *Gitanjali*

To Ruth

for her support and enthusiasm

CONTENTS

CONTENTS

CHAPTER 3

WAYS OF THINKING   **How Systematic Thinking Is Programmed**   **108**

CHAPTER 4

WAYS OF KNOWING   **How New Definitions and Understanding Affect Knowledge**   **174**

CHAPTER 5

TO THE USERS
OF THIS BOOK

You have a right to read *Thinking about Thinking* as you would any other textbook, but you will be missing a good bet if you do. Pains have been taken to structure the material for a much richer experience. You don't have to follow the suggestions, but you will be delighted with your results if you do.

STYLE AND TONE

The book is easy enough to read. It is written in plain, conversational English. But it is not a simple book. The ideas are not common. *Thinking about Thinking* combines a variety of philosophical and linguistic systems. And these in turn are intertwined with learning theory, biology—well, any number of academic disciplines. The structure and style make these ideas accessible and, if the guidelines are followed, meaningful and practical, too.

One reviewer said that the book is *layered*. The information and ideas can be picked up on a fairly superficial level, but then as you explore an idea and as you progress further into the book, the idea develops in a richer and richer context. Some religions say there are very old souls and very young souls on the planet. Well, maybe. But certainly the depth and extent to which an idea can be examined by an individual will depend on heritage and prior environment more than on raw intelligence—if there is such a thing.

DIALOGUES

The dialogues for the forty-five or so suggested class experiences help to create an environment in which all these different mind-sets can get comfortable with new material at their own rate and still not hold anyone back. It is vital for each participant to wrap his or her own language structure around these commonly shared concepts. In other words, we don't really know how well we grasp an idea until we try articulating our understanding in our own words. The dialogues are a powerful influence on readers' understanding of *Thinking about Thinking*. You can experiment with finding just the right mix of small-group and large-group discussion. Do give it a try the first couple of days at least.

It took me years to pay attention to what students had been writing in their evaluations of my undergraduate course in critical thinking. What came out over and over as the most valuable part of the course was the chance to talk with each other about course ideas. Not my scintillating expositions or brilliant observations, not any particular material. I suppose I just couldn't believe it, but when I deliberately built these dialogues into the structure, the course got more and more exciting. It was absolutely amazing.

FORM AND STRUCTURE

Don't jump to conclusions about the format of the book. It may look a bit gimmicky at first glance. But take a second look. You will find more than enough content to satisfy any introductory course on thinking and an abundance of ideas to think about for the rest of your life. I get fresh insights and clarification every time I go through the course. It is much like listening again to music or rereading an exceptionally well written novel. In fact, the book is constructed on the model of a musical composition with major and minor themes, rising and falling movements, rhythm and melody.

EXPERIMENTS AND ACTIVITIES

True, the book does involve readers in hands-on activities and dialogue *before* follow-up commentary and supporting materials by other writers. It is set up that way because it happens to work. You will see that it does, if you try it. We have to be actively curious about ideas before we read about them. It's a question of motivation. Some theorists call it readiness. Whatever it's called, it works for my students and it works for me. Once we have invested some of our own energy in any idea—no matter how well or poorly we do—we are fascinated with the ensuing conversation. Asking readers to *do* something before they read about it is backwards from conventional textbook formats, but it fits learning theory much better. After a few days the results will be all the proof you will need.

THE TITLES

There are dual titles for the chapters and many of the sections. One title is intended for the left brain and the other for the right. One describes and the other gives the feel. You can figure out which. As you develop your sensitivity to language, fewer and fewer titles will seem merely left brained.

MUTUAL AID

One thing students love about class dialogues is hearing other people's opinions. Right from the beginning they are asked to explore each other's biases and not to try to find fault.

For example, consider the following:

Steve: That's the dumbest idea I ever heard.

Me: Wait a minute, Steve. Jane's not going to want to talk about her idea if you put her on the defensive. How about rephrasing your concerns so that she is going to *want* to tell you all about her idea. Make her feel comfortable.

Steve catches on right away, and everybody gets the message: We are not here to attack each other. Everybody's view is worth considering. Some readers will recognize a little communication theory at work here.

The syllabus for my undergraduate course encourages students to

> participate cheerfully and supportively. You will need an eager mind and a thoughtful heart and a willingness to explore new ideas. Be willing to search the sources of your present ideas and beliefs. Share your views but resist the temptation to defend them. Take notes.

Within the first session the tendency to argue vanishes. The way questions are asked and what is meant by an answer make all the difference in producing this enthusiastic, positive response. Questions are always probes, not of the person but of the idea. Answers are always tentative possibilities. Finding ways to integrate diverse views into one encompassing view is one object of the game. Neil Postman's "Teaching into the Future" explores the art of question asking (see chapter 3). The way a question is phrased sets up the limits of possible answers. Garbage in, garbage out.

THE COMMENTARY

You will find commentary following most of the experiments and activities. I considered putting it somewhere else, maybe in the back of the book or in a booklet. I didn't want it to interfere with readers' opportunities to do their own reflecting first. I know, certainly, that once they catch on, most groups will generate plenty of material, much of it quite sophisticated, often, I am happy to say, sharper than my own ideas.

But those who aren't used to the possibilities may want to sneak a peek once in a while, especially at first. I think they have a right to do this if they need to, until they develop confidence. I know readers don't want these crutches once they are on their own feet. If they do, well, that is one kind of experience. It will be no worse than what one would get in a conventional approach. But after one has done some first-hand investigation, secondary sources do become welcome and do enrich and expand ideas developed in discussion and reflection.

THE LEARNING LOGS

Students don't have to keep learning logs, but my experience is that they will multiply their results significantly if they do. The give-and-take of class dialogues generates plenty of raw material, but it needs to be synthesized regularly and for a sustained duration. Half an hour works for most readers. It takes about that long to let the material organize itself and to give it meaning. Make regular entries for a couple of weeks and see what happens. Developing a habit reinforces the effect. It shouldn't surprise you that readers rank the logs second only to class discussions. Notice that what they value most are the things they themselves do. That fits perfectly with the psychology of growth and development.

NOT A WORKBOOK

Thinking about Thinking is not in any sense a workbook, though it does encourage active participation by readers. The time is long overdue for books purporting to be textbooks to use learning theory principles in their structure. A book about thinking has no alternative.

THE CONTENT

Thinking about Thinking is about thinking in general and not merely about logic. Critical analysis is a major theme throughout, but considerable groundwork is laid before it becomes a dominant motif in chapter 3. By the time readers reach that point they have prepared the ground well for a direct examination of inductive and deductive reasoning.

This book considers thought a natural biological function of human organisms. Whatever specialists do with aspects of thought is an intensification of what all physiologically normal humans can do. Rational thought is the linguistic component of the larger, complex, whole-brained thinking machine, which includes among other things input from our senses, from our genetic code, from our neocortex, and from our mammalian and reptilian brains.

Whole-brained thinking is always fascinating, but there is a practical outcome, too: Possibilities of deliberately applying it in problem-solving situations increase. A book about whole-brained thinking should be so designed that readers have to use that kind of thinking. This is such a book.

If you look, you will find a balanced menu of these thinking modes arranged rhythmically throughout, with an explicit synthesis in chapter 5. So readers have to use their minds in the way we know (so far) works best while they investigate how their minds do work. That sounds a bit like a snake swallowing its own tail, but it works in this book, as you will see.

IN A NUTSHELL

The foregoing boils down to a simple approach to *Thinking about Thinking* that you can use or not use according to your best lights. You can ignore the apparatus, if you wish, and you will still have a textbook unique in its field. You will find stimulating material that isn't available in any other textbook—so far.

If you use the apparatus, it comes down to this:

1. First do some hands-on work with a fundamental concept.
2. Once you get involved, get some raw material worked up in small groups and then as a whole class.
3. Take time to do some individual reflecting and synthesizing in learning logs.
4. Finally, follow up with my commentary and with the supplemental materials I have provided.

You will find this to be an effective and productive approach.

BOOK LEARNING

This book is intended for use in colleges. I hope you will consider it the most valuable book you've ever read. But if you try to get lessons from it, or if you try to learn from it, you will be approaching it in a stupid way. And you will fail. Your mind will reject that approach, as it always does, and everything will seem difficult.

But if you let curiosity and pleasure be your guides, your mind will hang on to all sorts of things you will treasure. What you retain will be what your mind and body need. No two of you will select the same things or process them in the same way. Isn't that marvelous?

That goes for your teacher, too. He or she will have to accept that his or her view is one of many and will have to relish all the diversity, even cherish it. That way, you will have much to say to each other. Your viewpoints will enrich and expand each others' ideas. If you were clones, that would not be true. Many college students seek refuge in pretending they are clones. But no one is.

If you feel a tingling sensation along the back of your neck and if you are eager to get to class each day, as you become involved in thinking about thinking, you will know things are going properly.

Joy is essential to learning. No joy, no learning. So enjoy yourself. That is the only way to grow and change. You have it on the best authority.

Let's get started.

ACKNOWLEDGMENTS

Pages

v   Excerpt from *Gitanjali* by Rabindranath Tagore (New York: Macmillan, 1913. Macmillan, London and Basingstoke).

12–15   "The Corner of the Eye," from *Late Night Thoughts on Listening to Mahler's Ninth Symphony* by Lewis Thomas. Copyright © 1981 by Lewis Thomas. Reprinted by permission of Viking Penguin Inc. and Oxford University Press.

23–25   "We May Be Brothers After All" by Chief Seattle (*Outdoor California*, November–December 1976).

45, 185   "The Pasture" and "For Once, Then, Something," from *The Poetry of Robert Frost* edited by Edward Connery Lathem. Copyright 1923, 1939, © 1967, © 1969 by Holt, Rinehart and Winston. Copyright 1951 by Robert Frost. Reprinted by permission of Holt, Rinehart and Winston, Publishers, the Estate of Robert Frost, and Jonathan Cape Ltd., Publishers.

52   Lines from "Chelsea Morning" by Joni Mitchell. © 1967, 1973 Siquom 6 Publishing Corp. (BMI). Used by permission. All rights reserved.

69–73   "The Three Brains" by Robert Bly from *Seventies #1*, Madison, Minn. Copyright © 1972 by Robert Bly, reprinted with his permission.

81–85, 181–182   Excerpts from *The Mind Parasites* by Colin Wilson. Copyright © 1967 by Colin Wilson. Reprinted by permission of Alev Lytle.

95–97   Excerpt from *The Origin of Consciousness in the Breakdown of the Bicameral Mind* by Julian Jaynes. Copyright © 1976 by Julian Jaynes. Reprinted by permission of Houghton Mifflin Company.

102   Haiku from *An Introduction to Haiku* by Harold G. Henderson, copyright © 1958 by Harold G. Henderson. Reprinted by permission of Harold G. Henderson.

103   "Simply Assisting God," from *Grooks* by Piet Hein.

104   "Your Poem, Man . . ." from *Some Haystacks Don't Even Have Any Needle* by Edward Lueders. Copyright © 1969 by Scott, Foresman and Company. Reprinted by permission.

108   "This Is Just to Say" by William Carlos Williams from *Collected Earlier Poems of William Carlos Williams*. Copyright 1941 by New Directions Publishing Corporation. Reprinted by permission of New Directions Publishing Corporation.

114–117   "Why the Geese Shrieked," from *A Day of Pleasure* by Isaac Bashevis Singer. Copyright © 1963, 1965, 1966, 1969, by Isaac Bashevis Singer. Reprinted by permission of Farrar, Straus and Giroux, Inc.

125   "Assumptions" by Indries Shah from *The Pleasantries of the Incredible Mulla Nasrudin*. By permission of Designs & Communications Ltd.

131–138   Max Shulman, "Love Is a Fallacy," from *The Many Loves of Dobie Gillis*. Copyright 1951, 1979 by Max Shulman. Reprinted by permission of Harold Matson Company, Inc.

156–162   "Teaching into the Future," An address given to the National Council of Teachers of English Convention in San Francisco, November 24, 1981, by Neil Postman.

171   Paul Reps, "Captured Snowflakes, Suffering," from *Zen Telegrams*. Charles E. Tuttle Company, Inc., Tokyo, Japan, 1969. Reprinted by permission of the publisher.

173   "A Reason for Writing" by Theodore Spencer, *The Paradox in the Circle*. Copyright 1941 by New Directions Publishing Corporation. Reprinted by permission of New Directions Publishing Corporation.

174   "Once More, the Round" by Theodore Roethke. Copyright © 1962 by Beatrice Roethke as Administratrix of the estate of Theodore Roethke, from the book The Collected Poems of Theodore Roethke. Reprinted by permission of Doubleday & Company, Inc.

184   "In the Caves of Ice" by Eugene Guillevic, *Selected Poems*. Copyright © 1968, 1969 by Denise Levertov Goodman. Reprinted by permission of New Directions Publishing Corporation.

194–200   Abridgment of "Big Week at Big Sur," from *The Dancing Wu Li Masters* by Gary Zukav. Copyright © 1979 by Gary Zukav. By permission of William Morrow & Company.

203–204   "In the Cathedral," from *The Trial*, by Franz Kafka, translated by Willa and Edwin Muir. Copyright 1937, © 1956 and renewed 1965 by Alfred A. Knopf, Inc. Reprinted by permission the publisher and Shocken Books, Inc. Copyright © 1925, 1935, 1946 by Schocken Books Inc. Copyright renewed 1952, 1963, 1974 by Schocken Books Inc. Permission also granted by Martin Secker & Warburg Limited, 54 Poland Street, London.

210–211   "Liberal-Arts Majors in Business." by Sam Bittner from *The Chronicle of Higher Education* April 14, 1982. Copyright 1982 by *The Chronicle of Higher Education*. Reprinted with Permission.

219–233   "The Pleasure of Finding Things Out" an interview with Richard Feynman on "Nova," broadcast on PBS January 25, 1983.

237–239,   Excerpts from *Never Cry Wolf* and *People of the Deer* by Farley Mowat.
252–255   *Never Cry Wolf* copyright © 1963 by Farley Mowat. By permission of Little, Brown and Company in association with the Atlantic Monthly Press and Farley Mowat Limited. *People of the Deer* copyright 1951, 1952, by Farley Mowat. By permission of Little, Brown and Company, in association with The Atlantic Monthly Press. Permission also granted by Farley Mowat Limited.

243   Drawing and words from *The Tao of Pooh* by Benjamin Hoff, illustrated by Ernest H. Shepard. Copyright © 1982 by Benjamin Hoff. Reprinted by permission of the publishers, E. P. Dutton, a division of New American Library, and Methuen Children's Books. Line illustrations by E. H. Shepard copyright under the Berne Convention, reproduced by permission of Curtis Brown Ltd., London.

244   "I Tell Them I'm a Liberal Arts Major" by Carol Jin Evans, abridged from *The Chronicle of Higher Education*. Reprinted by permission of Carol Jin Evans.

277   "El Viaje Definitivo" by Juan Ramon Jimenez, from Three Hundred
       Poems, 1903–1953 by Juan Ramon Jimenez, translated by Eloise Roach.
       Copyright © Francisco H-Pinzon Jimenez 1962. By permission of the
       University of Texas Press.

inside   Charles Demuth, "I Saw the Figure Five in Gold." Reprinted by permis-
backcover sion of The Metropolitan Museum of Art.
art

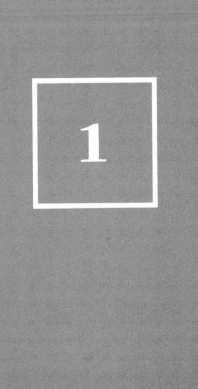

AN OVERVIEW OF THINKING PROCESSES

*One needs a clear sense of
one's self before one can
really understand. Critical
thinking supposes some kind
of background of wisdom.*
—David Scott, Student

CHAPTER ONE

WAYS OF BEING

KITTEN WATCHING

One reason "lessons" are so hard to learn is that they are chewed and digested by someone else and handed over to you like a used wad of gum with all the juice sucked out. Of course you are bored and your mind shuts down. It wants a piece of the action itself. It is an explorer, not a soggy sponge. If you want to learn history or calculus or welding, don't start with book learning. Mess around awhile first until you are suddenly and thoroughly intrigued with the subject. There are no boring subjects, just boring ways of approaching them. (Try not to blow up the chemistry lab. However, the only kid among my classmates in high school who ultimately became a good chemist was the one who did just that.) Once you have become intellectually excited about a subject, then turn if you must to textbook stuff. Only then will it stick. You will learn your "lessons," and they won't even seem difficult.

Watch how your mind functions as you go along reading and thinking in this chapter. Its purpose is to get you to become conscious of everything that is involved when you think. But don't start writing down facts. Instead, run your hands over the facts or ideas until you can feel them on your nerve endings, as if you were a safecracker. Play with them. Fit them together with others. Stand back and observe what your mind chooses to do with them. You will see that the process is a lot like watching a kitten. You will see that you are the most amazing creature in the universe. (So am I, so is an ant.) That may sound grandiose now, but if you don't agree by the end of this chapter, your investment will be cheerfully refunded.

TELLING LIES

KOAN ONE

Whatever you say a thing is, it isn't.

Don't read the commentary about Koan One until you find at least three ways of showing the koan is true. (You don't have to agree.) Talk it over with other students. Don't rush to a conclusion. Pool your ideas. We are not playing the "right" or "wrong" school game here.

Here is what to do: Form groups of four or five; don't make this complicated. Just do it. Allow five to ten minutes this time. (Later you will learn to adjust the duration for this initial session to fit the needs of the investigation.) Jot down as many possible supportive views as you can. It doesn't matter at this point how farfetched they are. In fact it is better to have a few that are off the wall.

You can stay seated where you are, but next confer as a class and share as many ideas from the groups as you can and investigate what lies behind any ideas that aren't clear. This part of your discussion can take ten to forty or fifty minutes, depending on what emerges. Stay with it as long as new insights keep coming.

At some point try for a general overview. But don't beat it to death. You will get a feel for the timing after you have done a few sessions. You will want to be flexible.

Just remember that all your dialogues should be considered open-ended. You will continue to expand the possibilities as you continue your investigation throughout this book.

Finally, as I recommended earlier, spend half an hour on your own writing your reflections on this first session in your learning log.

Then you can read my commentary.

(If you are dying to know what a koan is, you can ask or look it up. Usually some student will know. But the real way to know a koan is to solve one.)

ALL BEGINNINGS ARE DIFFICULT
Small-Group Discussion and Follow-up

My critical thinking classes often start with Koan One on the chalkboard. (Sometimes I will throw in what my wife's brother said to me years ago: "Clark, you just think you're thinking." If you take it seriously, a thing like that can turn you into a philosopher.) When we work in small groups and try for as many as we can, we are doing what Edward DeBono calls lateral thinking—trying to break free of the habit of one-directional, "correct" thinking. Students ask, "Well, which is right?" They all are. Every idea ever uttered is "right" within the context in which it evolved. You will have a lot more pleasure in life trying to achieve the speaker's frame of reference than trying to find fault with it.

Every time we do refute a view the possibilities of our world have been diminished just that much. You can see from this what is meant by a narrow mind and how tiresome it must be to have one. The more intriguing and more stimulating game is to find some way to incorporate all viewpoints into one big, inclusive view. In other words, make everything—*everything*—fit together. That is the game of every thinker. Nothing can be excluded.

You will be surprised at how much raw material a class will generate about this one statement on the first day. And while they are at it, the students are getting used to each other in a mutual-aid atmosphere essential for exploring ideas.

Keep a Learning Log

The next step is to go back to wherever you think best and do some more thinking on your own. What are the implications of the koan on you as a thinking creature? I ask students to keep a learning log, a record of their thoughts as they emerge, coming as close as possible to what actually passes through the mind, including random thoughts. This gives them a chance to reflect on how they actually do think. They have a physical record to examine. Not only are they thinking, but they are watching themselves while they are at it.

That is a good trick, isn't it, to watch yourself while you are thinking, as if there are several selves inside there. In fact, I can think of four selves right off the bat: the one who is physically putting these words on paper, the one who is telling it *what* to write, the one who's watching all this (amused), and the one, now, studying the process itself. And it is all so effortless.

This writing-while-thinking process should take about half an hour. It takes about fifteen minutes to get properly warmed up. I suggest students start as soon after every class session as possible at a regular time and place. Keeping a log is most productive when it has become a habit, like brushing your teeth.

COMMENTARY

Don't read the following paragraphs about Koan One until you have done all you can with other students and on your own.

About Names and Things

"Whatever you say a thing is, it isn't"? Most of my students think that is a crazy idea, but after they discuss it awhile and play with it, they begin to see possibilities. As teachers and some students know, it is the cornerstone of a field of study called semantics. On one level it simply means that a word and what it points to are two quite separate things with no necessary connection whatsoever. But knowing that and having the experience of it are two totally different things. That's why it's important to play with ideas on your own—before you read about them. That is not the way classes and textbooks usually work. And no doubt that is why so many students find school excruciatingly boring.

Let's play with the idea a bit. Bend your ear down to that object you are sitting on and you will not hear "chair." "Chair" is something linguistic, something in people's heads. Whatever it is, what you are sitting on is not "chair." "Then what the hell is it?" Well, see . . . uh . . . that is . . . um. I couldn't *say* anything that would help, could I? People who think that object really is "chair" have a lot in common with Archie Bunker. I will leave it to you to figure out why.

"Chairness" was invented out of thin air by us humans. And it doesn't exist anywhere in nature outside of human minds, furniture stores notwithstanding. This fascinating concept is fundamental to all that goes on in your mind, and hardly anyone ever really considers it. So once you grasp it, you are already miles ahead of just about everyone in the world. It may please you to know that people who are conscious of how words work have an easier time solving all sorts of problems.

Most classes settle for students being able to repeat, "Whatever you say a thing is, it isn't." Students may become champs at separating "symbol" from "referent," and all that. But that is the difference between knowing and knowing about. "Knowing about" is not accompanied by that tingling along your spine. The full feel of the implications of a concept is always

5

your intellectual payoff: the intense awareness of this totally made-up piece of fiction called language through which we create the only world we can know and our only true home. We live a linguistic life. It is indeed wonderful, but do not lose sight of the fact that it is *imagined*, made up, fiction, a big fib, a lie.

Whatever you say a thing is, it isn't. Suppose someone says you are lazy, or you say that about yourself. You are neither lazy nor not lazy. "Lazy" is an idea in people's heads. It doesn't exist in things. But if you act as if "lazy" is actually a physical trait you have, you can't change your behavior. You are trapped by your concept. In fact, you are free to behave any way you want no matter how long you may have been acting some other way. But you can only do it if you don't let the label control you. Treating an object or creature as if your label for it is actually a physical aspect of it is a good working description of a bigot. A bigot thinks things *are* their labels.

Thus, there are no murderers in nature or whores or thieves. There are no good people or bad people either. Knowing this allows us to think of ourselves and others in any way we choose. It is more fun and certainly more productive. A tea kettle is free to be a steam engine. Lightning can become an electric light or take the place of a team of horses. The sun may be a big bias machine.

These are a few of the ideas generated by Koan One. They are not new ideas, but few people are conscious enough of them to be able to use them on purpose. Most have to wait until alternative labels "come" to them. They don't know they can go after them deliberately.

TIME OUT

A Fact Is Not a Fact

Let's take time out here to investigate the importance of facts. I recall feeling uneasy one day in class early one semester when an argument got started on what chalk was composed of. I had thought it was composed of fossils, but there was disagreement about what mineral—or whatever—science says it is made of.

What I didn't like was the slight trace of smugness when someone would "set the record straight." I heard that tone several times in that early discussion. A lot of the responses were the showing-off sort of thing. I didn't like it because I know that if "experts" take over a group they can be destructive.* You are not going to want to think or take risks if there is that censorship hanging over your comments. No wonder shy students sit silently.

But there is a much more important implication. The facts are the least important part of our dialogue. I realize that this statement may set some readers' teeth on edge, especially if those readers think linearly. As you progress through the book, it will become clear why I make such a statement. (*Chalk* wasn't the subject of our discussion anyway. What it is made of had no real bearing on the "truth" of the point being illuminated.) The point is that the kind of thing we were getting at did not require that chalk be classified precisely or that *epistemology* be given a dictionary definition or that the exact number of legs on a spider be stated. If it really were crucial, we could always stop and check.

It is not that we want to be sloppy, but we must keep in mind what the purpose of thinking together is, and *that* is to get a feel for how life is, how it works, really works. And it is quite possible to do that even if half your "facts" are "wrong." You can get insight even with a whole garbage-canful of incorrect information. For that matter, history is a record of just such a situation. It shows that the world in which any genius of the past lived was full of incorrect information. And it didn't matter a bit. People went ahead and gained wisdom nonetheless. We are always having to rewrite the "facts."

***The Fat Lady Hasn't Sung.** You should not take textbook writers as experts either. Any texts, any ideas, including all those in this text, and there are hundreds, must never be taken at face value. They are for you to reflect on and explore and have fun with. But it would defeat the book's purpose if you simply accepted them. Please don't.

This book is the product of over thirty years of teaching and the materials in it are drawn from such fields as linguistics, semantics, rhetoric, learning theory, biology, physics, mathematics, neuroscience, and music. The sum is what seems to me to be the case, based on current evidence, but all knowledge is tentative. Nothing could be worse than to accept the ideas in this book, or *any* ideas, unquestioningly.

Indeed, it is humanity's condition to be ignorant. It is inherent in our situation that we have most of the facts somewhat or totally screwed up. We carry on our thinking in that atmosphere. But it would be ludicrous if all our efforts *therefore* were pointless and absurd. We can do *anything*—even under such adverse conditions. And, really, isn't that the whole point—to be in total chaos, a totally confusing situation, and yet to give it order, one's own order?

So that's it, the old idea decked out anew: Our function is to give the inherent chaos order. That is what *mind* and *meaning* are for. It is quite brazen of us, but heroic and wonderful, too, that we even undertake the task. Maybe it is all to the good that we don't realize too much at first, that we assume everything is sensible and that there are indeed facts on this planet. We use them, and they work. But they are more like magic tokens or talismans than objects or physical entities.

So, Plato, here we are again. Our facts, all facts, are fabrications. Even the roots of the two words attest to this. *Fact,* "something made, created." And therefore its relation to that other word, *fiction,* emerges. For *fic* means "made-up," too. Fact, fiction, fabrication—they are all the same thing. That is our shadow world and the only world we can ever "know." Knowing the facts means knowing shadows, and that is hardly something to be smug about.

LANGUAGING

Koan One has innumerable implications. Many will emerge as you progress through this book. But now it is time for a corollary.

**COROLLARY ONE
FOR KOAN ONE**

Whatever you say a thing is, it is.

There is a point of view from which any idea is "correct." Find some for Corollary One. You don't have to destroy Koan One to do it.

DIALOGUE AND REFLECTION

Don't read the following comments until you and your classmates have done what you can on your own. Do some reflecting in your learning log, too.

COMMENTARY

Don't read this page until you have done all you
can on Corollary One with other students and on
your own.

On Languaging

All ideas have alternative, valid hypotheses. So there are alternative ways
of talking about Koan One, too. And they are also true. One way to think
about "Whatever you say a thing is, it is" is to recall that the world, as far as
you are concerned, is a linguistic world. There may be some world *out
there*, but you look at "it" and think about "it" in language terms. It is language you look at. There may be something out there you throw waste-
paper into, but *it*, as I said earlier, is not "wastebasket." "Wastebasket" is an
idea in human heads.

But, and this is an enormous *but*, you are the godlike creator who
decides artificially inside yourself—not "out there," because that would be
impossible—how everything in your universe is to be labeled.* You and the
people in your language community also decide the relationships among
the labels. Normally, you have no need for all the things that object with
the crumpled paper in it could also be. You all "agree" it is "wastebasket,"
and laugh like crazy if someone wears it on his head. So, for practical purposes, we agree to limit that object to "wastebasketness" and ignore all its
infinite other aspects. In your linguistic world, once you invent "wastebasket," wastebasket has entered into existence. Whatever you say a thing
is, it is. And that just about annihilates, as far as we are concerned, whatever that infinite thing out there might have been for us. We filter out all
other possibilities through the "wastebasket" screen. In fact, we don't
really "see" the thing, we see a wastebasket. Slippery idea, isn't it?

All 450,000 words in your unabridged dictionary are like "wastebasket,"
never mind the interrelations we invented to glue them together. That
indeed leads to wonderland. The world that each of us perceives is made
of thin air, since physically, speech is puffs of air sculpted by lips, teeth,
tongue, larynx, nose, and so forth. Something fantastic is going on here.
We are all wizards of ahs.

Both Koan One and Corollary One are true. It all depends, doesn't it, on
what lies *behind* the words. You don't find out what lies behind a statement
by picking an argument with the speaker. You will find what is meant by a

---

*About "languaging": What else can we call it? Making nets or structures to catch and hold
wriggling ideas seems to be what we are doing. The word *thinking* doesn't take us very far. We
are languaging.

statement by exploring the speaker's idea with him or her. And you are not so inclined to get ulcers or cancer.

> *Our revels now are ended. These our actors,*
> *As I foretold you, were all spirits and*
> *Are melted into air, into thin air.*
> —Shakespeare, *The Tempest*

ON NOT MAKING EYE CONTACT

Following is a chapter from research pathologist Lewis Thomas's Late Night Thoughts on Listening to Mahler's Ninth Symphony. *Thomas has taken up several ideas that are also found in* Thinking about Thinking *and given them his own unique meaning. For example, take the idea that meaning is what lies behind and between words. Thomas takes up the same theme when he notices that some things can be seen only when you don't look directly at them. This is physically true, but it also has a philosophic implication. The same goes for music. "The real meaning," he says, "comes from tones only audible in the corners of your mind." I would go further and say that the real meaning is something that happens in my head and spirit and that Bach is the stimulus that triggers it. Otherwise, everyone would have the "same" experience when listening to Bach.*

Look at what Thomas does with computers, too. He says their major shortcoming is that they cannot be ambiguous. *These know-it-alls always have to be correct. The strength of your mind, by contrast, is its sloppiness, its ability to work with sloppy data. Chapter 3 of this book explores the part of your mind that does use computerlike thinking. It is a valuable part—but only a part—of the whole thinking process.*

Finally, I hope you enjoy reading Thomas's tracing of some fundamental words: earth, human, adam, word, chaos. *Notice how what he does with his material fits the reflective kind of writing recommended for your learning log and how his ideas themselves extend and enrich concepts developed in this chapter.*

Think of Thomas as a new voice in our dialogue on thinking. I suggest that you zip through fast the first time to catch on to his point of view and then go through again taking your own sweet time so that you get the feel of his ideas as well as the "facts." Our purpose of course is to fit Thomas's views into our developing picture of how our minds work.

THE CORNER OF THE EYE
Lewis Thomas

There are some things that human beings can see only out of the corner of the eye. The niftiest examples of this gift, familiar to all children, are small, faint stars. When you look straight at one such star, it vanishes; when you move your eyes to stare into the space nearby, it reappears. If you pick two faint stars, side by side, and focus on one of the pair, it disappears and now you can see the other in the corner of your eye, and you can move your eyes back and forth, turning off the star in the center of your retina and switching the other one on. There is a physiological explanation for the phenomenon: we have more rods, the cells we use for light perception, at the periphery of our retinas, more cones, for perceiving color, at the center.

Something like this happens in music. You cannot really hear certain sequences of notes in a Bach fugue unless at the same time there are other notes being sounded, dominating the field. The real meaning in music comes from tones only audible in the corner of the mind.

I used to worry that computers would become so powerful and sophisticated as to take the place of human minds. The notion of Artificial Intelligence used to scare me half to death. Already, a large enough machine can do all sorts of intelligent things beyond our capacities: calculate in a split second the answers to mathematical problems requiring years for a human brain, dráw accurate pictures from memory, even manufacture successions of sounds with a disarming resemblance to real music. Computers can translate textbooks, write dissertations of their own for doctorates, even speak in machine-tooled, inhuman phonemes any words read off from a printed page. They can communicate with one another, holding consultations and committee meetings of their own in networks around the earth.

Computers can make errors, of course, and do so all the time in small, irritating ways, but the mistakes can be fixed and nearly always are. In this respect they are fundamentally inhuman, and here is the relaxing thought: computers will not take over the world, they cannot replace us, because they are not designed, as we are, for ambiguity. [*Isn't it fascinating that it is only when things have more than one possibility that a productive possibility emerges? Our power lies in our capacity to create relationships that aren't logically possible.*]

Imagine the predicament faced by a computer programmed to make language, not the interesting communication in sounds made by vervets or in symbols by brilliant chimpanzee prodigies, but real human talk. The grammar would not be too difficult, and there would be no problem in constructing a vocabulary of etymons, the original, pure, unambiguous words used to name real things. [*Many linguists argue that words, by their very nature, were as ambiguous from the very beginning as they are today. More on that in chapter 2.*] The impossibility would come in making the necessary mistakes we humans make with words instinctively, intuitively, as we build our kinds of language, changing the meanings to imply quite different things, constructing and elaborating the varieties of ambiguity without which speech can never become human speech.

Look at the record of language if you want to glimpse the special qualities of the human mind that lie beyond the reach of any machine. *Take, for example, the metaphors we use in everyday speech to tell ourselves who we are, where we live, and where we come from.* [*Italics added*]

The earth is a good place to begin. The word "earth" is used to name the ground we walk on, the soil in which we grow plants or dig clams, and the planet itself; we also use it to describe all of humanity ("the whole earth responds to the beauty of a child," we say to each other).

The earliest word for earth in our language was the Indo-European root *dhghem,* and look what we did with it. We turned it, by adding suffixes, into *humus* in Latin; today we call the complex polymers that hold fertile soil together "humic" acids, and somehow or other the same root became "humility." With another suffix the word became "human." Did the earth become human, or did the human emerge from the earth? One answer may lie in that nice cognate word "humble." "Humane" was built on, extending the meaning of both the earth and ourselves. In ancient Hebrew, *adamha* was the word for earth, *adam* for man. What computer could run itself through such manipulations as those?

13

We came at the same system of defining ourselves from the other direction. The word *wiros* was the first root for man; it took us in our vanity on to "virile" and "virtue," but also turned itself into the Germanic word *weraldh,* meaning the life of man, and thence in English to our word "world."

There is a deep hunch in this kind of etymology. The world of man derives from this planet, shares origin with the life of the soil, lives in humility with all the rest of life. I cannot imagine programming a computer to think up an idea like that, not a twentieth-century computer, anyway.

The world began with what it is now the fashion to call the "Big Bang." Characteristically, we have assigned the wrong words for the very beginning of the earth and ourselves, in order to evade another term that would cause this century embarrassment. It could not, of course, have been a bang of any sort, with no atmosphere to conduct the waves of sound, and no ears. It was something else, occurring in the most absolute silence we can imagine. It was the Great Light.

We say it had been chaos before, but it was not the kind of place we use the word "chaos" for today, things tumbling over each other and bumping around. Chaos did not have that meaning in Greek; it simply meant empty.

We took it, in our words, from chaos to cosmos, a word that simply meant order, cosmetic. We perceived the order in surprise, and our cosmologists and physicists continue to find new and astonishing aspects of the order. We made up the word "universe" from the whole affair, meaning literally turning everything into one thing. We used to say it was a miracle, and we still permit ourselves to refer to the whole universe as a marvel, holding in our unconscious minds the original root meaning of these two words, miracle and marvel—from the ancient root word *smei,* signifying a smile. It immensely pleases a human being to see something never seen before, even more to learn something never known before, most of all to think something never thought before. The rings of Saturn are the latest surprise. All my physicist friends are enchanted by this phenomenon, marveling at the small violations of the laws of planetary mechanics, shocked by the unaccountable braids and spokes stuck there among the rings like graffiti. It is nice for physicists to see something new and inexplicable; it means that the laws of nature are once again about to be amended by a new footnote.

The greatest surprise of all lies within our own local, suburban solar system. It is not Mars; Mars was surprising in its way but not flabbergasting; it was a disappointment not to find evidences of life, and there was some sadness in the pictures sent back to earth from the Mars Lander, that lonely long-legged apparatus poking about with its jointed arm, picking up sample after sample of the barren Mars soil, looking for any flicker of life and finding none; the only sign of life on Mars was the Lander itself, an extension of the human mind all the way from earth to Mars, totally alone.

Nor is Saturn the great surprise, nor Jupiter, nor Venus, nor Mercury, nor any of the glimpses of the others.

The overwhelming astonishment, the queerest structure we know about so far in the whole universe, the greatest of all cosmological scientific puzzles, confounding all our efforts to comprehend it, is the earth. We are only now beginning to appreciate how strange and splendid it is, how it catches the breath, the loveliest object afloat around the sun, enclosed in its own blue bubble of atmosphere, manufacturing and breathing its own oxygen, fixing its own nitrogen from the air into its own soil, generating its own weather at the surface of its rain forests, constructing its own carapace from living parts: chalk cliffs, coral reefs, old fossils from earlier forms of life now covered by layers of new life meshed together around the globe, Troy upon Troy.

Seen from the right distance, from the corner of the eye of an extraterrestrial visitor, it must surely seem a single creature, clinging to the round warm stone, turning in the sun.

DIALOGUE AND REFLECTION

To illuminate Lewis Thomas's article, form discussion groups of about four or five people and connect his ideas with ideas developing in *Thinking about Thinking*. Try for several connections in each group.

Pool your discussion group findings in your large group.

Then in your learning log do some more thinking on your own, adding your own connections and reflections, tying all this in with your own experiences. Spend about half an hour on thinking-writing. Don't worry about proofreading this draft. You should generate between two and three pages in half an hour.

MAKING SENSE

> **KOAN TWO**
>
> We think by feeling.

Let's work backwards on this one. Ignore Koan Two as much as you can for now. We will get back to it later. But first try this experiment.

> Take a half-speed walk.

Do everything at half speed for about fifteen minutes and let whatever happens happen. Just register what goes on in you and around you as you go along. Don't sit down; keep on the move. If you must speak, do it at half speed too. You may feel somewhat conspicuous at first, but if you are on campus, people will assume you are doing some experiment for psychology. Besides, college students are supposed to do odd things. How else could they learn anything?

When you get back to class, pool your observations.

COMMENTARY

Don't read this page until you have taken the slow
walk and discussed it with other students.

The Significance of the
Half-Speed Walk

Some of my students get nervous walking around at half speed. It does
take a few minutes to get into the slower rhythm. But after they do, most
report a feeling of serenity and heightened sensitivity. They calm down—
they hadn't realized before how frenetic the usual pace can be—and they
sense things much more intensely. (We will get to what this has to do with
Koan Two soon.) In short, for most people, the slow walk results in an
enriched sensate world. Every perception is heightened—fallen petals,
cracks in the pavement, traffic music, students' voices, the sun on one's
face, the smell of grass. Something else happens, too. That inner tape
recording most of us have running all the time shuts up or at least stops
chattering and lets us listen and see and smell. Students are surprised that
all this was going on all along but they had been too busy to notice. The
world glows in a way many hadn't experienced since childhood. Not only
does the world around them shimmer, but they themselves feel more alive,
more attuned, more at one with their surroundings.

What this means is that most of us live in a world up ahead somewhere,
beyond where our bodies actually are. To walk fast without stumbling, we
have to focus on a point some distance ahead—at the expense of noticing
where we really are. Speeding up means we are never quite "there." To
hurry is to rob ourselves of most of the information available to our senses.

But so what? So I don't feel everything, so I don't see the new buds on the
trees or the lines of worry on a friend's face, or register the classroom
smells of books and chalk. I have more important matters on my mind:
tests, homework, car payments (all *future* events, please note). Where is
the payoff in being here, in this moment, now?

DIALOGUE AND REFLECTION

Now it is time to get back to Koan Two: We think by feeling. As before, discuss the koan with classmates. Find as many ways as you can come up with

to confirm the statement. Find several points of view from which it is true. (You don't have to agree.) Afterward, do some reflecting in your learning log.

COMMENTARY ON KOAN TWO

Don't read the following paragraphs until you have tried Koan Two on your own.

On Thinking by Way of the Senses

We think by feeling. The senses, our sensorium, are information collectors. What would our minds have for raw material without them? Our genetic inheritance, of course, supplies us with a huge, undetermined amount of prepackaged data. We are born with this information, tons of it, and we decide to be human creatures instead of a stalk of corn because of it. But without interacting with our surroundings by means of our senses, we would die. Thus, feelings, feelings of all sorts, are essential to thought. We think by means of our nerve ending data—and not just for survival either. We need affection, feelings of belonging, of touching others, of caressing, too. We do not think well without having these feeling needs gratified, as is clearly shown by experiments with baby monkeys and data from orphanages and clinics dealing with deprived children.

Computers—which are developed on the model of the human mind— are getting smarter. They will do better. But until they develop feelings, emotion, they will remain outclassed. Emotionless intelligence is idiotic. Around most colleges you will find examples of it. But nothing is known, nothing understood, without being registered first on the nerve endings.

To think as we humans do, for the purposes we have, a computer would have to become human itself. We think by feeling. Intellect without feeling is impossible. It would be like a car going down the highway without a driver.

Inevitably, such considerations lead to the question, What is the purpose of life? That is the big koan everyone gets to work on during his or her lifetime. No one knows. But biologically, almost by definition, life involves feeling, *requires* feeling in order to *be* life at all.

The slow walk suggests that each moment is rich with information we can absorb—if we slow down. It would appear that the faster we go, the more we should get. But it is just the opposite. Going fast, we get superficial impressions, and these lead to gross errors in thought. That is to say, we don't really understand things until we feel them, get the feel of them.

18

They don't "make sense." You can see the implications of that expression for thinkers. You will see that even abstract thinkers such as the great quantum physicists must get the "feel" of concepts they are working with; they must get them on their nerve endings. Ideas have to make sense. Even the apparent chaos inside the atom or the behavior of light waves or particles had to "feel" right to their discoverers. We think by feeling.

Nature has designed us humans as it has other mammals—dolphins, whales, chimps, lions, wolves—with an emotive component, that is, feelings. Emotion is the rich, warm sensor that powerfully guides and directs the biological organism. In fact, what we have learned to call thought— which seems to some so mechanical and matter-of-fact—is never objective, and in the biological sense it must not be. For the heart of the mammalian computer is spirit. When the spirit is not engaged, the biological computer stays "down."

Koan Two has infinite implications, as do all ideas. It certainly explains why this section of *Thinking about Thinking* uses koans. "Knowing" is having the experience of the idea. You have to feel it, and you cannot do that with the intellect alone. That is why zen masters developed koans in the first place. There are no multiple-guess tests in the zendo.

Soon you will see these koans begin to interrelate and influence each other. Let them. That is the whole idea. All thoughts must eventually integrate into one encompassing view, your own idea of what being on this planet in this cosmos is all about.

But for now, let's move on to Corollary Two.

FEELING ON PURPOSE

COROLLARY TWO
FOR KOAN TWO

We feel by thinking.

DIALOGUE AND REFLECTION

Try some lateral thinking on this concept with your classmates, and then reflect on your observations and their implications in your learning log.

COMMENTARY ON COROLLARY TWO

Don't read the following paragraphs until you have
worked on the koan on your own and with your
classmates and reflected on it in your learning log.

On Feelings Directed by the Mind

We feel by thinking. Contradictory ideas are not necessarily contradictory. They only seem so when we go too fast. Here is an idea to chew on: We wouldn't have feelings if we didn't intend to. Feelings take place in the mind and are the result of a purposefulness sent out to the nerve endings from the center of your organism. We actually choose to feel (or not to) and then decide what label to affix to that feeling and what it means. You can see that this idea is closely related to Corollary One, Whatever you say a thing is, it is.

Thus, something touches my nerve endings, say, *heat*. But it is not "heat" at the finger tips. The sensation becomes "heat" through a process of sorting and classifying in the mind. It becomes "heat" because we think it so. And so it is with all other nerve ending data. They are raw assaults on the senses until given meaning by the mind. That is how one man's junk can be another man's art or how an olive can be distasteful one day and become a delicacy the next. We interpret what happens on the tongue by way of thought. We feel by thinking.

That accounts for the philosopher's observation that there are those who would never have been in love if they had never heard of love. That is, we would not register what is going on out there at the nerve endings at all if the mind were not prepared to acknowledge it and give it meaning. You cannot give a hotfoot to someone who has no functioning nerve endings in his foot. You might burn his toe, but he will be serenely indifferent. Under hypnosis, you feel or don't feel according to what your mind decides. But hypnosis merely emphasizes the way your mind works all the time. The things you feel are images your mind makes up. No two people have the same reality. "What's going on" is always an interpretation. We filter out more than we let in. Isn't it amazing that we dare to form ideas about the universe based on such flimsy evidence?

Thus, the mind, because it is designed that way by the genetic code, creates whatever feelings it permits us to register. In that sense, feelings ultimately are concepts, ideas, interpretations. And of course concepts ultimately are feelings. These seeming contradictions exist because it is the nature of the mind to separate things that in the physical world are not really separate. Heredity and environment, for example, are part of an integrated whole; they are not really separable. The same is true of feelings and concepts. They are not separate but are part of each other with no actual break or separation. Through language we create an artificial separation that enables us to think about things. But we must not lose sight of the deeper wholeness. The separation is not really there.

It follows that we ourselves deliberately choose our behavior and the labels for the events that touch us. There is no absolute connection between an event and how we feel about it. One useful application of Corollary Two is to realize that we are not stuck with our anger, embarrassment, and fear and that awareness of how feelings are created opens the way for alternative, equally valid responses, a more deliberate interaction with our world.

A slow walk helps. At half speed, because I am not "going somewhere," I have time for you and you and you (trees, people, ideas). I am less judgmental. I have time for the melody.

THE FEEL OF IDEAS

Following is a profound example of the effects of a lifelong slow walk. When President Franklin Pierce in 1854 offered to buy Indian land and provide the Indians a "reservation" in place of it, Chief Seattle wrote the following reply. You will see several connections with ideas developing in Thinking about Thinking.

Seattle's words might make you want to go out and tear down billboards. Most of my students are saddened. The letter makes me feel sorry for our planet. But that is not my purpose in including it. Rather, I would like you to consider his idea that all things really are connected, in fact, are all one thing. If you don't think so, consider your belly button. But also notice that Seattle's feelings are a part of his words. His ideas are feelings. His feelings are ideas. No separation. You can feel the strength that his centeredness gives him.

The first step in highway beautification is to know billboards as well as Seattle knows "the soft sound of the wind darting across the face of a pond." You and the ad agency may be brothers after all.

WE MAY BE BROTHERS AFTER ALL

Chief Seattle

How can you buy or sell the sky, the warmth of the land? The idea is strange to us. If we do not own the freshness of the air and the sparkle of the water, how can you buy them?

Every part of this earth is sacred to my people. Every shining pine needle, every sandy shore, every mist in the dark woods, every clearing and humming insect is holy in the memory and experience of my people. The sap which courses through the trees carries the memories of the red man.

The white man's dead forget the country of their birth when they go to walk among the stars. Our dead never forget this beautiful earth, for it is the mother of the red man. We are part of the earth and it is part of us. The perfumed flowers are our sisters; the deer, the horse, the great eagle, these are our brothers. The rocky crests, the juices in the meadows, the body heat of the pony, and man—all belong to the same family. [*Seattle isn't just using sweet expressions here. He means what he says literally. Biologically, what he says fits Western science accurately.*]

So, when the Great Chief in Washington sends word that he wishes to buy our land, he asks much of us. The great Chief sends word he will reserve us a place so that we can live comfortably to ourselves. He will be our father and we will be his children. So we will consider your offer to buy our land. But it will not be easy. For this land is sacred to us.

The shining water that moves in the streams and rivers is not just water but the blood of our ancestors. If we sell you land, you must remember that it is sacred, and you must teach your children that it is sacred and that each ghostly reflection in the clear water of the lakes tells of events and memories in the life of my people. The water's murmur is the voice of my father's father. [*Instead of speed-reading this paragraph, go back and slow-walk it. Find points of view from which we can make his statements literally true.*]

The rivers are our brothers, they quench our thirst. The rivers carry our canoes, and feed our children. If we sell you our land, you must remember, and teach your children, that the rivers are our brothers, and yours, and you must henceforth give the rivers the kindness you would give my brother.

We know that the white man does not understand our ways. One portion of land is the same to him as the next, for he is a stranger who comes in the night and takes from the land whatever he needs. The earth is not his brother but his enemy, and when he has conquered it, he moves on. He leaves his father's graves behind, and he does not care. His fathers' graves and his children's birthright are forgotten. He treats his mother, the earth, and his brother, the sky, as things to be bought, plundered, sold like sheep or bright beads. His appetite will devour the earth and leave behind only a desert.

I do not know. Our ways are different from your ways. The sight of your cities pains the eyes of the red man. But perhaps it is because the red man is a savage and does not understand.

There is no quiet place in the white man's cities. No place to hear the unfurling of leaves in spring, or the rustle of an insect's wings. But perhaps it is because I am a savage and do not understand. The clatter only seems to insult the ears. And what is there to life if a man cannot hear the lonely cry of the whippoorwill or the arguments of the frogs around a pond at night? I am a red man and do not understand. The Indian prefers the soft sound of the wind darting over the face of a pond, and the smell of the wind itself, cleansed by a mid-day rain, or scented with the piñon pine.

The air is precious to the red man, for all things share the same breath—the beast, the tree, the man, they all share the same breath. The white man does not seem to notice the air he breathes. Like a man dying for many days, he is numb to the stench. But if we sell you our land, you must remember that the air is precious to us, that the air shares its spirit with all the life it supports. The wind that gave our grandfather his first breath also receives his last sigh. And if we sell you our land, you must keep it apart and sacred, as a place where even the white man can go to taste the wind that is sweetened by the meadow's flowers.

So we will consider your offer to buy our land. If we decide to accept, I will make one condition. The white man must treat the beasts of this land as his brothers.

I am a savage and I do not understand any other way. I have seen a thousand rotting buffalos on the prairie, left by the white man who shot them from a passing train. I am a savage and I do not understand how the smoking iron horse can be more important than the buffalo that we kill only to stay alive.

What is man without the beasts? If all the beasts were gone, man would die from a great loneliness of spirit. For whatever happens to the beasts, soon happens to man. All things are connected. [*The connectedness of all things is a dominant theme throughout* Thinking about Thinking.]

You must teach your children that the ground beneath their feet is the ashes of our grandfathers. So that they will respect the land, tell your children that the earth is rich with the lives of our kin. Teach your children what we have taught our children, that the earth is our mother. Whatever befalls the earth befalls the sons of the earth. If men spit upon the ground, they spit upon themselves.

This we know: The earth does not belong to man, man belongs to the earth. This we know. All things are connected, like the blood which unites one family. All things are connected.

Whatever befalls the earth befalls the sons of the earth. Man did not weave the web of life; he is merely a strand in it. Whatever he does to the web, he does to himself.

Even the white man, whose God walks and talks with him as a friend to friend, cannot be exempt from the common destiny. We may be brothers after all. We shall see. One thing we know, which the white man may one day discover: our God is the same God. You may think now that you own Him as you wish to own our land, but you cannot. He is the God of man, and His compassion is equal for the red man and the white. This earth is precious to Him, and to harm the earth is to heap contempt on its Creator. The whites too shall pass; perhaps sooner than all other tribes. Contaminate your bed, and you will one night suffocate in your own waste.

But in your perishing you will shine brightly, fired by the strength of the God who brought you to this land and for some special purpose gave you dominion over this land and over the red man. That destiny is a mystery to us for we do not understand when the buffalo are all slaughtered, the wild horses tamed, the secret corners of the forest heavy with scent of many men, and the view of the ripe hills blotted by talking wires. Where is the thicket? Gone. Where is the eagle? Gone. The end of living and the beginning of survival.

DIALOGUE AND REFLECTION

In your small groups connect Seattle's message with the slow walk, "The Corner of the Eye," and the role of language in our thinking. Any other connections will be fine—the more lateral thinking the better.

In your large group, pool your ideas. Tie them all together.

Later, do your own reflecting in your learning log.

COMMENTARY

Be sure to do your own reflecting before reading
this page.

The Limitations of Feelings

Now let's do some crossover work between the ideas that whatever you say a thing is, it isn't and the idea that we think by feeling. Let's try to integrate, to connect, the uses of the sensorium (our senses) and the creation of "facts" in our computer minds. There can be no doubt that we live in a cloud of ignorance. Our facts are all fabrications, and no two creatures have identical sense impressions. Ignorance, yes, but it is a luminous ignorance. If the electrons in that luminous cloud coalesce, merge, correctly, we get *lightning, enlightenment.* We know that our facts are faulty at best. But if, in William Blake's phrase, our senses are cleansed, as Chief Seattle's certainly were, we get a closer, a richer, mix for the mind to process. A student said that we can't get enough information at half speed. But that isn't true. I can only be where I am, so hurrying doesn't help. The only thing I can do to enhance my life is to look around and relax into the here-and-now and become one with it.

Getting more and more knowledge doesn't help. We need to process the more-than-enough data we already have. I don't need more; I need to use what I already have more sensitively. What I need is a "critical mass," to borrow a term from atomic fission research. If you bring together a certain minimum of stuff, it will take over and complete the process on its own. How much do I need? Enough to spark synthesis, a critical mass. We apparently have all the help we need built right into our genetic code. This idea will be developed several more times in *Thinking about Thinking*.

(We will discuss, for example, the "hundredth monkey" phenomenon. It was found that when monkeys on a Japanese island taught themselves to wash the sand off their sweet potatoes, monkeys hundreds of miles away with no contact began washing their sweet potatoes, too. Subatomic physicists, too, are encountering the same sort of simultaneous change in matter, changes that cannot be explained by conventional mathematics.)

The senses are filters as well as collectors. They filter out more than they let in. That doesn't seem to matter. We are designed to work with limited information. If my biology is not a joke, the situation must be just as it should be.

There is another complication to the problem. Whatever the *senses* say a thing is, it isn't—the same problem again as with any other labeling. Thus, if I ever expect to deduce a world, I will have to do it with hints and traces. No one ever lets this situation stop him or her. Everyone creates a view of the world willy-nilly. The secret is never to *conclude* anything. Whatever my world view is at this moment, it is an approximation. Since everything is changing constantly, the view must constantly grow and change as well.

That should not disturb anyone. For there is a music to all this, a melody. As with trees and rocks, the universe may well be realizing itself (becoming real) through you. It may be the mind-body's main task simply to be, to experience the music intensely. Questing after knowledge may not be nearly as crucial as learning to dance. (Gary Zukav discusses the importance of learning to dance in *The Dancing Wu Li Masters*, which deals with the new science of subatomic physics. An excerpt is included in chapter 4.)

TIME OUT

An Intense Vision of the Facts

If what I see "out there" were really out there, perceptions would be identical for all humans—for that matter, all creatures. But they are not. For example, Brad Lemley describes people whose perceptions are so extreme that there can be little doubt that they experience a different reality.* Michael, a client of neurologist Richard Cytowic, is such a person. Michael sucks a lemon and reports, "There are points like small spears against my hands. It's almost as if I put my hands on a bed of nails." When Michael tastes food, he also feels geometric forms. Roast beef feels like long, marble archways. Spearmint feels like cool, glass columns. This taste-touch crossover has been given the name synesthesia (*syn,* "joining"; *aisthesis,* "sensation"). It is a rare condition in which perceptions commonly confined to one sense overlap with two or more senses.

You can see the advantages of such a sense crossover, say, in cooking. While other cooks must test a recipe by taste alone, Michael can also "add some points to the chicken if it's too round."

Of course, as Lemley observes, we all do mingle the senses all the time, as when we say red is a warm color or green is cool. Someone has a sour disposition or feels blue today. The difference is that synesthetes experience such sense crossovers as real, intense experiences. According to Lemley, Cytowic believes that synesthesia is a vestige of the way early humans viewed the world before the new brain mass overgrew the old mammal brain and "carefully fenced off the senses from each other." (Your three brains are described in chapter 2.)

The rest of us can take a lesson from these sense specialists. When we use metaphors, our thinking will be much more productive if we learn to allow ourselves the time and quietude to get the feel of them. This sense crossover allows us to "understand" more completely.

While synesthetes experience these crossovers spontaneously—B-flat is green, roast beef is an archway—we may learn to develop the knack deliberately and thus share with the synesthetes their different universe, a richer way of feeling. We can learn how to use metaphor to evoke a stronger interaction with our perceived world and thereby gain a more intense vision of the "facts," essential to accurate interpretation of our experience.

Nature has all sorts of surprises for us. Things are not so settled as they appear to be.

Psychology Today, June 1984.

SENSE OUT OF NONSENSE

KOAN THREE

The medium is the message.

Below is a warm-up exercise to get you ready for Koan Three. The koan is a statement by Marshall McLuhan, who annoyed a lot of settled thinkers back in the sixties with the idea that the TV set in the living room is more meaningful than anything that appears on the screen, air is more of a message than anything that breathes it, print is more significant than all the books ever written, and so on.

To catch on to that concept, try this. Make one English sentence using all seventeen words listed below. Work together with two or three other students if you can.

beamish	reppix	ludder	sudally	up
conded	nectles	the	ronky	frangled
had	when	the	and	cerded
her				the

After you have made a sentence, see what you had to know to produce it and pool your findings.

Next, try to make an English sentence out of these words and compare your results with your first attempt.

hat	dove	phor	vorsh	taph
narl	created	div	nin	gical
finally	baker	wrote	curly	nerves
laughed				elib

The second sentence is tougher than the first even though there are more familiar words in this group. You can figure out why. It has something to do with the koan. Now you can work on it. The medium—in this case, the English sentence structure—is the message. The structure is the deep meaning. Find as much support as you can for the koan by considering the implications of the nonsense sentences. You don't have to agree.

DIALOGUE AND REFLECTION

It is always a good idea to work first in small groups and then in your large group. Follow up with your own reflections in your learning log. Let this procedure become a habit.

SOME STUDENT REFLECTIONS

Washing the Dishes
and Exploring the Atom

Below is an excerpt from a student's unpolished reflections after the discussion of Chief Seattle's letter in class and after the slow walk.

I believe we would be different people if we took that slow walk daily, stopped to smell the flowers, watch the sunset, watch the birds. The animals are our teachers. But I believe we can make changes within ourselves right where we are now. It's not necessary to move to the country. Just that slow walk showed me how we can "get away" yet be very close. Besides, many may live in the country and not enjoy the beauty. Their thoughts may be so inward that they cannot see the external beauty.

What to do about it? If each person did what was right for him— took time to enjoy the beauty—the inner peace that would come from that would be spread to others by osmosis.

Chief Seattle's quote, "the end of living and the beginning of survival," is unfortunately just where we are now. There is more for me in life than survival. We all must learn that on our own. We cannot be taught that. Gentle suggestions are useful and do make an impact. The medium is the message. This letter makes me think more; it makes a difference. It was written so poetically but has such a strong message.

Here is an excerpt from another student:

Now, when I'm about to litter, I think about Seattle's letter. How could I have been so ignorant about the world I live in. At least now I can begin and others will follow. . . . You know, when we humans get mad at the world, throw rocks or kick the chair, we are hurting ourselves. Why pick on something that can't defend itself? How about just giving life another thought instead? I don't see how I could get mad at the world's energy.

Everything is one, and the things on earth are components. The universe is an organism, and the planets, stars and comets are the major organs. The life of these organs is the cells that make it up. This table I am writing on is a cell and so am I. We all work together to benefit our environment. Criminals are probably the bacteria and the parasites of the whole system. Everything *is* connected, and life is a continuous chain of events, just like our own bodies, where one thing affects the other.

This is such a tremendous thought. Maybe we could go even deeper and dare to say our universe, our organism, is only a cell of an organ of an even greater organism. That organism would have to be just so vast and so huge and powerful. Just think of all that energy. It is true that we are energy. I mean, chemistry has proven that. People are energy and they radiate energy. People absorb energy and everything has an aura. "Everything is connected" really summed it up.

COMMENTARY

Don't read the following paragraphs until you have done all you can with Koan Three.

On Invisible Structure

One thing that ought to emerge from making nonsense sentences is the realization that you are an expert at English grammar. As a native speaker, you have mastered a tremendously complex structure system for thought. Any foreign student would envy your mastery of English syntax. Never let anyone suggest that you don't know your grammar. You are brilliant at it—and have been since you were five.

The medium-message idea is subtle, though. It is difficult to realize because it has become so much a part of us that we don't even notice it. You have to turn things upside down to see what has been going on out of awareness. Robert Frost said that a sentence is a sound in itself. Even when you can't make out the words, you can tell an English sentence from French or German or Chinese by the rhythm and melody. The music of English is the first thing infants absorb, long before they fit words into the patterns. English is much more a musical structure than a mechanical one.

Indeed, a whole unabridged dictionary full of words remains gibberish until fitted into an English structure, a pattern that isn't really there physically. It is an idea in your mind waiting to be given physical existence through the words you fit together. A dictionary of English tells us little of how English speakers think. The English sentence tells us everything. If you want to know our bedrock view of how the world works, look at the structure of the sentence, not its content.

This structure is nonphysical, and meaning isn't on the lines or even in the words. That is, words don't really mean anything at all until they are put into relationship with other words. You give words their meaning by the way you fit them together with other words, as you did with the nonsense words. They have possibilities, potentials, but that is all.

What happens is that you have a "thought" or some sort of perception, a *conception*, and then you express it by stuffing it into forms you have available. All of that has been worked out a long time ago. For example, here is one tiny thing you had to master before you were five. $D\text{-}O\text{-}L\text{-}L_1$ is the same sort of thing as $D\text{-}O\text{-}L\text{-}L_2$. When Helen Keller's teacher tried to palm off a substitute doll in an attempt to show her grouping, Helen smashed the intruder. There was no connection in her mind. She wasn't buying the con. On the other hand M-U-G and W-A-T-E-R were one event to her, one thing going on, so why confuse her by trying to make two things of *mug* and *water?* You can see the problem this craziness must have presented to Helen or any eighteen-month-old child. It is a subtle thing a child has to grasp very early.

On top of that, even if you do grasp grouping (a doll is a doll is a doll) and separating (mug, water), that doesn't get you very far without the English sentence structure itself. This pattern and all its possible variations have been internalized (it could just as well have been Japanese or Tagalog), and now you can automatically slot your thought into it. Once you have grasped the English way of shaping what you have perceived, does that structure in turn begin to affect what thoughts you will be able to have and how you will think them? Surely it does. You begin selecting out of the infinite continuum that which lends itself to the structures you have available to you. (It is the same with the sun, air, TV. You function within the structures they make available to you.) Of course we *can* introduce "foreign" ideas into our idea bag, but it is difficult, and while English may bend some, it won't exceed certain limits. So back beyond language there is a perceiving-conceiving organism that is much more inclusive than the forms it is stuck with. These structures prune the continuum down to manageable size.

Think of the wonder of it. As little kids, we take into ourselves—and we do this on our own, not at the urging of parents or teachers—a system, a program, like software for a computer. We program ourselves with the English structure system: word order, affixes, plurality, form classes and their rules for interchangeability, agreement, topics, subjects, all that.

For familiar (cliché) events, we can generate spontaneous statements, but for new feelings or those not yet made conscious, those finally asking to be born, we have to sort through the program for analogs (something already recognized that is similar). Until something clicks, the holistic (whole) self is dissatisfied. It seems that all our objective, conscious, codified, and physical messages are the physical substitute for nonphysical *feelings*. We think by feeling. So whatever we see in language structures is about something truly nonphysical. You cannot touch anything stored in linguistic forms. Language, then, is a manifestation of spirit. The job of the nonsense sentences is to help us to realize this deeper mystery. The whole universe is chaos, nonsense—nonsense until we "make sense" of it. Structuring makes sense out of nonsense. When we work with these sentences, that is what we are probing for, the magic. The work of any language is the same, to give spirit a physical form. The deep structure, the medium, is the message.

To experience how hard it is to think outside your conventional structures for thought, find the sum of 8 and 9 in base 12 and then find their product. Your head will hurt.

L'AUTRE MOI

KOAN FOUR

Who are you?

Skip your name, sex, age, occupation, address, and so on. Who are you fundamentally, beyond those surface features? What is your deep structure? Give yourself a look at your unique self. Who is it who is running the show?

To get warmed up for Koan Four, try this class project. It should take less than one session to complete.

Draw a mandala.

Bring colored construction paper and Cray-Pas colors to class and draw a mandala. All you need to know about a mandala for now is that it is a figure with a center and any sort of lines or shapes you wish radiating from it or surrounding it. The outer boundaries of your figure may be of whatever shape pleases you.

While working, avoid noticing, as much as you can, what other students are drawing. As soon as you finish, put your name on the back of the drawing. Those who finish first should begin looping tape on the backs and tastefully mounting the drawings on a convenient wall, as in an art gallery.

When you are all finished, take a look at your selves.

DIALOGUE AND REFLECTION

Pick out one drawing to discuss together. Describe what is there, with as little interpretation as possible. Just observe what colors were used, the kind of configurations, shapes, locations. Let everyone point out one thing about the drawing. Then do some guessing about what the person is like who drew it. Let the artist critique your observations. Do the same thing with a few more drawings.

Explore the implications of the drawings. They are fingerprints.

Reflect in your learning log.

COMMENTARY

Read the following after you have had time to view
and chat about your drawings.

The Many Masks of Mind

When my students display their mandalas all together, the array is gorgeous, like a wonderful flower garden. No two are alike. It is a visible reminder of the uniqueness I like to engage in each student. It is touching to come face to face with a naked self and suddenly to discover the rich mix of human beings who have been sitting so politely in the hard classroom chairs. I never met a self I didn't like. Each has his or her own genetic code to actualize, and each must become more and more himself or herself—and consequently less like anyone else—through growth and change. That is what education is. I mount my mandala along with theirs and use it as a barometer to check up on my own development.

I tell my students, "These drawings are *you,* and what we see in the chairs around the room are your masks. There is a lot more of you visible in the mandalas than in the façade of appearances you have built around your selves." *Personality,* of course, comes from the Latin, *persona,* "mask," which goes back to *per sona,* "through sound"—in other words, through talking, language. *Person* also derives from this root. Who *are* you?

C. G. Jung, a contemporary of Freud and a pioneer investigator into genetic memory and the collective racial unconscious, used mandalas extensively in his work to help his clients see what they were really like and how they were feeling. "Only gradually did I discover what the mandala really is," Jung wrote. "Formation, Transformation, Eternal Mind's eternal recreation."

You can use your mandala to see your self better. We are clever at using language to conceal our selves. But the drawings come more directly from the right brain, the part that usually advises us out of awareness. It is almost impossible to keep the hand from putting on paper what the mind dictates. Your drawing is your outerance, *utterance* as we now spell it. You did it, and whatever is there is you. It is your fingerprint.

My students usually complete the mandala sessions by selecting a few drawings, without knowing who the artists are, and describing what they see. Then they make some guesses about what the self is like who drew them. If you take your time and let the drawing speak, it will tell you everything. To read a mandala, you have to approach it with humility and gentleness. You have to let the mandala tell you things—what it wants to say, not what you feel like imposing on it.

37

Be patient and be willing to stand quietly and just look. Gradually an interpretation should emerge, but of course, it will always be tentative, an educated guess. You can begin by describing precisely what's there, without interpretation. Color choice, light or heavy lines, precision, bold solid colors or light shading, every square inch filled or just a few geometric forms, closed or open figures, arrows or circles, symmetry, balance, clutter, erasures, and so on. After you describe as much as you can, then step back and ask, What is the person like who drew this?

Everyone loves this activity, which is quite uncommon in left-brained academia—especially the person whose drawing is being examined. The most interesting topic in the world is one's own sweet self. The artist then gets to correct any errors. Ultimately the result is that the creator, through the art, sees himself or herself more clearly, and everyone gets to know everyone else much more intimately. We like that. The atmosphere of the classroom is richer and warmer, like basking in the sun on the beach. This exercise more than any other reduces the competitive tone of class dialogues and fosters a genuine interest in the unique views of each participant. The mandalas make it clear that there is no one right answer. There are thirty (four billion) unique views, all valid and essential to the clear thinking of the rest of the group. I don't need to go on. Once you have done this exercise, you can see for yourself the value for the group and for each person. Each view I can incorporate helps enrich and clarify my own view.

That may suggest what this exercise has to do with clear thinking. If I do not really know myself, I just think I'm thinking. That is, there are numerous sides to our selves not directly accessible to our consciousness. We need to realize the full range of resources involved in our decisions and in our problem solving. We have to incorporate the right hemisphere of our brain, which the mandalas make available to our deliberate use, as well as our overvalued left-hemisphere, logical side. In addition, there are depths as well, a genetic memory that contains the biological (and possibly the cultural) history of human creatures. When we think, conscious of it or not, we use the whole package, environment and heredity, sense and mind, genes and abstract structures. We can think blindly or we can learn to think in harmony with the universe in which thought takes place. Taking as many peeks at ourselves as possible, from all angles, increases the potential for satisfying results. We feel much more actively involved, more alive, more joyous.

Is the mandala a valid picture of you? A lot of what you see in your drawing *is* acculturated, comes from the surroundings you happen to find yourself in. We have internalized certain color preferences, certain color-emotion patterns, warm colors, restful colors, and so on. But the *Luscher Color Test* suggests that psychological states have predictable color associations, at least in Western societies. (Your mandala might be a mental weather forecast.) Nonetheless, your drawings over the months and years will have an essential uniqueness that can only come from you—like your handwriting. There seems to be a fundamental self at work on top of which the spiritual weather shifts from day to day. If you listen to your drawing you can discover your emotional state and the effect it is having on your thinking.

In my own mandalas, for example, I have observed a gradual change, perhaps because the drawings helped me recognize certain needs and drives. My drawings do have different surface features now. But the deep structure, the self that wants to be actualized, remains constant. The drawings used to be busier, but there was always an attempt at symmetry, even an urgency for balance. But to compensate, I deliberately made the figure a bit asymmetrical. I continue to prefer bright solid colors. I have picked up a few techniques to make the figure more crisp. I never like vague, spiderwebby drawings without clear order. I don't like chaos. What artist would? Clearly, as my spiritual weather shifts, the exterior features alter to reflect it.

The nonconscious aspect of ourselves, the bulk of the iceberg, remains fundamental and strong. The drawings make that obvious. We need access to what is going on inside. All thought is holistic, and most of it is under the surface. We need to realize that. The thinker who has achieved some mental-physical integration is healthier. Most textbooks on critical thinking separate clear thinking from style or from creative thinking and ignore the unconscious or dismiss it as unfathomable. But these things are all interconnected. When we look at one or the other, we are looking at aspects of the same thing, one thing going on all at once.

Conscious thought is not independent of what else is going on. We think well only if the whole mental process is involved. Some of the neat systematic approaches look ludicrous to semanticists or linguists.

*Critical thinking is not
just coming up with contrary
ideas or finding fault. Critical
thinking is placing in perspective
an idea and shaping it to fit in
with what else we know.*
—David Scott, Student

39

VALID INFERENCE
Dotting i's and Crossing t's

KOAN FIVE

Proof is linguistic.

Once you have thought up the most wonderful idea in the world, how do you prove that it is right or *valid,* even to yourself? Logicians have some standard methods for validating conclusions. See if you and your classmates do, too.

    A. If all con artists are amiable
       and all realtors are amiable,
       does that mean that all realtors are con artists?

When you are satisfied with your answer, jot down the steps you took and the tests you used to reach certainty. Are there differences in your lists, or do you all use the same criteria?

Next work on question B but also keep one eye on your mind as it works its way through the question. See what is involved. After you have discussed B, do the same with C.

    B. If some lenders are compassionate
       and all compassionate people are easy touches,
       does that mean that some easy touches are lenders?

    C. If all deliberately cruel people are unforgivable
       and some selfish people are not unforgivable,
       is there anything wrong with concluding, therefore,
       that some selfish people are deliberately cruel?

Now you can work on the koan. If you are like my students, by now you have pushed the word *proof* around a bit and no doubt the words *true* and *truth* also. You probably questioned most of the statements in these thinly disguised syllogisms*, too—what they *assume*, what their *assumptions* are.

So now find some ways to show that proof *is* linguistic.

DIALOGUE AND REFLECTION

As usual, I suggest that you discuss the koan in class and follow up with your own reflections in your learning log. If you have made this routine a habit, it is probably already feeling comfortable and pleasant.

COMMENTARY

Read the following only after you have done all
you can on Koan Five on your own.

On the Nature of Proof

Left-brain thinking is examined in chapter 3. For now, let's simply open the subject. First, it may well be that we only *think* proof comes from our conscious mind. As you figure out what the issues are in syllogism A, you feel your certainty coming on, confusion or fuzziness clearing up, before you actually formulate the words. You sense you are "right" before you verbalize it. We use logic not to figure things out but to nail them down. More accurately, there is a dynamic mix between the metaphoric, holistic material from your right hemisphere and the sequential, systematic material developed on the left side. (That is, assuming your wiring is typical. More on right-brain/left-brain thinking in chapter 2.)

Most thinkers agree that the intellect, the logical mind, *must* be the servant to the whole mind and never the master. It is too limited, too ignorant, ever to be placed in charge. "Our view is limited, being objective," says a private detective in a Fellini film.

You no doubt noticed that your analysis of the syllogisms hinged on linguistic terms (words) and that consensus could only be reached when you

---

**Syl·lo·gism*, from Latin *syl* (*syn*), "together," and *logismos*, "to reason." *Logos* means both "word" and "logic" or "reasoning." A syllogism consists of a pair of statements and the logical conclusion it is possible or not possible to draw from them. Syllogisms are explored in more detail in chapter 3.

agreed on what you meant by those terms. Words like *all, every, only, never, not, any* are crucial. So are words like *some* and *sometimes.*

Did you also notice words like *are* and *is,* the linking words that make things equal to each other? We are back to *is*ness again. One thing is the *same as* something else, a physical impossibility. That is the metaphoric process, and it is pure fiction. Good heavens! Can that mean that *logic* rests on *metaphor,* which is right-brained, poetic, and holistic? You already know that things are or are not what you say they are, depending entirely on the angle from which you wish to view them.

So it emerges, then, that the rules of proof have to be agreed upon by the participants, as in any well-constructed game. Tennis isn't much fun with the net down. Most of us pick up the rules of logic informally as participants in the culture that couches its views in English language structures. Linking verbs like *is* and *are* are common to a whole family of Western languages, but languages like Chinese, Hopi, and Futuna structure thought differently and find our logic faulty.

Your skill at working your way through problems like the three provided here is a matter of practice. By the time you got to the third one you were probably already speeding up. If you did one or two such analyses every day, in a month or so you would develop a system to streamline your results. In fact you could reduce the process to something akin to algebra and wouldn't even have to get emotionally involved. You could do it mechanically. You will have to decide whether the investment would be worth it to you.

One practical use occurs in taking multiple-guess and true-false tests. Often you can figure out what answer is wanted even without having studied the material. The more practice you have, the higher your score.

How well you do with these logic exercises is not a matter of how well you think but what you prefer to think about. Your mandala can help you realize which way your preferences tend. If you prefer a more spontaneous, right-brained approach to "truth," you can be grateful that others don't. Computer software would be a shambles without programmers who love sequential, deliberative reasoning, who can recognize ambiguous statements and those that don't fit the patterns of thought being developed. Real estate contracts hinge on this kind of thinking, and so do small-claims court judgments.

Logic can be used to test ideas you already have and to organize them. When I deduce or induce something, I have to check it out. Seeing that it "computes" is a critical part of the process. Logic, "the theory of valid inference," is a set of rules invented to do that.

There is a parallel to all this for right-brained thinking. The mind produces a metaphor*—strictly right brained. How do I validate a metaphor? There is a never-ending process I go through. First of all, the metaphor is "correct." That is, my self has made its statement, an accurate reflection of my inner view. I validate it by getting the feel of it through the use of my conscious thinking process. I work it into language forms until it clicks and I say, "I see." The right brain gives me an accurate statement, but I don't know what this "dream" (metaphor) means until I cast about for the language to match, left-brained language. "It's like . . . it's like . . . ," and then, click, "*That's* it. I see."

So I have these two ways of knowing, metaphoric and linguistic, and they have to match up before the whole process may be considered complete.

We do have to keep in mind that the "facts" we use in this process are always faulty and incomplete and tentative, regardless of whether they are right or left brained. No matter, by the process of validation, I make clear. I work back and forth between the two sides, using the one to validate the other. The mind no doubt is biologically structured for order. If I behave myself, I will do all the things I should be doing.

So I have ways of making clear what my conscious mind has seen and what my metaphoric side has seen. They are two different processes, but they do overlap and in essence boil down to the same process. Thus, if you work very carefully through a syllogism, you will get an insight or a click at some point, an orgasmic, poetic feel.

Likewise, if you fiddle around with a full-blown metaphor, at some point you will get a click or orgasmic feeling, and you will say, "I see."

The task is to get these two processes working back and forth flexibly and fluently.

---

*You will know all you need to know about metaphor by the end of chapter 2.

A SYNTHESIS

Now What?

If you have tried the koans, kept a learning log, and read my follow-up comments, take time out now to pull your thoughts together. Reread the chapter quickly and reread your learning log. Then reflect on the whole experience in your log.

You can use reflective writing to discover or bring to the surface what you know and feel. Trying to fit the bits and pieces together will put you in charge of your own learning. No one can synthesize this material for you. Others can do it for themselves but not for you, no matter how good they are. Your own mind and spirit are the only ones who can. If things have gone well, no two students will come up with the same views. You will select different aspects to emphasize and will organize them in your own special way. Your results should provide stimulating subject matter when you get back to class.

Two hours or so for this entire effort should give enough time to get a good grip on the experience you have been through and to give it your tentative meaning. I consider chapter 1 an advance organizer, as reading specialists might describe it, for the rest of the book. It is intended to contain a minimum number of aspects of thinking to suggest the complex whole.

If you would like to emerge with a polished essay, your log can serve as your prewriting material. Your tone and style are probably just what they should be just as they are. Be careful not to edit out your best qualities. In case you hadn't noticed, your writing, as well as your drawing, is a mandala of your self. It is important. Keep it.

But you may want to do some cutting and pasting, clear up anything that might be confusing to someone else, cut out any clutter that makes your ideas fuzzy, and make sure the spelling and punctuation are all right.

From log to final version will take a minimum of three drafts. For many writers eight or more minor to major rewrites are typical. It depends on how important the final product is and how much you care about being clear.

THE PASTURE

I'm going out to clean the pasture spring;
I'll only stop to rake the leaves away
(And wait to watch the water clear, I may):
I sha'n't be gone long. —You come, too.

I'm going out to fetch the little calf
That's standing by the mother. It's so young
It totters when she licks it with her tongue.
I sha'n't be gone long. —You come, too.

—Robert Frost

2

HOW MEANING IS CREATED

He who bends to himself a joy
Doth the winged life destroy.
But he who kisses the joy as it flies
Lives in eternity's sunrise.
                    —William Blake

CHAPTER TWO

WAYS OF MEANING

FALLING PETALS

The mind refuses to think about topics assigned to it. But you can't stop it from exploring ideas it has gotten involved in and is curious about. Hence, the koans in chapter 1. All the lovely abstract ideas about beauty and truth, predestination, logical proof, form and function, fallacious argument remain dull, dull, dull until the thinker somehow or other is inflamed with curiosity. Koans are sometimes the match, sometimes the fuel.

As Gary Zukav explains in *The Dancing Wu Li Masters,* the Master will not discuss the theory of gravity until the student stands in wonder at a petal falling. He will not discuss laws of gravity until the student exclaims that a light stone and a heavy one, dropped simultaneously, strike the earth at the same moment. If the student says, "There must be some way to say this more simply," then the Master can speak of mathematics.

Only when one's own mind is engaged is there any value in abstract discussions. At that point the discussion will no longer seem dull; nor will it any longer seem "abstract," even when poorly written. When we pan for gold, we have to sort through lots of sand and gravel.

A koan is an instrument for thought. Ultimately, it is not a thing at all; it is an attitude, a *manner* of thinking. Once you get the knack, anything can serve the purpose: the way rods and cones in the retinas of our eyes are arranged, the mushroom gardens African termites cultivate, the fact that large blocks of concrete develop cracks. The atom, as you will see later in this book, is jam-packed with koans.

If you approach the articles, poems, stories in *Thinking about Thinking* as if they were koans, they will work that way for you. For thinkers, anything will serve.

It is hopeless to try to memorize facts. They won't stick. When you study history or algebra you will get much further *playing with* than *working at.* "Life is too important to be taken seriously," said Oscar Wilde. Once you understand, or *grok,* as Robert Heinlein termed it in *Stranger in a Strange Land,* memory is biological and automatic.

A key is to turn whatever you want to think about into koans. The rest follows. Please consider all the topics in this chapter koans.

A koan a day keeps senility away.
—Doug Gerber, Student

FROM COCKSURE IGNORANCE TO THOUGHTFUL UNCERTAINTY

What is the meaning of meaning?

"Silly question. Meaning is . . . what do you mean, what does it mean? It's obvious . . . isn't it?"

You have noticed, I'm sure, how it puts people in a snit when you say it's obvious and they don't think so. Even worse is "Any fool can see . . ." If everything were obvious, there would be no dialogue. The piece of the pie that is obvious to you is not obvious to me. *Obvious* is another name for cocksure ignorance. "Education," said Henry David Thoreau, "is the journey, *not the destination,* of going from cocksure ignorance to thoughtful uncertainty." *Certainty* is another name for bigotry.

To get your exploration of meaning going, consider the following:

Do things mean? Is meaning some sort of physical stuff out there, immutable and solid as rock?

If not, *is meaning manufactured, created?* If so, by whom? Is there *the* meaning of a painting or *a* meaning, or are there innumerable meanings? *Once meaning exists, is it permanent?*

What is the purpose of meaning? Is it essential? Could we get along without it?

Where is meaning located? Does it exist wherever there is intelligence? (What is intelligence?) Do all intelligent organisms generate it? Is there a cloud of collective intelligence uniting the entire community of intelligences? Whatever the answer(s), isn't this a wonderful subject to contemplate?

If you have meaning, *where do you store it?* Is there a physical aspect? A nonphysical one?

What is the meaning of meaning? Imagine not having any at all. What would that be like? What do we do with it?

DIALOGUE AND REFLECTION

Use any of these questions that interest you to get your dialogue started. Explore *meaning* in small groups and pool your findings. Later reflect on your observations in your learning log. To be a clear thinker, must you have thought about what meaning is?

Wasting Time

And he went back to meet the fox.

"Goodbye," he said.

"Goodbye," said the fox. "And now here is my secret, a very simple secret: *It is only with the heart that one can see rightly;* what is essential is invisible to the eye."

"What is essential is invisible to the eye," the little prince repeated, so that he would be sure to remember.

"It is the time you have wasted for your rose, that makes your rose so important."

"It is the time I have wasted for my rose—" said the little prince, so that he would be sure to remember.

—Antoine de Saint Exupéry, The Little Prince

COMMENTARY

Read the following observations only after you
have explored the meaning of meaning as much as
possible on your own.

Making a Scheme of Things

Things don't have meaning. They are given meaning and given it by
thinkers. Even one-celled creatures *give* meaning to stimuli and move
closer or farther away accordingly. Some people think that we humans are
exactly the same as those creatures but simply process more data, and that
process boils down to a binary computer program, on-off, yes-no, start-
stop, farther-closer. As you know, a binary system can generate millions of
possibilities in short order. Out of these: meaning. We are meaning
makers, meaning-generating organisms.

Each moment along the continuum spawns new data, which don't just
pile up but get processed and digested so that the meaning one sees now is
not the same as the meaning one saw yesterday. The new stimuli are like
dye dropped into water and stirred: It is not like adding more and more
pigeonhole data. (Pigeonhole thinkers end up fact heads.) Every part of the
meaning balloon is affected and changed. Because of the process by which
data are assimilated, meaning grows and changes all the time. But cocksure ignorance tries to prevent the process, indeed, tries to remain ignorant. (*Ignorant*, "to ignore," "not pay attention to," "discount as irrelevant.")
When we try to use yesterday's meaning in a world in which everything
has altered overnight, we stumble and bump into things. When our right
brain knows one thing and our left thinks something else, we are schizoid
(*schizo*, "split," "divided"). We are all schizoid to some extent.* In fact our
task on the planet may be to pull ourselves together, to bring into harmony
what we know out-of-awareness and what we think we know. We can nur-
ture this process, go along with it, or fight it. Semanticist Neil Postman's
idea of good schooling is "the nurturing of student intelligence." That
sounds healthful, doesn't it?

To put it another way, the mind is a connecting organ and the structure
it makes is meaning. If we ignore anything the mind needs, we will get
meaning that doesn't fit very well, sleeves too long, collar too tight. We all
know (how we know is a good question) when something doesn't fit. One
of my selves must be a tailor.

---

*I am not using *schizoid* in the technical sense here. *Schizophrenia*, as used in the narrow
technical sense, refers to a specific kind of illness that seems to be caused by chemical
imbalance in nerve cells.

Each of us makes his or her own meaning. And we now know that we do it intentionally, on purpose. As Leslie Hart puts it, "The human brain is intensely *aggressive.* Each brain is highly individual, unique; it seeks out, demands, and will accept only what it *needs* to make sense of surrounding reality, as it perceives that reality."* Think what this means to teaching methods commonly practiced. Thirty people do not learn one thing. They learn thirty different things.

Each of us makes his or her own meaning, but together we form a group meaning, too. Even when we squabble, we Americans share a world more like each other's than like that of any other society. Even if you have just stormed out of your father's house, you share more meaning with your family than with anyone else—as you will gradually come to realize. If you hurry, you can make it back home for Thanksgiving.

Physically, meaning is *electrochemical.* Sense data and linguistic data are translated instantly into electrical impulses, which produce a chemical change in the data-bank brain; in other words, they become *encoded.* The whole meaning package is like a laser hologram. As input continues, the hologram, or scheme of things, constantly alters, like the weather. "There's a sun show every second" (Joni Mitchell). This process will go on whether we like it or not. But we are more adroit and resilient when we go along with the process.

Meaning, then, is dynamic, not static. Think what that does to the durability of "facts" and "truth."

Now let's take a look at what researchers are discovering about how the brain is put together to accommodate the process of making meaning.

How the Brain Works (New York: Basic Books, 1975).

WHO'S MINDING THE STORE?

Please don't read the next section describing your brain as though it were a school assignment. There is a practical, useful purpose for having an overview of brain structure, but don't try to memorize all the names of the parts and their definitions. Those parts that will be important to you will become absorbed by your mind as you go along. I would not like you to be tested on anything technical in this section. Don't sweat over it. Later on, if you need to refresh your understanding, you can come back to that part and review it. It will still be here waiting for you. As you read, discuss, and reflect, you will pick up what you need. Learning is normal. It is what you do all day long. So trust your biology. Don't turn something you are good at into drudgery.

Thinking about Thinking is about being able to think on purpose—when you want to. The structure of your brain and what each part does are a key to that deliberate control. You already are in control, but you may not realize how much. You get angry on purpose; in fact, you choose all your feelings, including shame, joy, and depression. You damp down your sense blanket when you decide to fall asleep, but you always know you are asleep. That's why you don't wet the bed. Who puts dreams into your head? You do. You deliberately create everything that pops into your skull, even if you aren't consciously aware that you do. You give yourself measles. You deliberately patch up scratches good as new. You shoot adrenaline through your system when you need to be supra-human. You choose shock when the going is too tough.

In short, things don't happen to you; you happen to things. You create the world; you create your self. Once you know that, you can begin doing it consciously, not fighting your nature but joining in with it. To do this you need to know what your nature is. Your many selves would like a captain. Your new brain, which you will be reading about, provides you that opportunity. That is why a short section on your brain is included in this book, as an introduction to your wetware.

A Reading Experiment

If you would like to see how easily your mind can read and absorb without the pain dutiful students typically suffer, here is a foolproof method you can use on any reading assignment.

1. Quickly browse through the whole assignment a couple of times, just to get an idea of what is involved and what the writer wants to tell you. Play around with the parts.
2. Read any part that catches your eye, as deeply or lightly as suits your own curiosity. Don't mark anything or try to learn any new words.
3. Step back and see what you still have to do to get a complete enough understanding *for your purposes*. Then fiddle around again until the whole section comes clear.
4. Go back and highlight or underline key ideas. If you get more than five main ideas, you are marking too much. In this section on the brain there are only three main topics, and each is divided into two or three subtopics.
5. Jot down from memory what you now understand, twenty-five to fifty words or so. Abbreviate. Write fast. If anything is still fuzzy, go back over that part.

That is all there is to it. Try it. You will see that you have absorbed more understanding and more vocabulary than you would have had you just started at word one and sweated and struggled through sentence by sentence. Once you make a habit of this kind of approach, you can cut your study time by two-thirds. That is a guarantee.

The BFAR Reading Method

■ Browse.   Do this as if you were browsing through a magazine or newspaper. (If the reading seems too tough, come back several different times but only a few minutes each time. Your right brain will work on it for you in the meantime, and it will begin to clear up.)

■ Focus.   Once you see what the writer wants you to understand, try for a general overview without worrying about details.

■ Absorb.   And *then* mark. The fewer things you mark the easier it will be to review later.

■ Reinforce.   Write out from memory what you have just learned. Go back and clear up anything that is still fuzzy.

Try the BFAR method on the section on the brain. You will see how effective it is.

THE GEOGRAPHY OF CONSCIOUSNESS

The two halves of your brain handle stimuli quite differently. This chapter is about right-brain thinking. You can guess what chapter 3 is about.

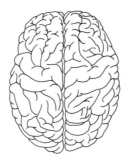

The Infinity Within

Three pints of greyish-yellow organic matter, weighing about three pounds. Viewed from above, it resembles a cauliflower split down the middle. That's *your* brain, the one you are using at this moment to read this sentence, the one right there behind your eyes cheerfully processing billions of bits of data just to read this sentence. Does it hurt your head? Does it take effort? When you realize how much has to go on just to twitch your little finger, how could you ever seriously consider yourself stupid? As you read this, you are using your brain to think about your brain. Or we could say you are using your consciousness to think about the laws of consciousness. (That is the phrase novelist Colin Wilson uses to describe *phenomenology*, the study of how things appear or look, "the geography of consciousness.")

The brain you are thinking with right now is made up of between 100 billion and 1 trillion cells (one for each dollar in the national debt—at this writing). Over 15 billion of these, called *neurons*, do the work. The rest provide support for these little thinking cells. These service workers, called *glia*, handle the biochemical tasks and provide support and nourishment for the neurons, who send chemical messengers, called *neurotransmitters*, back and forth across narrow chasms, called *synapses*. (*Neuro*, "nerve," "sinew," or "fiber"; *glia*, "glue"; *synapse*, from *aspis*, "to join," and *syn*, "together.") *ha ha !*

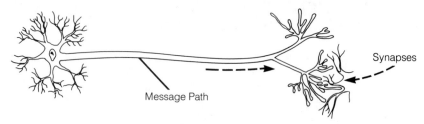

Model of a Neuron (Nerve Cell)

The chemical messages are being processed by the billions all the time, flowing from and to the sense organs, muscles, and other organs and nerves throughout your body. "Why, who makes much of a miracle?" wrote Walt Whitman. "As for myself, I know of nothing but miracles." Please take time right now and get the feel of your brain miracle. Once you have accessed the wonder of it and of you, read on.

> This space and time provided for reflecting on the amazing process of scratching an itch.

YOUR THREE-COMPUTER HOOKUP

> ### Your brain is a koan.

We will get back to the right brain and how it and the left hemisphere take tests for you and help you decide who you are in love with. But there is much more going on than takes place in the brain we can see from above. You have two more brains tucked away in there underneath and nestled inside that divided cauliflower.

Viewed from the side, the three brains look like a toadstool or a fat question mark.

Each of your three brains is a unique computer with its own kind of program. They "think" differently and carry out significantly different tasks. Nevertheless, they are linked together and affect each other profoundly. At this moment, you are processing information in three distinct ways simultaneously.

Depending on your purpose, when you want to reflect on your three brains, you can choose from several models or concepts. And you can do it in Latin or English. (If you want to make a career of neuroscience, you will have to get used to the Latin. But if you look at the roots, you will see a number of associations with common words, and that will make it easy to get used to them.)

Form: The Physical Structure

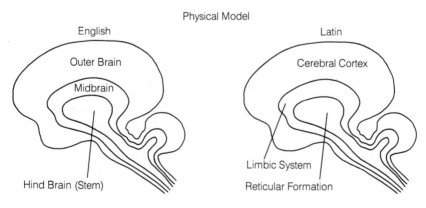

Physical Model

English / Latin

Outer Brain — Cerebral Cortex

Midbrain

Hind Brain (Stem) — Limbic System / Reticular Formation

57

In the physical model identifying the location and appearance of the three brains, they are labeled the *reticular formation*, the *limbic system*, and the *cerebral cortex*. English translation:

1. *Reticular*, "netlike." Thus, an intricate network of nerves the size of your little finger at the top of your spinal cord, also called the *brain stem* or *hind brain*, all synonyms.
2. *Limbic*, "border." (Limbo is the region between two worlds.) Thus, the brain structure surrounding the brain stem like a cap, the *midbrain*.
3. *Cerebral cortex*, from *cerebrum*, "brain," and *cortex*, "bark" or "skin." Thus, outer layer.

Got that?

Function: What Each Brain Does

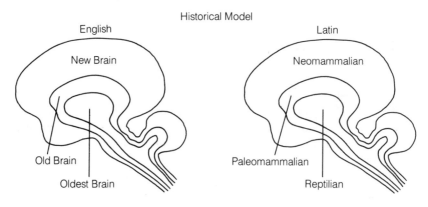

Historical Model

Now consider the historical model developed by neuroscientist Paul MacLean (Director of the Laboratory of Brain Evolution and Behavior of the National Institute of Mental Health). MacLean's is an attractive theory because it enables us to get a handle on how thought, or meaning, gets created. It gives us a chance to influence our own thought deliberately.

The midbrain functions much like the brains of "lower" mammals. The hind brain or stem works like those of cold-blooded reptiles. And the outer brain is the preserve of *primates* like apes, chimps, and humans, with a few extra features in the human.

"In the evolutionary sense," says MacLean, these three formations "are eons apart."

Our Reptile Brain

If you observe the behavior of lizards, snakes, and crocodiles, you will see how your reptilian hind brain operates: In matters of self-preservation and survival of the species, we react much like them. This area may also be the storehouse for tribal lore, archetypal images that come to us in dreams, ancestral memory. We still carry with us the brain structure of our forgotten ancestors.

In our rituals, class systems, and awe of authority, as well as in many of our unexplainable compulsive neuroses, MacLean thinks our behavior is like the *unlearned, preprogrammed behavior* of reptiles. When the brain stem is stimulated or damaged, our behavior changes fit those we find in reptiles. This brain still uses ancient forms of mentation (thinking) and has its own kind of intelligence, its own sense of time and space, its own memory, and so on.

Our Old Mammal Brain

Experiments in which the midbrain is stimulated or blocked lend further support to MacLean's theory. Our midbrain resembles the completely developed brain of mammals other than primates. The earlier mammal types appeared on the planet after the reptiles and before us human types. So MacLean calls the middle brain paleomammalian, the old mammal brain. (*Paleo,* "ancient," "old," "archaic.") Mammals, of course, are all of us warm-blooded creatures who nourish our young with milk. (*Mammalia,* "breast.")

Our old mammal brain, the lower fifth of our brain mass, is the area where we generate *feelings and emotions.* As Richard Restak* puts it, the midbrain is the "center for the four F's—feeding, fighting, fleeing, and sexual behavior." The reptilian brain functions compulsively almost as a reflex does, but the old mammal brain appears to process data according to the emotional content it associates with the stimulus. Its computer program is *feeling directed.* If a ninety-eight-pound woman sees her child pinned under a car, she might lift it off with her bare hands, something she could never do if she took time to consider. She moves directly from feeling to action. The midbrain doesn't have to mull things over. On the other hand, since there would be nothing in the scene to activate its circuits, the reptilian brain would watch the life being crushed out of the child without blinking an eye.

The Brain, The Last Frontier (New York: Doubleday, 1979), 66. A discussion of the historical model can be found more fully developed in chapters 3 and 4 of Dr. Restak's book.

In addition, the old mammal brain seems to be the center of our sense of self. We run our experience through our feelings to see if it's "really" happening, if it "makes sense," if it feels correct. ("Sense of self" is not the same as *awareness of self* or *consciousness of self*. Sense of self is a unified feeling, a centeredness. All mammals seem to have it. Consciousness of self seems limited to animals with the "new" brain.) The midbrain could also be the center in which the eye of wisdom, the "third eye" of Eastern philosophy, is situated. (Of course, like any other computer, this one can screw up, too. It can be damaged or get too much or too little of certain chemicals and show you a "real" world that is totally internal.)

Our New Brain

State of the Art. You can see where this discussion is leading. With only our reptilian and old mammal brains we would be in perfect harmony with our environment. We would be locked into an automatic response to stimuli, and it would not occur to us that there might be other ways of behaving—all those wonderful and horrible dilemmas we humans enjoy.

Instead, all of a sudden, this 5-billion-year-old planet spawned the new brain, which constitutes four-fifths of our entire brain mass, the surface of which is so extensive it has to be wadded up to fit into a decent-sized skull. Our new brain is barely dry behind the ears. It has been here perhaps 2 million years. That is one twenty-five-hundredth ($1/2500$) of the earth's lifetime. No wonder we are still trying to figure out what to do with it and even *how* to use it. It is as if Apple came up with a fabulous new computer and didn't send the instruction manual. If the brain stem is radar and the old mammal brain is black and white TV, to use Restak's image, the new brain goes far beyond color TV. It is laser holography and a whole lot more.

It has only been in the last thirty years or so that a biologically based theory of how we think has been put forth. Even now our geniuses have no choice but to use the new brain intuitively. They really don't know *how* they are able to produce the "Ode to Joy" or E = mc². Nevertheless, some of what has been discovered is already opening possibilities for deliberate thought. In this case a little bit can make a tremendous difference. Our new brain has a new way of "computing" information. We want to explore this new way of thinking in chapters 2 and 3. Coupled with the reptilian and mammalian computers already in place, the new brain gives living matter a whole new ball game.

(I hope you are finding this as fascinating as I think it is. If not, go back and give each paragraph a chance to sink in. Play with the concept long enough to get the feel of it. For example, it takes some doing to get the feel

60

of a million years and then five thousand times that. Unless you do, though, there is not much point in looking at such figures—or in studying anything for that matter.)

We do know now that the two clearly divided halves of the brain you can see from above do "compute" in very different ways. But they pass the results back and forth to each other over a bridge of 20 million nerve fibers called the *corpus callosum*. In English that would be "thick (or callused) body," a network of fibers uniting the two hemispheres.

Each hemisphere is wired to nerves on the opposite side of the body. If you have damage in your right hemisphere, the left side of your body is affected and vice versa. (In some instances the other hemisphere can learn to take over, as when a right-handed person learns to write with the left hand. The right brain develops circuitry to carry on this function and so on. Also, both sides do possess some of the characteristics of the other. Both sides, for example, do have their own hookup to the midbrain, which you will recall is the seat of your feelings. Without feelings, we can't even get the new brain to fire up. "My heart's gone out of it," we say. "The fun's gone out of it.")

As for processing information, most of us are wired so that "conscious" thinking is done by the left brain. Out-of-conscious-awareness thinking is done by the right brain. But do keep in mind that genuinely left-handed people are wired just the opposite. This chapter describes typical wiring. The whole package, right and left, is the realm of knowledge, ideas, concepts. The middle and hind brains simply have no place to carry on this sort of symbol creating and manipulating. It is a matter of design. But the two sides "know" in different ways. They have two distinct ways of obtaining data, organizing, understanding (giving meaning), and expressing results. Together they give us a unified concept or idea of the world, a perfect yin yang of consciousness.

The Order-Seeking Left Hemisphere. The *left hemisphere* uses language. One part of the left brain (called Broca's area after the French surgeon who discovered it) converts thoughts into structures of sequential sounds—in other words, speech patterns. Another area of the left hemisphere, discovered by German neuroscientist Paul Wernicke, gives these word patterns their meaning. Damage in Broca's area still allows one to produce conscious meaning, although with painful slowness. Damage in Wernicke's area lets one string together faultless but meaningless sentences. When we use the left-brain linguistic circuits, we have a certain amount of conscious awareness of ourselves in action. We can see ourselves working our way through a math problem or reasoning our way through an argument. This is the "logical" side of our new brain.

If you want to know what kind of thinking occurs in your left hemisphere, review your work on nonsense sentences in chapter 1.

In short, your left brain is *linguistic* (from *lingua*, "tongue," "speech") and *logical* (from *logos*, "word"). The left brain is *systematic*, conscious of *time* and *sequence*, not much good at space. One thing leads to another. It *analyzes* step by step, part by part. It draws conclusions based on "facts." It *describes*, *defines*, counts up. The left brain is *linear.*

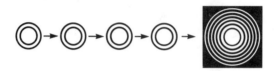

Left-Brain Thinking

(Formal logic, the science of "correct" reasoning or the theory of valid inference, is strictly linguistic and left brained. It proceeds by building mutually exclusive statements one by one until an airtight conclusion can be stated.)

The Structure-Seeking Right Hemisphere. The left brain takes things one at a time. The right brain takes them in as a bunch. The left brain analyzes, the right *synthesizes*. That is, it sees overall patterns and thus appears to solve problems all at once. (if not all at once, certainly with lightning speed), making leaps of insight, the "aha" feeling you are familiar with. It can do perfectly well with sloppy, incomplete, or even "wrong" data, and works happily with *hunches* and *feelings*.

Your right brain also uses words but in a much different way than the left, and words are only part of its raw material. It has almost no use for sentence structure or sequential thought. It is not "reasonable" at all. That is, it operates *holistically* (as a whole, all at once), metaphorically, and analogically. (Metaphor is next on our agenda. Analogy is the process of taking a new image and scanning the data bank for a similar pattern, even though "logically" the two might come from quite separate realms of experience.)

The right hemisphere is *visual* and *spatial*. It has no *sense of time or tense*. Everything is *now*. It is nonjudgmental and amoral, doesn't give a damn about what "should be," has no sense of decency. It is play oriented rather than game oriented and has no use for external rules of order. Sound like you?

Thus, perceiving a figure at the end of the block as "Jim" is right brained, the result of an all-at-once synthetic process of *pattern recognition*. You don't have to go through billions of bits of visual information to arrive at your conclusion. "Jimness" is taken in as a cluster. (In fact, it may well be that all your thoughts have to be of this sort sooner or later.) You "recognize" (*re-cognize*, "to know again") the pattern instantly and pass the information to your language center over in your left brain for translation into language and cognitive meaning. But you already knew all of this metaphorically. One picture isn't worth a thousand words. It's worth a billion words.

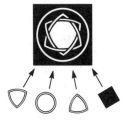

Right-Brain Thinking

CREAM-OF-WHEAT PERCEPTION

Try this.

Richard M. Jones, in his *Fantasy and Feeling in Education* (NYU Press: New York, 1968), asks this question: If a student's answer to the question "What is infinity?" is that infinity is like the box cover of Cream of Wheat, is that a right- or a left-brained answer? Figure out whether the student answered "correctly."

When the student was asked about his answer, he explained that the man on the box of Cream of Wheat is holding a box with a picture of the same man holding the same box with a picture of the same man holding the same box and so on. "You can't see them all just like you can't see infinity. You just know they're all there, going on and on forever."

Cream-of-Wheat perception is virtually ignored in American schools, even though it is a much surer indicator of concept mastery than is a parroted dictionary definition. The obsession with ordered, step-by-step, linear thinking shuts off direct access to the incredible power of our right brains. This brain comes out to play only in a supportive, warm, and loving environment. Judgment, threat, and pressure send it scurrying for cover. It always plays hooky on test days.

But our two brains need to be on friendly terms. If either is subordinated, our thinking is incomplete, and we feel fragmented. The trick is to see that each side is encouraged to do what it does best.

THINKING ON PURPOSE

The preceding ideas on your three brains are information, raw data, but they are not meaningful (not full of meaning), at least not as far as you are concerned. I give these ideas meaning, my meaning, but how do I get my meaning over the net to you? The answer is that I can't. No one can. But *you* can. You can work up this information and give it your own meaning. But if you try to force the data into your memory banks, you will fail.

That is why it is necessary periodically to take time out to talk about and play with the implication of what you have been reading and then to reflect on it. If you do, you will go through a process of seeking parallels between the new ideas and areas of meaning already stored in your data banks. You must fool around until each idea "computes" or somehow fits. You will always be able to do this. There is always some area of experience, however far afield, that will match up. "It's like, it's like"—click!

Once you get your analogy, or comparison (an image), you can complete the process of making it conscious by fitting into language structures (nets for holding meaning, sentences) what you have already discovered all of a sudden, in a burst of insight. If you don't get busy and wrap some language around your insight, it will slip through your mental fingers like a dream, and it won't "make sense."

I can offer you this guarantee: There is no such thing as an idea so alien to your experience that you cannot find an analogy to make sense of it. You can, if you wish, understand anything, *anything*. Surely one idea you will have grokked (using Robert Heinlein's term for complete understanding) by now is that you have an extraordinary, miraculous capacity to perceive and process patterns and make them mean.

DIALOGUE AND REFLECTION

Now would be a good time to give significance to your *triune* (three-part) brain. After all, so what if you do have a brain that functions with icy detachment, another full of fury and affection, and another spinning out abstract worlds of its own devising? Do you think any better knowing that? And what can you do with such knowledge? Work with three or four other students and explore implications and possibilities and what they may add up to. Pool your results and later reflect on your own in your learning log.

COMMENTARY

Read this after you have pooled your observations
with other students and after you have done your
own reflecting in your learning log.

Brothers, Maybe

The triune brain—what am I going to do with it? Maybe nothing. Maybe being awake to my own amazing selfness is plenty. Who can say that simply bearing witness to the phenomenon of this bright light of intelligence that has found its way into living matter and is now looking all around at itself in wonder is not enough? What's the use of a mud pie; what's the use of hopscotch? Quantum physicist and Nobel Prize winner Richard Feynman says the reason he explores the rich broth of stuff inside the atom is for the fun of it, "the pleasure of finding things out." That, no doubt, is why he is so good at his work: He is having such a good time.

Sniffing through intellectual garbage dumps does have its uses. A good day of piling things together, rearranging them, seeing if you can build some sort of palace, sends you home with an appetite. You sleep well, and you feel great. The next day you feel better and work better still. It builds. When you behave like that, you know more about your business than anyone else. So you usually do get the prizes—though you are so absorbed in your play you hardly notice.

That is a roundabout way of saying that thinking about thinking is its own reward but that if anyone really cares, pleasure is good insurance for top scores on tests. In fact, the less pleasure you experience, the less likely you will be to grasp the concepts.

The triune brain really is a new wrinkle. "All things are connected," said Chief Seattle. And the image of the triune brain with its reptile-mammal-supra intelligence provides the appropriate symbol. Thinkers use the neo-cortex as evidence of the separation of human beings from everything else, but they have it backwards. The triune brain demonstrates, instead, the connectedness of living things. Through the brain stem and the flow-ering of the limbic system and the neocortex emerges the unity of all life. "The perfumed flowers are our sisters. The deer, the horse, the great eagle, these are our brothers." The new brain enables life to witness itself and, through mentation, is the means by which all things are reunited into one whole. Seattle knew that. It is as if life has been steadily working toward consciousness of itself. The neocortex gives the reptile and the mammal their eyes.

The triune brain is a model of how this is possible. We sometimes must downshift to reptilian directness to preserve our lives; most of the time we function under the power of our mammalian feelings; but occasionally we transcend both and live momentarily in the airy brilliance of the new brain—and take everything else with us when we do.

But, and this is the point, the new brain is meaningless and useless without the full incorporation (from *corpus*, "body") of the rest of itself. In fact, without the stimulus of mammalian intention and reptilian wakefulness and the drive of the reptile brain to keep on living no matter what, it would sit there idle. When we see how much our behavior is like that of other creatures, it is easy to join Seattle in the brotherhood of all things, including rocks and trees, all interconnected and interdependent, all one.

Human, *from the Latin* humus, *"earth"*

INTERLUDE

A student's response to the question, "What would you do if you knew you had only a couple of hours to live?"

In a white, bare hospital room:

"But, Mr. Maher, I realize this is difficult for you—but I said you're dying. You don't have a very good chance to make it through tonight. Who can I call for you?"

Wow. Dying. What do I feel now? I wasn't even fully aware that I was alive yet. Did I live? I mean really live? It seemed like real living was always in the next room or the next state or the next day or something. What happened?

Hey! I can demand anything I want now, not unreasonable stuff, but all the reasonable stuff I was always so meekly willing to go without for someone else's wants. Get my father and brother in here, and my ex-wife— I want to ask them some things I was always too polite to ask before.

What about the muscles and bones and stuff? What about this brain? All the things I prepared for? College and stuff? I'm not nearly in shape yet. I could have developed a lot more speed and strength. What about all that I've learned? I haven't had time to teach anyone yet. I gotta have more time to teach!

What about glorious, beautiful lovemaking? Sweet, warm communion on the grass in the sun—time to love. I need time to love.

My daughter—doesn't she need a father who will hear her laugh and check her homework? Pony rides.

Who can you call for *me*, doctor? What me? There is no me, doctor. Call them, but call them for *them*. I am no one except what I *do*, and I will never again *do* anything except lie in this bed and watch that clock on the wall laugh at me. There is so much to *do*, doctor, and one trivial little ingredient is about to call off the whole show. Some little bit of tissue in my gut that won't do this or that or whatever. Who gave that bit of tissue all this authority? My joy, my love, my growth, my career, my capacity to live. LIVE! Passionately, exuberantly, free, joyfully, intensely, loud, rich, high, peak, alive, now! Who gave all this away so capriciously, so wantonly, to a tiny bit of meat in my gut? Where is it now? Ethereally it vanishes; a mighty beacon like the sun, it burned ferociously, as though fire and heat were eternal. And now you say it's vanishing, all an illusion? How could I have wanted to live so large and lie here dying so small? Why this joker card? *You're* all not dying!

Tomorrow morning you will all wake up and maybe remember me who died so angrily—and slip right back into your narcosis of illusion of safe, secure, eternal, invincible, mediocre reality. You fools! Get out of here! Get out of here! Go out and DO! Get out on the grass, in the sun, in the water, in your homes, and in the streets, shout it, for crissake! This is your LIFE! Every one of us is dying. It's going, rolling off the counter one day at a time! Get out and LIVE IT. I hate you for your blind stupidity.

I hate every second of my life that I ever gave away to someone because I was afraid that if I didn't, they wouldn't like me. . . .

—*Bill Maher, Student*

ON READING
WITH YOUR THIRD EYE

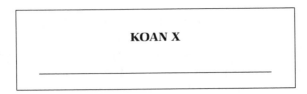

KOAN X

By now you will have been thinking about your triune brain and its implications and will have reflected on it in your learning log. If you wrote
down your thoughts as you went along with minimal editing, you would
have written three or so pages in half an hour. We need to do this. We need
to use ideas actively in order to work them into our own scheme of things.
That means we have to use our third eye.

The little prince knew that he needed all three of his brains to see
rightly. Onitsura in seventeenth-century Japan put the same idea into a
haiku poem:

> *To know plum blossoms,*
> *one's own nose*
> *and heart*

We need both.

Your next koan, Koan X, is the article on the three brains that follows.
The introduction contains suggestions for your nose and heart. Decide for
yourself what should be written in the blank space under Koan X above.

WHAT IT IS LIKE TO LIVE IN THE THREE BRAINS

The poet Robert Bly read about the work of Paul MacLean on the three brains and did some reflecting on his own, just as you have been encouraged to do in Thinking about Thinking. *If Bly had been in your class, his learning log might have contained an unpolished version of the article that follows.* Even though the biology of the brain has been known for some time, it was really just a pile of bricks until people like MacLean took thought and made some kind of house (structure) out of them. MacLean gave the data meaning.*

Then Bly looked at MacLean's theory and took off on his own, as I would like you to do, too, throughout this book. Bly more than likely said to himself, "Let's see what I can do with these ideas." What do theories on armament, politics, religion, and philosophy look like in terms of the reptile, mammal, and new brains? Here is what Bly came up with. As I always recommended in Thinking about Thinking, *let yourself find a point of view from which Bly's theory is "right." Then, if you have concerns, express them to your discussion group and find some way to settle them. You will get much more pleasure from your reading using this approach than in immediately seeking flaws. Ask yourself how Bly would like you to read him, and then read him that way. Try the same approach with your loved ones.*

THE THREE BRAINS

Robert Bly

MacLean's map of the head isn't psychological, as Freud's Ego, Id, and Superego, but geographical—the three brains are actually in the head, and brain surgeons have known for a long time what they look like. MacLean's contribution has been to suggest that each of these brains is to some extent independent. During evolution, the body often reshaped the body—fins, for example, in us, turned utterly into arms, but the forward momentum in evolution was apparently so great that the brain could not allow itself the time to reform—it simply added.

The reptile brain is still intact in the head. . . . The job of the reptile brain appears to be the physical survival of the organism in which it finds itself. Should danger or enemies come near, an alarm system comes into play, and the reptile brain takes over from the other brains—it takes what we might call "executive power." In great danger it might hold that power exclusively. It's been noticed, for example, that when mountain climbers are in danger of falling, the brain mood changes—the eyesight intensifies, and the feet "miraculously" take the right steps. Once down the climber realizes he has been "blanked out." This probably means that the reptile brain's need for energy was so great that it withdrew energy even from the memory systems of the mammal and new brains. The presence of fear produces a higher energy input to the reptile brain. The increasing fear in this century means

---

*I find numerous koans buried in Bly's article. Find at least one intriguing idea for you. See how many your whole group finds. Then see how many koans you can solve together.

that more and more energy, as a result, is going to the reptile brain: that is the same thing as saying that the military budgets in all nations are increasing.

MacLean himself speculated, in a paper written recently for a philosophical conference, that the persistent trait of paranoia in human beings is due to the inability to shut off the energy source to the reptile brain. In a settled society, if there are no true enemies, the reptile brain will imagine enemies in order to preserve and use its share of the incoming energy. John Foster Dulles [*Secretary of State under Eisenhower*] represented the reptile brain in the fifties. . . .

The mammal brain has quite different functions. When we come to the mammal brain we find for the first time a sense of community: love of women, of children, of the neighbor, the idea of brotherhood, care for the community, or for the country. "There is no greater love than that of a man who will lay down his life for a friend." Evidently in the mammal brain there are two nodes of energy: sexual love and ferocity. (The reptile brain has no ferocity: it simply fights coldly for survival.) Women have strong mammal brains, and probably a correspondingly smaller energy channel to the reptile brain. They are more interested in love than war. "Make love, not war" means "move from the reptile brain to the mammal brain." Rock music is mammal music for the most part; long hair is mammal hair.

The Viking warrior who went "berserk" in battle may have experienced the temporary capture of himself by the mammal brain. Eye witnesses reported that the face of the "berserk" appeared to change, and his strength increased fantastically—when he "woke up," he sometimes found he had killed twenty or thirty men. The facial expression is probably a union of the concerns of all three brains, so if one brain takes over, it is natural that the shape of the face would change.

What does the third brain, the "new brain," do? In late mammal times, the body evidently added a third brain. Brain researchers are not sure why—perhaps the addition is connected to the invention of tools, and the energy explosion that followed that. . . . Curiously, the third brain seems to have been created for problems more complicated than those it is now being used for. Some neurologists speculate that an intelligent man today uses $1/100$ of its power. Einstein may have been using $1/50$ of it.

The only good speculations I have seen on the new brain, and what it is like, are in Charles Fair's new book, *The Dying Self,* Wesleyan University Press. Fair suggests that what Freud meant by the "Id" was the reptile and mammal brain, and what the ancient Indian philosophers meant by the "self" was the new brain. His book is fascinating. He thinks that the new brain can grow and that its food is wild spiritual ideas. Christ said, "If a seed goes into the ground and dies, then it will grow." The reptile and mammal brains don't understand that sentence at all, both being naturalists, but the new brain understands it, and feels the excitement of it. The Greek mystery religions, and the Essene cult that Christ was a member of, were clear attempts to feed the new brain. The "mysteries" were the religion of the new brain. In Europe it was at its highest energy point about 1500, after knowing the ecstatic spiritual ideas of the Near East for 700 years. Since then, "secularization" means that the other two brains have increased their power. Nevertheless a man may still live if he wishes to more in his new brain than his neighbors do. Many

70

of the parables of Christ, and the remarks of Buddha, evidently involve instructions on how to transfer energy from the reptile brain to the mammal brain, and then to the new brain. A "saint" is someone who has managed to move away from the reptile and the mammal brains and is living primarily in the new brain. As the reptile brain power is symbolized by cold, and the mammal brain by warmth, the mark of the new brain is light. The gold light always around Buddha's head in statues is an attempt to suggest that he is living in his new brain. Some Tibetan meditators of the thirteenth century were able to read books in the dark by the light given off from their own bodies.

If there is no central organization to the brain, it is clear that the three brains must be competing for all the available energy at any moment. The brains are like legislative committees—competing for government grants. A separate decision on apportionment is made in each head, although the whole tone of the society has weight on that decision. Whichever brain receives the most energy, that brain will determine the tone of that personality, regardless of his intelligence or "reasoning power." The United States, given the amount of fear it generates every day in its own citizens, as well as in the citizens of other nations, is a vast machine for throwing people into the reptile brain. The ecology workers, the poets, singers, meditators, rock musicians and many people in the younger generation in general, are trying desperately to reverse the contemporary energy-flow in the brain. Military appropriations cannot be reduced until the flow of energy in the brain, which has been moving for four or five centuries from the new brain to the reptile brain, is reversed. The reptile and the new brains are now trying to make themselves visible. The reptile brain has embodied itself in the outer world in the form of a tank which even moves like a reptile. Perhaps the computer is the new brain desperately throwing itself out into the world of objects so that we'll see it; the new brain's spirituality could not be projected, but at least its speed is apparent in the computer. The danger of course with the computer is that it may fall into the power of the reptile brain. Nixon is a dangerous type—a mixture of reptile and new brain, with almost no mammal brain at all.

We do not spend the whole day "inside" one brain, but we flip perhaps a thousand times a day from one brain to the other. Moreover we have been doing this flipping so long—since we were in the womb—that we no longer recognize the flips when they occur. If there is no central organization to the brain, and evidently there is not, it means that there is no "I." If your name is John there is no "John" inside you—there is no "I" at all. Oddly, that is the fundamental idea that Buddha had thirteen hundred years ago. "I have news for you," he said, "there is no 'I' inside there. Therefore trying to find it is useless." The West misunderstands "meditation" or sitting because, being obsessed with unity and "identity," it assumes that the purpose of meditation is to achieve unity. On the contrary, the major value of sitting, particularly at the start, is to let the sitter experience the real chaos of the brain. Thoughts shoot in from all three brains in turn, and the sitter does not talk about, but *experiences,* the lack of an "I." The lack of an "I" is a central truth of Buddhism (Taoism expresses it by talking of the presence of a "flow"). Christianity somehow never

71

arrived at this idea. At any rate, it never developed practical methods, like sitting, to allow each person to experience the truth himself. Institutional Christianity is in trouble because it depends on a pre-Buddhist model of the brain.

Evidently spiritual growth for human beings depends on the ability to transfer energy. Energy that goes normally to the reptile brain can be transferred to the mammal brain, some of it at least; energy intended for the mammal brain can be transferred to the new brain.

The reptile brain thinks constantly of survival, of food, of security. When Christ says, "The lilies do not work, and yet they have better clothes than you do," he is urging his students not to care so much for themselves. If the student wills "not-caring," and that "not-caring" persists, the "not-caring" will eventually cause some transfer of energy away from the reptile brain. Voluntary poverty worked for St. Francis, and he had so little reptile brain paranoia the birds came down to sit on his shoulders.

If energy has been diverted from the reptile brain, the student, if he is lucky, can then transfer some of it to the mammal, and then to the new brain. Christ once advised his students, "If someone slaps you on the left cheek, point to the right cheek." The mammal brain loves to flare up and to strike back instantly. If you consistently refuse to allow the ferocity of the mammal brain to go forward into action, it will become discouraged, and some of its energy will be available for transfer. Since the mammal brain commits a lot of its energy to sexual love, some students at this point in the "road" become ascetic and celibate. They do so precisely in order to increase the speed of energy transfer. The women saints also, such as Anna of Foligno, experience this same turn in the road, which usually involves an abrupt abandonment of husband and children. Christ remarks in the Gospel of St. Thomas that some men are born eunuchs; and some men make themselves eunuchs in order to get to the Kingdom of the Spirit. However if a man is in the reptile brain at the time he begins his asceticism, then the result is a psychic disaster, as it has been for so many Catholic priests and monks.

The leap from the reptile to the new brain cannot be made directly; the student must go through the mammal brain. St. Theresa's spiritual prose shows much sexual imagery, perhaps because the mammal brain contributed its energy to the spiritual brain.

"Meditation" is a practical method for transferring energy from the reptile to the mammal brain, and then from the mammal to the new brain. It is slow, but a "wide" road, a road many can take, and many religious disciplines have adopted it. The orientals do not call it meditation, but "sitting." If the body sits in a room for an hour, quietly, doing nothing, the reptile brain becomes increasingly restless. It wants excitement, danger. In oriental meditation the body is sitting in the foetal position, and this further infuriates the reptile brain, since it is basically a mammalian position.

Of course if the sitter continues to sit, the mammal brain quickly becomes restless too. It wants excitement, confrontations, insults, sexual joy. It now starts to feed in spectacular erotic imagery, of the sort that St. Anthony's sittings were famous for.

Yet if the sitter persists in doing nothing, eventually energy has nowhere to go but to the new brain.

Because Christianity has no "sitting," fewer men and women in Western culture than in oriental civilizations have been able to experience the ecstasy of the new brain. Thoreau managed to transfer a great deal of energy to the new brain without meditation, merely with the help of solitude. Solitude evidently helps the new brain. Thoreau of course willed his solitude and he was not in a reptile city, but in a mammal or "mother" nature. Once more the truth holds that the road to the new brain passes through the mammal brain, through "the forest." This truth is embodied in ancient literature by the tradition of spiritual men meditating first in the forest and only after that in the desert. For the final part of the road, the desert is useful, because it contains almost no mammal images. Even in the desert, however, the saints preferred to live in caves—perhaps to remind the reptile brain of the path taken.

To return to poetry, it is clear that poets, like anyone else, can be dominated by one of the three brains. Chaucer is a great poet of the mammal brain; clearly St. John of the Cross and Kabir are great poets of the new brain. The reptile brain seems to have no poet of its own, although occasionally that brain will influence poets. Robinson Jeffers is a man with an extremely powerful mammal brain, in whom, nevertheless, the reptile brain had a slight edge. His magnificent poems are not warm towards human beings, On the contrary, he has a curious love for the claw and the most ancient sea rocks. Every once in a while he says flatly that if all human beings died off, and a seal or two remained on earth, that would be all right with him.

Bach makes music of new brain emotions; Beethoven primarily out of mammal brain emotions. Blake is such an amazing poet because he talks of moving from one brain to another. His people in "the state of experience," after all, have been pulled back into the reptile brain.

> *The invisible worm*
> *That flies in the night,*
> *In the howling storm,*
> *Has found out thy bed*
> *Of crimson joy,*
> *And his dark secret love*
> *Does thy life destroy.*

When we are in a state of "innocence," Blake says, we are feeling some of the spiritual ecstasy of the new brain. The industrialists, as Blake saw clearly, are in a state of "experience," trapped by the reptile brain.

I think poetry ought to take account of these ideas. Some biological and neurological speculations are marvellous, and surely that speculation belongs in literary criticism as much as speculation about breath or images or meter. A man should try to feel what it is like to live in each of the three brains, and a poet could try to bring all three brains inside his poems.

EXTEND, DEEPEN, CHANGE

In small groups explore the meaning Bly gives the structure of the brain. You can start with the koans (intriguing ideas) you found. See what implications you can come up with and use these to change, extend, or deepen ideas you already have. Pool your thoughts in your large group. Later reflect in your learning log.

COMMENTARY

Don't read this section until after you have done
your group work and reflected on your results in
your learning log.

Gear Shifting

Concerning how one should read an article like Bly's, I must tell you about an experience I had when I showed it to an anthropologist who had an office next to mine. Mark would frequently bring me articles and books on the human brain, articles about chemical changes in the brains of schizophrenics, new ways of doing brain scans, laser surgery, all very scientific.

So when I ran across Bly's article on the three brains in a literature anthology and found it intriguing, I gave it to Mark to read. When he returned it, there was a quizzical look on his face. Here's why:

Mark had tried to read Bly's article as if it were one of the "scientific" articles he was used to, and of course it wasn't. It was literature. What that means is that literature tries to get at truth in a different manner than is used in science. At least it reports its findings in a different style, a different frame of reference. Literature is not even looking for the same kind of "truth." To go from his customary way of reading to Bly, Mark would have had to change gears.

For example, when Bly says, "St. Francis had so little reptile brain paranoia the birds came down to sit on his shoulders," it doesn't matter at all whether it is really the lack of brain-stem influence that allows the birds to trust St. Francis. Not at all. What the statement means is that the situation is *like* that. Certain things we do *as if* we were reptiles, some *as if* we were mammals, some *as if* we were dominantly new brained. Bly uses the *idea* of the three brain types as a means of examining how we do behave and as a means of determining how we *can* behave. He is using them as metaphors, tools for examining the human situation.

Thus, when Bly says the real value of sitting (meditating) is to "let the sitter experience the real chaos of the mind," he may at first seem dead wrong. Maybe he is. But so what? If we gave his idea a chance, we may see more than we bargained for. Certainly there is tremendously more chaos in the universe than most people have an inkling of. The mind is usually a terrible chatterbox with thoughts running rampant most of the time—at least on the surface. If you sit quietly and try to focus on one thought, you will see how right Bly is. If it turns out he is wrong, however, the consideration is just as valuable. You will see yourself better.

So Bly could be wrong about the facts—he could even have some things mixed up technically—and still use the metaphor quite productively. Before we had the three-brain information, other models had to be used, the conscious-unconscious analogy or the id, ego, and superego, or the collective unconscious and the racial memory. These are all metaphors, too, and can all be used to get at the "truth" of what we humans are "like." One advantage of the triune-brain metaphor is that it has a physiological basis. Chief Seattle got at the same "truth" but with another set of metaphors.

These metaphors aren't <u>the</u> truth. It is what they get us to look at and get the feel of that is important. If we had to wait for all the facts to come in, we would never get started piecing together our pictures of reality. People would have had to sit on their hands for the past two million years. Ancient Chinese thinkers, the Greeks, the Hindus, modern physicists, Newton—all used the metaphors available to them. It makes no difference. Their tools of thought all lead them to the same deep center. The universe has always provided enough hints and enough tools. Most of us don't choose to use them, partly because we don't know we can or don't know how. Many don't think it is really possible, and then of course it isn't.

Whatever the comparisons Bly uses, this article is really about how to take control of our mental processes and how deliberately to set into motion desirable states of mind. Since that is his aim, we would waste our time to dwell upon the facts. The point is to examine any new message— essay, article, short story, lab report—from the point of view of the person who generated it. How does he or she want to be read? After we have seen it through his or her eyes, we are free and welcome to make use of whatever we want of the material.

Reading well is a matter of changing gears.

Education: The time wasted on plum blossoms

METAPHOR
A Dancing Lesson from the Right Brain

> *Metaphor* is defined in some dictionaries as an *implied comparison,* that is, one thing seen as though it were the other.

The exploration below is designed to bring your right-brained thinking to your conscious awareness. Go through the list together in a large group or work with three or four other students. Spend just enough time on each item to get the feel of the implied comparison. Make sure everyone grasps (groks) each item as you go along. There is a reward waiting for you at the end.

Example: Figure out why paper or metal is a metaphor for (*stands for* or *takes the place of*) sheep or cows.

Key: In a simpler society, what would your large herd of sheep mean to your neighbors? Right, wealth. The herd *represents* wealth, *stands for* wealth. An "implied comparison." And if you don't want to drag all your sheep with you to Katmandu to show how rich you are or to pick up a few rugs, you find something to stand in for your sheep, maybe some of that rare yellow metal that's so popular. So metal becomes a metaphor for cows or sheep, easier to haul around. Pretty soon, the way metaphor works, you can forget the sheep and all that manure and deal directly with gold. You never have to set eyes on a sheep. When even the metal gets too heavy, you can use a piece of paper (properly certified) to take its place. Pretty soon a wallet full of paper feels terrific and you never have to think about actual gold. An implied comparison. Of course, plastic feels even better these days.

Now work your way through each of the following.

1. *Bread* is a metaphor for money.
   Make sure you all grasp that and move on.
2. *Key* and *grasp* used above are metaphors.
3. "The sun poured in like butterscotch and stuck to all my senses" (Joni Mitchell, "Chelsea Morning"). *Like* and *as* make the comparison more explicit. It is "stuck to all my senses" that I like. "Chelsea Morning" is a metaphor, too.
4. "I'm sorry, honey, I can't kiss you. I have diabetes." (There is a bonus metaphor in this one, sweetie.)

5. How about each of these: *foot* of the hill, *head* of the class, *leg* of a table, nerves of *steel, hare* lip, *haywire, eye* of a needle, *eye to eye, tête á tête, Montana, Colorado.* The metaphor in number 4 above is more alive than any in number 5. These are called *dead* metaphors. You can figure out why. *Dead* metaphor is a dead metaphor, too, isn't it? How about a *dying* fire?

6. *Daisy* is an implied comparison. Check its etymology (origins). It's a triple comparison.

7. Richard, Leonard, Kathleen (check *catharsis*), Patricia (check *patrician*)

8. *Budget,* from French *bougette,* a small leather bag.

9. *Per·son·al·i·ty,* from Latin *persona,* "actor's mask." Your personality is a metaphor, an implied comparison, for you. Be sure to get the feel of that. Further back, *per·sona* meant "through sound, words"—another implied comparison.

10. My heart is a *pump.* A pump is a pump is a pump?

11. Trace "mad as a hornet," the word *mad* here meaning crazy.

12. Realize that *real·ize* is a metaphor. *Real·ity,* too.

13. metaphor for a box.

14. metaphor for a box.

15. If you bring to class one of those things you call a box, it, too, is a metaphor for a box.

16. Your name and all the words you use to describe yourself are metaphors for you: *woman, young, five feet four, me, student, sweetheart, liberated.* Who are you really? Whatever the answer, that will be a metaphor, too, won't it?

Usually at about this point in the exploration, one of my students will blurt out, *"Everything* is a metaphor!" I have always been lucky that way.*

Finally, let's see if we can push it so far as to say that treating metaphors as if they were real is making believe. And reality, in the most positive sense, is make-believe.

---

*In literary criticism, metaphor is considered just one of several kinds of figures of speech. When you are discussing literature, you will have to narrow your meaning of the term to the technical sense that is in common use. When the comparison uses *like* or *as,* call it a simile: "He's just *like* a bear this morning." "You dog" would be called a metaphor.

DIALOGUE AND REFLECTION

Now take time to discuss the implications of this exercise and reflect on your ideas in your learning log. Connect metaphor with other ideas developing in *Thinking about Thinking*.

This exercise is a koan.

COMMENTARY

Don't read this until you have done your own reflections.

Title: _____

_____

When you finish reading these pages, create a dead-metaphor title and a live one. If you have time, put everyone's on the chalkboard and discuss them. Don't label the titles as dead or alive in advance. Poll the class to see what they think, and why. You will find some titles that are semicomatose and some will change categories right before your eyes.

At first when we discuss metaphor, many of my students find it keeps slipping through their fingers. It is a curious situation. We all generate metaphor twenty-four hours a day. We do it continuously. But metaphor itself is hard to talk about. Maybe it is because the process is so much a natural part of us. It is like trying to scratch the tip of your finger with the tip of the same finger. You can't see the eye you are seeing with.

But I want to drive the point home if I can. If we can grasp what a word really is and does, it opens all sorts of doors to how we think, and that is exciting.

Here is a key idea from I. A. Richards, who devoted much thought to metaphor during the middle decades of this century. "Words," he said, "are the meeting points at which regions of experience which can never combine in sensation or intuition, come together." Let's see what that means.

Consider the idea "The fire is dying." In the lower mammal brain and in the reptile brain, you can watch a fire change to no-fire all day long. And you can watch creatures stop breathing all day long. But they are entirely separate events with no relationship whatsoever. There isn't any place in your brain to link these two regions together. They are permanently isolated from each other. Nature needs a computer designed to connect these two events, and it needs some kind of *byte* to store this connection in once the fusion takes place: *words*.

So this new kind of brain looks back and forth, back and forth, between the fire and things that quit living. "Hey," says the new brain, "creatures *die*, and the fire is doing the same sort of thing. The fire is *dying*." In nature, of course, such a blatant disregard of the actual situation is ridiculous. But the new brain is designed to do exactly that, to set up these impossible connections, connections that simply aren't in nature. The senses themselves are physically unable to do this. The mammal and reptile brains can't do this. Only the new brain can do it, because it is the kind of computer designed for it. (This is not to say that other creatures don't think and think well. Theirs is a different *kind* of thinking, an excellent kind of thinking. It would be wonderful someday to crawl inside your dog's brain and experience its world, and the spider's and the elm's. Different kinds of computers, that's all.)

If you look into nature for something like "love," you will search in vain. For "love" is an idea created in the new brain *about* a whole bunch of observations it has made. "Love" is a concept, a metaphor, a word. Life, unprocessed through the new brain, contains no such thing.

This new computer we are learning to play with has an area, the right brain, that looks back and forth between dissimilar events, feelings, even words themselves, and searches for links. When the gap is bridged, one piece of the picture it is building fits in. Connecting things that nature keeps separate is the whole idea of the new brain.

Of course, moving back a stage, the *idea* of death is itself the result of a bunching of aspects the right brain thinks it sees. It is, of course, a big liar. It says "same" when even "similar" is quite farfetched. Really, how similar is what happens to a fire and what happens to a person? The fire *died?* Come on!

But notice how useful. Amusingly, what the right brain decided about fire and death long before modern science came along turns out to be a good guess after all, only we got it backwards. What is easy to observe in the fire, because it takes place so fast, is indeed exactly what happens in animals: oxidation. Another synapse bridged! Paper dies too, then, and we could extend the metaphor to anything that comes apart, de-structures.

79

We end up with dying empires, a dead sea, even dead metaphors. Rocks can die and so can stars.

So we create these artificial situations, these purely *non*inevitable connections. We take an aspect here, an aspect there, and wad them together. Every word is the result of such a coupling together of imagined likenesses.

I said "useful" because this business of seeing sameness where it really isn't is what enables us to see a bicycle as a pump for an irrigation system. It enables us to imagine heart transplants: "That thing over there is enough like this sick thing over here to take its place." The metaphoric process.

Your right brain is the site of this amazing activity. It goes on automatically. Your right brain is constantly scanning for these possibilities. It then sends these vital nuggets across that bridge of neurons to your left brain where they are strung together in patterns such as sentences for storage. (Actually, it is much more dynamic than that. The two sides feed back and forth constantly, correcting, refining, rearranging, consulting.)

One more note on "dying." Once the concept comes into existence, the brain keeps working it over and refining and expanding it. More and more aspects are added. "Dying" becomes a living entity, indeed a thing of nature now, and goes through all the growth and change of any living matter.

I don't want to bleed this idea to death. Some readers probably "got" it rather quickly and some didn't. It depends on how much spade work you brought to the idea before you ever started reading these words. Why not take time here and explain metaphor to each other so that everyone "gets" it? Students are known to be better at this sort of thing than teachers anyway.

To repeat: The point of intersection of one plane of experience with another is a *word.* That is another way of defining a metaphor. All words are metaphors. You will see in chapter 3 that *all language is metaphor* as well.

I. A. Richards observed that most people think that words are triggers that make you think of some physical thing out there that they stand in for. But the fundamental and major point is that nature is empty of meaning or significance until a word is provided. The word is what is meaningful (full of meaning). Mind-brain gives meaning through its ability to connect. Nature without mind has no meaning. (If you are getting this, please explain it to those who aren't.) But nature does provide itself with mind, the new brain, and thus everything has the potential of meaning. Mind has its work cut out for it. And all this time some readers thought they were on the planet just to enter the work force.

MIND

Opting Out of the Work Force

What are the possibilities of this brain we have been investigating? Why don't we all think like Leonardo da Vinci, and why don't we think like da Vinci all the time? After all, we know there is far more brain tissue available in any human head than has ever been used—even by da Vinci. He wasn't even using one one-hundredth of it.

Colin Wilson took up the question in his science fiction novel The Mind Parasites. *He asks, if we take everything we know about the brain-mind and integrate all the associated studies, including linguistics, the collective unconscious, DNA, parapsychology, and so on, what future can be envisioned for our minds, and what are the barriers that will have to be demolished?*

Following are four excerpts from The Mind Parasites. *Your metaphoric right brain will notice many connections with ideas explored in* Thinking about Thinking. *In fact, all four passages are built on metaphor: Humans are infinite; the mind is an unmapped territory; the mind is a vast electronic brain; ordinary thinking is a view through out-of-focus binoculars; the human brain is a searchlight or a laser beam. Figure out what mind parasites are and if there is an insecticide to eliminate them.*

Wilson says that using the mind deliberately is a knack. It is more like learning to ride a bicycle than mastering a set of rules. Thinking about Thinking *is your bicycle.*

From *THE MIND PARASITES*

Colin Wilson

THE SPACE BETWEEN TWO INFINITIES

[*Notice how a change in your metaphor, the comparison you choose to use, makes all the difference in your response to life's situations. Change your assumption and you can change your behavior.*]

At this point, I looked at the moon again—and was suddenly overwhelmed with an inexpressible fear. I felt like a sleepwalker who wakes up to find himself balancing on a ledge a thousand feet above the ground. The fear was so immense that I felt as if my mind would dissolve; it seemed impossible to bear. I tried hard to fight it, to understand its cause. It was connected with this world I was looking at—with the realization that I was a mere object in a landscape. This is extremely difficult to make clear. But I suddenly seemed to see that men manage to stay sane because they see the world from their own tiny, intensely personal viewpoint, from their worm's eye view. Things impress them or frighten them, but they still see them from behind this windshield of personality. Fear makes them feel less important, but it does not negate them completely; in a strange way, it has the opposite effect,

---

NOTE: *Subheads and bracketed commentary have been inserted by the author of this book.*

81

for it intensifies their feeling of personal existence. I suddenly seemed to be taken out of my personality, to see myself as a mere item in a universal landscape, as unimportant as a rock or fly.

This led to the second stage of the experience. I said to myself: "But you are far more than a rock or fly. You are not a mere object. Whether it is an illusion or not, your mind contains knowledge of all the ages. Inside you, as you stand here, there is more knowledge than in the whole British Museum, with its thousand miles of bookshelves."

This thought in a sense was new to me. It led me to forget the landscape, and to turn my eyes inside myself. And a question presented itself. If space is infinite, how about the space inside man? Blake said that eternity opens from the centre of an atom. My former terror vanished. Now I saw that I was mistaken in thinking of myself as an object in a dead landscape. I had been assuming that man is limited because his brain is limited, that only so much can be packed into the portmanteau. But the spaces of the mind are a new dimension. The body is a mere wall between two infinities. Space extends to infinity outwards; the mind stretches to infinity inwards. [Mind *could be a metaphor for the fusion of the physical and the nonphysical.*]

THE UNMAPPED TERRITORY

Where the geography of the human mind is concerned, the main problem is not to plunge into the realms below consciousness, but to learn to fit words to what we do know about it. With the use of a map, I could walk from Paris to Calcutta; without a map, I might find myself in Odessa. Well, if we had a similar "map" of the human mind, a man could explore all the territory that lies between death and mystical vision, between catatonia and genius. Let me put this another way.

Man's mind is like some vast electronic brain, capable of the most extraordinary feats. And yet unfortunately, man does not know how to operate it. Every morning when he wakes up, man crosses to the control panel of that vast brain, and proceeds to turn knobs and press buttons. And yet this is the absurdity: with the immense machine at his disposal, he knows only how to make it do the simplest things, to deal with the most obvious, everyday problems. It is true that there are certain men whom we call men of genius who can make it do far more exciting things: write symphonies and poems, discover mathematical laws. And then there are a few men who are perhaps the most important of all: men who use this machine to explore its own capabilities. They use the machine to find out what they can do with the machine. They know that it is capable of creating the Jupiter symphony and *Faust* and *The Critique of Pure Reason* and multi-dimensional geometry. Yet in a sense, these works have been achieved by accident, or, at least, by instinct. Well, many great scientific discoveries have been stumbled on by accident; but when they have been discovered, the scientist's first task is to learn the hidden laws that govern them. And this electronic brain is the greatest of all mysteries, for to know its secret would turn man into a god. So to what better purpose can consciousness be employed than to explore the laws of consciousness? And this is the meaning of the word "phenomenology," perhaps the most important single word in the vocabulary of the human race. [The Mind Parasites *was published in 1967. Since then man has been steadily mapping the mind. We still know very little, but even that gives us much more of a chance to think, not by accident, but deliberately.*]

OBJECTIVITY:
A BLURRED VISION OF THE FACTS

The fact, you see, is this. Once you have got the knack of using the mind properly, everything follows easily. It is a matter of breaking a habit that human beings have acquired over millions of years; of giving all their attention to the outside world, and thinking of "imagination" as a kind of escapism, instead of recognizing that it is a brief excursion into the great unknown countries of the mind. You had to get used to thinking how your mind worked. Not just your mind in the ordinary sense, but your feelings and perceptions as well. I found that by far the most difficult thing, to begin with, was to realize that "feeling" is just another form of perception. We tend to keep them in separate compartments. I look at a man, and I "see" him; that is objective. A child looks at him and says: "Ooh, what a horrid man." The child feels about him, and we say that is subjective. We are unaware of how stupid these classifications are, and how much they confuse our thinking. In a sense, the child's feeling is almost a "perception." But in a far more important sense, our "seeing" is also a feeling. [*We think by feeling; we feel by thinking.*]

Think for a moment of what happens if you are trying to adjust a pair of binoculars. You turn a little wheel, and everything is a blur. Suddenly, a single extra turn makes everything become clear and sharp. Now think what happens if someone says to you: "Old So-and-so died last night." Usually, your mind is so full of other things that you don't feel anything at all—or rather, your feeling is indistinct, blurred, just as if the binoculars are out of focus. Perhaps weeks later, you are sitting quietly in your room reading, when something reminds you of Old So-and-so who died, and quite suddenly you feel acute grief for a moment. The feeling has come into focus. What more is necessary to convince us that feeling and perception are basically the same thing?

A MENTAL FOG

As we realized when we thought about this matter, the chief weapon of the parasites was a kind of "mind-jamming device" that could be loosely compared to a radar-jamming device. The conscious human mind "scans" the universe all the time. "The wakeful life of the ego is a perceiving." It is like an astronomer scanning the skies for new planets. Now an astronomer discovers new planets by comparing old star photographs with new ones. If a star has moved, it isn't a star, but a planet. And our minds and feelings are constantly engaged in this process of scanning the universe for "meanings." A "meaning" happens when we compare two lots of experience, and suddenly understand something about them both. [*The point at which we "understand something about them both" is a metaphor, a word that contains them both.*] To take an extremely simple example, a baby's first

83

experience of fire may give it the impression that fire is wholly delightful: warm, bright, interesting. If he then tries to put his finger into the fire, he learns something new about it—that it burns. But he does not therefore decide that fire is wholly unpleasant—not unless he is exceptionally timid and neurotic. He superimposes the two experiences, one upon other, like star maps, and marks down that one property of fire must be clearly separated from its others. This process is called learning.

Now supposing the mind parasites deliberately "blur" the feelings when we try to compare our two experiences. It would be as if they had exchanged an astronomer's spectacles for a pair with lenses made of smoked glass. He peers hard at his two star maps, but cannot make much out. We do not learn clearly from experience when this happens. And if we happen to be weak or neurotic, we can learn entirely the wrong thing—that fire is "bad" because it burns, for example.

I apologize to nonphilosophical readers for these explanations, but they are quite essential. The aim of the parasites was to prevent human beings from arriving at their maximum powers, and they did this by "jamming" the emotions, by blurring our feelings so that we failed to learn from them and went around in a kind of mental fog.

THE BEAM OF ATTENTION

The secret is this: that the poor quality of human life—and consciousness—is due to the feebleness of the beam of attention that we direct at the world. Imagine that you have a powerful searchlight, but it has no reflector inside it. When you turn it on, you get a light of sorts, but it rushes off in all directions, and a lot of it is absorbed by the inside of the searchlight. Now if you install a concave reflector, the beam is polarized, and stabs forward like a bullet or a spear. The beam immediately becomes ten times more powerful. But even this is only a half measure, for although every ray of light now follows the same path, the actual waves of light are "out of step," like an undisciplined army walking along a street. If you now pass the light through a ruby laser, the result is the waves now "march in step" and their power is increased a thousand-fold—just as the rhythmic tramping of an army was able to bring down the walls of Jericho.

The human brain is a kind of searchlight that projects a beam of "attention" on the world. But it always has been like a searchlight without a reflector. Our attention shifts around from second to second; we do not really have the trick of focusing and concentrating the beam. And yet it does happen fairly often. For example, as Fleishman observed, the sexual orgasm is actually a focusing and concentrating of the "beam" of consciousness (or attention). The beam of attention suddenly carries more power, and the result is a feeling of intense pleasure. The "inspiration" of poets is exactly the same thing. By some fluke, some accidental adjustment of the mind, the beam of attention is polarized for a moment, and whatever it happens to be focused on appears to be transformed, touched with "the glory and the freshness of a dream." There is no need to add that so-called "mystical" visions are exactly the same thing, but with an accidental touch of the laser thrown in. When

Jacob Boehme saw the sunlight reflected on a pewter bowl, and declared that he had seen all heaven, he was speaking the sober truth.

Human beings never realized that life is so dull because of the vagueness, the diffuseness, of their beam of attention—although, as I say, the secret has been lying at the end of their noses for centuries. And since 1800, the parasites have been doing their best to distract them from this discovery—a discovery that should have been quite inevitable after the age of Beethoven and Goethe and Wordsworth. They achieved this mainly by encouraging the human habit of vagueness and the tendency to waste time on trivialities. A man has a sudden glimpse of a great idea; for a moment, his mind focuses. At this point, habit steps in. His stomach complains of being empty, or his throat complains of dryness, and a false little voice whispers: "Go and satisfy your physical needs, and then you'll be able to concentrate twice as well." He obeys—and immediately forgets the great idea.

The moment man stumbles on the fact that his attention is a "beam" (or, as Husserl put it, that consciousness is "intentional") he has learned the fundamental secret. Now all he has to learn is how to polarize that beam.

The secret of life is this: Consciousness is intentional.

DIALOGUE AND REFLECTION
Laser Thinking

Now take some time to work up Wilson's ideas about the mind. My own experience is that he is right in saying that life feels impoverished to the degree that our consciousness is asleep. "To him whose elastic and vigorous thought keeps pace with the sun," wrote Henry David Thoreau, "the day is a perpetual morning. . . . Morning is when I am awake and there is a dawn in me. . . . To be awake is to be alive. I have never yet met a man who was quite awake. How could I have looked him in the face?" The more focused our minds, the more stimulating the environment. You may have thought of some ideas about how to focus your beam of attention more deliberately, possibly by linking the idea of laser thinking with the use of metaphor. The learning log, you have probably discovered by now, helps to develop habits of "consecutive discourse," to use John Dewey's phrase. You have to hold an idea steady long enough to examine it. And certainly you will have to vanquish the mind parasites. Do you think Einstein had any? He must have; he wasn't using more than two percent of his new brain either. What antidotes to mind parasites can you come up with in your group? This is a wide open field.

Small-group discussions would be good at this point, along with your own reflections later in your learning log.

COMMENTARY

Don't read this section until you have discussed
The Mind Parasites and reflected on it in your
learning log.

Activating Symbols

Dead metaphors aren't really dead; they are just sleeping. You can revive any dead metaphor. They are like the sleeping princess waiting for your awakening kiss. You could start with a Leo Buscaglia hug. That is, if you waste time on a word, it will get very lively. Take Wonder Bread, for example. That was a trade name for some years and, of course, was just bread. But the artist Sister Corita decided to pay attention to the words. Being a religious person, she was quite aware of the rich significance *bread* has for Christians. And on top of that, *wonder* bread! Sister Corita got a big cardboard cube and pasted Wonder Bread wrappers on all six sides and hung it as a mobile in a gallery. She liberated "Fly the Friendly Skies" in the same way. Friendly skies!

These advertising expressions had become clichés, things we don't pay attention to anymore, the way it is with almost all words. But Corita took them back to their rich, full meaning and "unclichéd" them. You can do that with any word that has become matter-of-fact or obscure or stripped of its emotive content. All you have to do is give it your attention.

You have probably seen the effects of unclichéing ideas in your learning log. When you catch on to an idea, the realization usually pops into your consciousness in the form of a new metaphor. The more you become absorbed in your thoughts, the more you will find fresh, spontaneous metaphors sprinkled through your entries.

There is a good reason for resuscitating words. "It is only with the heart that one can see rightly," says the fox to the little prince. "It is the time you have wasted for your rose that makes your rose so important." Of course, if you unclichéd every word in this sentence, it would be impossible to read. You have to be selective. Usually it will be the idea you are currently curious about. Just remember that it is the feel of the idea that results in understanding.

This is a good place to explain Robert Heinlein's neologism *grok* (*neo*, "new"; *logos*, "word"). Heinlein invented *grok* because *understand* had become "dead" and was being taken too superficially. In *Stranger in a Strange Land*, to grok was to see the idea the word represents in exactly the same way as the speaker saw it and felt it. You had to become one with the speaker, merge with him or her, so that in effect you *became* the speaker, even became the idea itself. Only then did you grok it.

Heinlein's concern is reflected in the ideas of communication specialists like Carl Rogers. Rogers suggests that good listening and understanding prohibit expressing our own view until we can rephrase the speaker's idea to the speaker's satisfaction. Only then can you say your piece. By then, of course, most arguments fall apart. You risk being changed when you allow yourself to listen, to grok, but you will find yourself in a far richer environment. You accept more, and you will have a lot more fun.

Not only can you grok ideas but you can grok any structure. You can study animals and trees and rocks and galaxies and atomic particles this way. That is what Jane Goodall has done in her study of chimpanzees. It is the time she has wasted for the chimps that makes them important. Many scientists use the grokking approach now. Farley Mowatt did the same thing with Canadian wolves. Einstein did it with his thought experiments.

If you deliberately grok school subjects, you will find they are not difficult. It takes some fooling around with the vocabulary, for example, some hugging and kissing. Take a few jawbreakers to your dictionary. Look at the etymology (origins) of the words. A lot of mystery will dissolve right there. As for the ideas, sit quietly and let them tell you about themselves. Then imagine yourself asking the author or teacher, "Is this what you are saying?" See if that computes. Run the new idea through your analogy bank. You will come upon some area in your experience that the new idea will fit.

"Some people grok very easily," wrote a student. "It seems to take me longer. I usually don't grok something until I try grokking something else, and while I'm in the process, I grok the first idea. A lot of times I don't understand what's going on in class until I think about it quite a lot. I usually get it while I'm at work or in the car, and then before I write it here I lose it. No, I still have it, but the delicious words I used while it was still in my head are lost." We all have that experience. I suggest a pocket notepad.

When you no longer need the crutch of definition, when the new idea is part of your nervous system, you have understood it. It will be forever part of your picture of what reality is like. You will never lose when you understand completely; you always gain. You also feel good.

This sort of complete understanding, grokking, was described by philosophy professor Paul Weinpahl in his *Zen Diary:* "Walking back, I again have the experience of identification with the world. There is nothing to think about now. However this time the identification is with a bamboo tree. Standing before it, I first have a brotherly feeling for it. Then I feel that it and I are one. I merge with it. It becomes conscious." This is no doubt the same kind of feeling Chief Seattle described in his letter to Franklin Pierce. We may be brothers after all.

The language of academic courses is deliberately cold-blooded. You find a much higher frequency of Latin-based words than you ever encounter in ordinary life. The idea is to carry on clear, rational discourse with all feeling carefully purged. You can see that this approach is barking up the wrong tree. Abstract or technical language or vocabulary deliberately narrows words as much as possible to one meaning. (Actually, this is impossible.) The technical use of words does have its value, but not when you are trying to understand something. Once you do, then you can get as technical as you need to. People who are working together in anthropology can save their energy for new concepts by having standard restricted definitions for those already settled. For understanding and grokking, make new metaphors. For nailing down, use dead ones.

Do keep in mind, though, the uncertainty principle. All definitions are tentative. Studies of chimpanzees, termites, wolves, and whales have forced scientists to redefine *human* several times in the recent past. Quantum mechanics has turned the laws of physics upside down—or at least tremendously extended the frame of reference. It is the nature of life to grow and change. Our description of it, language, must follow suit and must grow and change as our understanding does. Dead metaphors aren't really dead. They are only sleeping.

HOME COSMOGRAPHY

KOAN

Define *dream.*

Your right brain contains all the possible meanings of the word *dream* that you ever encountered. It is perfectly happy to supply any of them for a particular situation. It doesn't care what your left brain thinks is logical. It sees any particular meaning as only one instance of the inclusive general meaning. Bigots never see more than one meaning at a time.

To begin work on this koan, look at all the definitions of *dream* available in a college-sized dictionary. Make them all fit, and then try your hand at creating a definition that encompasses them all—that is, what is the most general thing you can say about a dream? For example, from what point of view is what you are doing right now a dream?

After you have explored what it means to dream, try the experiment on the next page. When you have completed it, look at the suggestions provided for integrating the activity with ideas developing in *Thinking about Thinking.* But first concentrate as much as possible on the experiment itself.

REFLECTION

When you are finished, reflect on this investigation in your learning log and connect your observations with others you have been developing.

NOTE: *Cosmography,* from *cosmos,* "universe," "world," "order," "harmony"; *graphy,* from *graph,* "to write," "to depict."

Pilgrim's Progress

1. Have someone read the following directions to the class. Allow plenty of time to complete each step.

- Close your eyes; relax; imagine you are floating.
- You come to a hill. Float down to the top of the hill and land. Look around. What do you see down below? Keep in mind everything you see on this journey.
- Now float down to the path at the foot of the hill. What is it like?
- Start walking on the path. Notice your surroundings.
- After you have walked and walked, you come to a key. Describe it to yourself. What do you do with it?
- Continue walking. After a while you see a cup lying on the path. Look it over carefully and decide what to do with it.
- Next you come to a body of water cutting off the path, but you know the path continues on the other side. Describe the body of water and how you get across.
- Continue walking. You come to a bear blocking your way. What is it like? What do you do?
- After a while, you come to a house beside the path. What is it like? Would you stay there?
- Now leave the house. Continue walking. Finally you come to a wall. Examine the wall carefully and decide how you get to the other side.
- Now open your eyes.

2. Quickly write down your adventure from beginning to end with as much detail as you can remember. Don't take time to edit. A rough draft will do.

In groups of three or four, read and discuss one person's narrative at a time. Each narrative is the writer's self. So see what it tells you about that person—feelings, attitudes, self-image, tone, confidence, sense of humor, concerns, style, and so on. You can compare your results with those you got from your mandala. The two make a fairly complete picture of your favorite person.

3. In your large group, pool your observations to give this experiment as much significance as you can.

Find points of view that support the idea that this daydream is a message from your right brain. Remember, your right brain is spatial, holistic, synthetic, visual, metaphoric.

Find ways to show that your adventure is a
mirror, metaphor, myth, mandala.

COMMENTARY

**Don't read this until you have discussed the
significance of your walk through the forest and
reflected on it in your learning log.**

Movie Making

So what is a dream? What would be the most inclusive and productive definition? Something going on while I'm asleep? Yes. Thoreau "never met a
man who was quite awake." He was right. There is no difference, really,
between daydreams and night dreams. Sometimes our eyelids are up,
sometimes down. We make them all out of the same raw material. At night
your sensors are damped down so that the raw materials are chosen
mainly from already-stored data. But even in the daytime, once the raw
data are delivered to your right brain, the same process is used.

When we deliberately dream, as in the stroll you took in our experiment, there is more conscious involvement of the verbal left brain. Accidental daydreams, when something sets us off and we forget "where we
are," lie somewhere between deliberate imagining and night dreams. In
our most wakeful state, we manufacture visual imagery constantly. What
you see around you as you read this is a translation of electrochemical
impulses into a 3-D movie. This chaos of available data is filtered, and the
residue is given shape and significance, or meaning, by yourself, the film
director.

So there is a sense in which what you see is what you have made up. As
you know, the student next to you makes up a reality movie significantly
different from yours.

There is a continuum from the most wakeful "dream" right on through
to those we have in deepest sleep. (This is called REM dreaming in the ter-
minology of dream analysis. That is, Rapid Eye Movement takes place
when we are having the kinds of dreams analysts find most meaningful.)
I hope you can see that when you are walking around, driving your car,
carrying on your daily activities, you are having a vivid "dream." (If this
isn't coming through, stop here and talk it over until it does.) That is, your
sense of what is going on is just that, a "sense," an interpretation. You interpret, imagine (make a picture of) a story in which you are the principal
actor. Usually, you don't consciously think of yourself doing this. If you

91

were too conscious, you would flub your lines. You have to become the character you imagine for yourself to such an extent that you forget it is all made up. You don't want to direct a B movie. You have seen personnel directors, teachers, salespeople, playing the role too self-consciously— rotten actors. Con artists do a good job of it.

But the best performance goes further so that the actor merges with the role and the play is real. We dream twenty-four hours a day, and there is a continuum of dream states. (If you think you are awake right now, stop for a moment and think of what has been going on in you the past few minutes.) Paradoxically, the deeper the dream state, with your eyes closed, the more like our wakeful condition it seems. It feels so "real." What you are doing right now is so much more "real" that if you pinch yourself, you yell, "Ouch!" The best dreams are the most real. If this isn't clear, please take time out to explain it to each other so everyone sees it.

Thus, the best dream of all, the goal of your neocortex, is that laserlike beam of attention, that state of consciousness, in which we see what is going on to the nth degree. In other words, we "wake up." Being "awake" could be defined as dreaming with everything we've got—both right and left hemispheres of the new brain fully operative, all senses sandpapered to their most sensitive state, the reptilian and mammalian computers fully integrated, all systems go—that is, being fully conscious but in addition being fully conscious of this consciousness, and all this going on harmoniously and simultaneously. Some trick! To "know thyself" would take at least this much. And still we would not know how or why.

There is a productive use of extending the idea of the word *dream*. If everything that goes on in our processing banks is "dreaming," of different stages, intensity, and awareness, it opens the way for deliberately influencing both the tales that come to us at night and those we live during the day. It makes all this story material available for our reshaping and directing. You can make any kind of movie you wish, and you can make it as artistic or messy as you choose. We all make up our own story as we go along. If you don't like yours, rewrite it. Practice your lines, change the lighting or the sets. Or keep it all as it is but don't fight it. You can always like what you do, even the scary parts, the nightmares and the roller coasters. That way, you are always free to be doing what you like.

Let's translate this discussion of what a dream is into right- and left-brain language. Whatever you "dream," it is something you yourself made up. In other words, it is a metaphor. A dream is a metaphor. It is an implied comparison. As such it comes from your right brain. It is complete and accurate. And it has the potential of meaning—but not until it is made concrete through left-brain verbalization. You have to put some language around it. (Recall how your night dreams fade when you don't write them down or talk about them as soon as you wake up.) You say you don't know what it means? You do know. But since your right brain can't talk, speech being a function of Broca's and Wernicke's areas of your left brain, it has to wait patiently for you to wake up and give it a voice. If you insist on ignoring important messages from your right brain, it will give you recurring messages (flying, suffocating, having erotic adventures) until you do pay attention.

You have to fiddle with the persistent dream until you find the language to fit it. Meaning seems dim and vague until the right "name" for what you have already seen in your right brain crystalizes the whole matter. Again, paradoxically, it is the conscious activity of your logical, sentence-making left brain that seeks this fusion. The point of insight releases an emotive payoff, a sudden explosion, that unites both hemispheres and the whole organism. It is orgasmic. You could also call these insights epiphanies or moments of enlightenment or, as John Dewey put it, "the irradiating and illuminating function of language in mind." All readers have had this experience many times.

It is possible to do so deliberately. It could well be argued that clear thinking is the ability to bridge the gap between the metaphoric, dream-generating right brain and the conscious, language-generating left, the spirit and the flesh, the idea and its concrete representation merged.

When you took the stroll in our experiment, you generated a metaphor. When you discussed it with others, you began the process of giving it meaning. If you were lucky, you got a fusion of the right words with the images you had created, and you got the "aha" insight. Obviously, a lot of the language activity doesn't pan out. Maybe it's this; maybe it's that. But even this casting about for possibilities is profitable because it keeps your mind actively working on a self metaphor that will eventually be accurate and productive. You will find that an accurate metaphor of yourself is always comfortable and pleasant. I never met a self I didn't like.

Metaphor is both flesh and spirit. And so are you.

93

THE YIN YANG OF CONSCIOUSNESS
Two Persons in One Head

Tips on interpreting your excursion follow right after this passage from a book by Julian Jaynes. He gives such a clear description of how the two halves of your neo-cortex function that it should be added here. The title of Jaynes's book is almost an essay in itself: The Origin of Consciousness in the Breakdown of the Bicameral Mind. *It looks like a left-brained title, but examination shows it to be right brained or metaphoric.*

The title translates this way. According to Jaynes's theory, as long as humans could be defined as humans, they had a neocortex split down the middle with the two halves functioning, as now, in two distinctly different ways (analytic versus synthetic, and so on). But at first the corpus callosum, that bridge of nerve fibers, did not pass the findings of the two hemispheres back and forth as it does now. Each side had to work out-of-awareness of the other's activities. Furthermore, even though the "conscious" and vocal left side was conscious, it was not really aware that it was conscious. There was not nearly the kind of reflective analysis that is now available to us. Bicameral comes from bi, *which of course means "two," and* cameral *is from the root that also gives us the word* camera. Camera *means literally "chamber," "room," "vault," "box." Your great-grandmother's Kodak was a "box" camera. So* bicameral mind *means two-chambered, two separate vaults.*

Jaynes makes the fascinating case that in ancient times the split between the two chambers was so complete that one side literally did not know what the other was doing. If the right brain figured out something or realized something, it had a tough time telling the left about it. The left, never guessing that there even was a right side, figured out that the gods must be talking to it. All through Homer's epics, his heroes are having chats with the gods and getting instructions from them. Jaynes argues that these were messages from the right hemisphere. To Achilles the voice of Athene was as concrete as anything else in his reality.

Now there is much more feedback across the corpus callosum, and we don't normally hear voices, even though the academic world still pays hardly any attention to the input of the right brain. The deliberate integration of the two halves may be the new frontier in schooling.

In the passage that follows, Jaynes describes experiments in which the corpus callosum has been severed. These experiments demonstrate conclusively that the two hemispheres do function as if a person were two separate selves. Jaynes thinks that is probably how it was with ancient humans. The disruption of the flow of information over the corpus callosum bridge could also account in part for instances today of individuals' hearing voices, split personalities, and so on. The less the two sides talk with each other, the more split we become. But if the mind can break down the separation between the two vaults of your brain, you can become self-aware. More and more self-awareness seems to be the next stage in our mental development. Thus, The Origin of Consciousness in the Breakdown of the Bicameral Mind.

From *THE ORIGIN OF CONSCIOUSNESS IN THE BREAKDOWN OF THE BICAMERAL MIND*

Julian Jaynes

Is it possible to think of the two hemispheres of the brain almost as two individuals, only one of which can overtly speak, while both can listen and both understand?

The evidence that this is plausible comes from another group of epileptics. These are a dozen or so neurosurgical patients who have undergone complete commissurotomy, the cutting down the midline of all interconnections between the two hemispheres. [Commissure, *from* com, *"together," and* mittre, *"to put,"* *thus, "a band of fibers joining two symmetrical parts."*] This so-called split-brain operation (which it is not—the deeper parts of the brain are still connected) usually cures the otherwise untreatable epilepsy by preventing the spread of abnormal neural excitation over the whole cortex. Immediately after operation, some patients lose speech for up to two months, while others have no problem whatever—no one knows why. Perhaps each of us has a slightly different relationship between our hemispheres. Recovery is gradual, all patients showing short-term memory deficits (perhaps due to the cutting of small hippocampal commissures), some orientation problems, and mental fatigue.

Now the astonishing thing is that such patients after a year or so of recovery do not feel any different from the way they felt before the operation. They sense nothing wrong. At the present time they are watching television or reading the paper with no complaints about anything peculiar. Nor does an observer notice anything different about them.

But under rigorous control of sensory input, fascinating and important defects are revealed.

As you look at anything, say, the middle word of this line of print, all the words to the left are seen only by the right hemisphere, and all the words to the right only by the left. With the connections between the hemispheres intact, there is no partic-ular problem in co-ordinating the two, although it really is astonishing that we can read at all. But if you had your hemispheric connections cut, the matter would be very different. Starting at the middle of this line, all the print to your right would be seen as before and you would be able to read it off almost as usual. But all the print and all the page to your left would be a blank. Not a blank really, but a nothing, an absolute nothing, far more nothing than any nothing you can imagine. So much nothing that you would not even be conscious that there was nothing there, strange as it seems. Just as in the phenomenon of the blind spot, the "nothing" is somehow "filled in," "stitched together," as if nothing were wrong with nothing. [*Reread this definition of nothing. The kind of nothing we are familiar with is quite man-ageable. You can walk around and look at the hole it fills. The other kind is unthinkable. We have no way to approach it; we don't even know it's not there. A certified bigot simply cannot see what you are talking about. There is no place in his head for it to connect with. If you want to change this sort of mind, you will first have to build a whole new area of connections in his head so*

95

there will be someplace for the new idea to lodge.] Actually, however, all that nothing would be in your other hemisphere which would be seeing all that "you" were not, all the print to the left, and seeing it perfectly well. But since it does not have articulated speech, it cannot say that it sees anything. It is as if "you"— whatever that means—were "in" your left hemisphere and now with the commissures cut could never know or be conscious of what a quite different person, once also "you," in the other hemisphere was seeing or thinking about. Two persons in one head.

This is one of the ways these commissurotomized patients are tested. The patient fixates on the center of a translucent screen; photographic slides of objects projected on the left side of the screen are thus seen only by the right hemisphere and cannot be reported verbally, though the patient can use his left hand (controlled by the right hemisphere) to point to a matching picture or search out the object among others, even while insisting vocally that he did not see it. Such stimuli seen by the right nondominant hemisphere alone are there imprisoned, and cannot be "told" to the left hemisphere where the language areas are because the connections have been cut. The only way we know that the right hemisphere has this information at all is to ask the right hemisphere to use its left hand to point it out—which it can readily do.

If two different figures are flashed simultaneously to the right and left visual fields, as, for example, a "dollar sign" on the left and a "question mark" on the right, and the subject is asked to draw what he saw, using the left hand out of sight under a screen, he draws a dollar sign. But asked what he has just drawn out of sight, he insists it was the question mark. In other words, the one hemisphere does not know what the other hemisphere has been doing.

Again, if the name of some object, like the word "eraser," is flashed to the left visual field, the subject is then able to search out an eraser from among a collection of objects behind a screen using only the left hand. If the subject is then asked what the item is behind the screen after it has been selected correctly, "he" in the left hemisphere cannot say what the dumb "he" of the right hemisphere is holding in his left hand. Similarly, the left hand can do this if the word "eraser" is spoken, but the talking hemisphere does not know when the left hand has found the object. This shows, of course, what I have said earlier, that both hemispheres understand language, but it has never been possible to find out the extent of language understanding in the right hemisphere previously.

Further, we find that the right hemisphere is able to understand complicated definitions. Flashing "shaving instrument" onto the left visual field and so into the right hemisphere, the left hand points to a razor, or with "dirt remover" to soap, and with "inserted in slot machines" to a twenty-five-cent piece.

Moreover, the right hemisphere in these patients can respond emotionally without the left talking hemisphere knowing what it is all about. If a series of neutral geometric figures is being flashed to the right and left visual fields at random, which means respectively into the left and right hemispheres, and then a picture of a nude girl by surprise is flashed on the left side going into the right hemisphere, the patient (really the patient's left hemisphere) says that it saw nothing or just a flash of light. But the grinning, blushing, and giggling during the next minute contradicts

96

what the speech hemisphere has just said. Asked what all the grinning is about, the left or speech hemisphere replies that it has no idea. These facial expressions and blushings, incidentally, are not confined to one side of the face, being mediated through the deep interconnections of the brainstem. The expression of affect is not a cortical matter. [Affect *here means "feeling" or "emotion," a product of the midbrain.*]

Similarly with other sensory modalities. Odors, for example, presented to the left nostril only and so to the right hemisphere in these commissurotomy patients cannot be named by the talking hemisphere, though the latter can say very well whether the smell is pleasant or unpleasant. The patient may even grunt, make aversive reactions, or explain "Phew!" to a stench, but cannot say verbally whether it is garlic, cheese, or decayed matter. The same odors presented to the right nostril can be named and described perfectly well. *What this means is that the emotion of disgust gets across to the speaking hemisphere through the intact brainstem, while the more specific information processed by the cortex does not.* [*Italics added. Notice that the cortex gives the limbic region permission to express emotion. The cortex is the control center.*]

Indeed, there is some indication that it is the right hemisphere that commonly triggers the emotional reactions of displeasure from the brainstem. In test situations, where the right hemisphere is made to know the correct answer, but of course cannot speak, and then hears the left dominant hemisphere making obvious verbal mistakes, the patient may frown, wince, or shake his head. It is not simply a way of speaking to say that the right hemisphere is annoyed at the erroneous vocal responses of the other. And so perhaps the annoyance of Pallas Athene when she grasped Achilles by his yellow hair and twisted him away from murdering his king (Iliad, I:197). Or the annoyance of Yahweh with the iniquities of his people.

Of course there is a difference. Bicameral man had all his commissures intact. But I shall suggest later that it is possible for the brain to be so reorganized by environmental changes that the inferences of my comparison here are not entirely foolish. At any rate, the studies of these commissurotomy patients demonstrate conclusively that the two hemispheres can function so as to seem like two independent persons, which in the bicameral period were, I suggest, the individual and his god.

DIALOGUE AND REFLECTION
Wetware Storage

If you want to understand something you read and have it become part of your view of how things are, you have to play around with it until it clicks into place. You have to do that with any idea, not just your reading or school assignments but anything you give attention to. Otherwise it will fade rapidly from your memory banks; as much as nine-tenths will vanish overnight. A short period of reinforcement will produce the opposite result: nine-tenths or more retained.

When possible, talk about ideas with others, preferably in small groups so that you always get a chance to talk. You yourself have to put language around ideas; it is not nearly as effective just to sit and listen. But when there isn't time in class for discussions, you can always work up material in your learning log. Once you make this a habit and have a regular time, place, and duration, the routine will feel productive and good.

So, as usual, talk with others about Jaynes's ideas, and later reflect in your log.

THE PATH: METAPHOR AND DREAM

Now let's go back to your stroll along the path. You were on a *path* and encountered a *key, a cup, a body of water, a bear, a house,* and *a wall*. What is "the" meaning of each of these? The way to figure out your dream (and those you have at night, too) is to define these words or images in their most extended sense. For example, a key has innumerable extended meanings. It is an object you use to unlock a door of some sort. But we also give people the key to the city; there are keys to the kingdom; there are keys to puzzles or problems, keys to the future, and so on. Your right brain, as you know, treats a word like *key* as a metaphor. It looks at *key* holistically and sees all its meanings as *one* meaning. In your right brain, *key* is fat. In your left, it's lean.

When you find a key on your path, your left brain will provide a very specific definition, but every modifier it uses will have its own multiple meanings in your right brain. Discourse, reflective thinking, brings these two kinds of thinking into harmony. You need to see each specific word in its general right-brained context. In order to understand any idea, you need both its particular meaning and its general meaning. An academic education should center on the play between specific and extended meanings of fundamental words. In Freudian psychology, *key* stands for education. You can see that education as a key, something that unlocks doors (and closes just as many), is certainly one of the extended meanings of the word. In a general sense, the key you imagined is a *tool* for you. How much store did you set on it? Was it a practical key, like the one to your apartment, or was it ancient, gold, silver, jewel encrusted, tarnished, rusty, polished, a treasure to you? It is important how you feel about it, too. Your midbrain has to be in on this. Did you keep it? Play your specific description against general possibilities until a meaning that fits this particular situation emerges. You will see that the meaning of a word is always broader than you might at first imagine. That should help to calm you down in arguments.

Proceed in this manner with the other things you encounter on your journey. A *path*, a *road*, a *journey*, a *trip*—these kinds of words have associations with the course your life is taking, as it seems to you, and how you feel about it. Is it easy walking, arduous, beautiful, depressing? Is the day summery, overcast, hot, cool? Flowers, dark forests?

A *cup* is a container, a receptacle, a vessel, anything that can be filled. You can see that one of its extended meanings—one that your right brain is always aware of whenever you use the word no matter what the context—could be your sex life. But take *sex* in its extended meaning, too. That could be your creative life and your relationships, your *intercourse*, in its extended sense, with the possibilities along your path. Whenever you use the word *intercourse*, your right brain will always be aware of its sexual meaning along with all its other meanings. That's how metaphors work. Is your cup fine china, styrofoam, cracked, soiled, white, red, fragile? Do you keep it? How do you feel about it? Some people use it to refresh themselves from the water across their path.

The *body of water*? Difficulties along your way. What is your attitude about them? How do you deal with them?

The *bear* is threatening forces, your death, for example. How do you feel about it? What do you do?

In its extended, right-brained meaning, a *house* is a structure for sheltering organisms of any sort. Organized religion is a "house" for its followers, the "house of God." But *house* is any kind of protective shelter to shield you from the "elements" (life). Did you go in? Was it occupied? Was it ancient, elegant, plain? Would you stay there?

Of course, the *wall* across your path is what is up ahead, something you have to face. Your *future* is an extended meaning. Some people use their key to open a door they find in the wall. Some see the wall as insurmountable. Some climb it with no trouble. How do you feel about your future?

By the way, it is not in the instructions, but did you take a peek over the wall? I hope you saw a wonderful, magical place. If not, the real payoff of this exercise is that everything along your path can be reprogrammed. You can deliberately work on a new dream that suits what you would like. You are free to change or reinforce any part of it. It is a bit like Dickens' *A Christmas Carol*. The stroll gives you a chance to see how things are. It is not how things have to be.

One implication of the entire preceding discussion of metaphor and dreams is that you can examine any material that pops into your head the same way we examined your stroll along the path. That includes recurrent dreams you have at night, daydreams, and even the picture you have of

99

daily life, your real-life dream. This will enable you to bridge categories you ordinarily keep separate in your conscious mind so that you can discover alternatives and possibilities. Manipulating metaphor is a technique for solving problems.

REFLECTIONS ON DREAMS

This is a good place for discussion and an entry in your learning log. What would it be like if there were not a picture of reality in your head (which of course is another name for a *vision* or *dream* of reality)? Try to imagine *emptiness*, indeed *nothingness* of the kind Julian Jaynes describes in this chapter. That's what would happen if your memory banks aborted. Whew! With memory would also go history. Would you still be "alive"?

Imagination is more important
than knowledge.
　　　　　　　—Albert Einstein

THE MEANING OF THE FACTS

Following is a transcript of a talk given to English teachers and students in Salem, Massachusetts. If you keep your eye peeled, you will find that virtually every idea in the talk can be found somewhere in the first two chapters of Thinking about Thinking, *either fully developed or suggested. This transcript is about the implications of what you have been exploring—one person's combining of ideas into one complete view that holds them all.*

If you have been thinking about the meaning of the thoughts in chapters 1 and 2, a view of how your mind works has been growing. It will be different from the transcript that follows but will have similarities, too. You can set up a dialogue with the author. (That is what good reading is.) It should be a stimulating discussion.

Afterward you will have a chance to pull your own developing thoughts together in an extended entry in your learning log.

METAPHOR, BOTH ONE'S OWN NOSE AND HEART

Metaphoric process is central in the universe: in all *human* beings and in all else as well. The process of abstracting out some item, of finding some other, different, item somewhere else in the same way, and of bringing those two things together at some point of contact, which fuses them forever in association, is the very nature of all creation. To create is to be alive; anything else has the feel of nonliving or death about it. To be metaphoric, to create analogies, is the very nature of that living process. If we can say that life is creation, we can say that creation is metaphor. It is, as Robert Frost has said, feats of association, little or large accomplishments of association. Things that never existed together in the continuum of the universe are suddenly brought together in a warm synaptic flash. These warm spots are the *matter* of the universe. Space, emptiness, is the major element of everything. Even in the atom there is infinitely more space than matter. *The matter in the universe gets together,* as Frost has said, *in a few terribly isolated points and sizzles.* And sizzles.

Even well-schooled people commonly think that metaphors are something used in poems and that only specialists in the field would have anything to do with them. Metaphor, they think, is some sort of window dressing that people created to make the world look nicer. It doesn't occur to them how far-reaching this process is. It also seems like a mechanical thing. Anybody can toss them off as soon as he or she knows the principle and can go around making up metaphors. And that is actually true. One can do that. Anybody can do it. One can say, "I am a typewriter. John is a lead pencil." This kind of thing is done in an impersonal way by clever verse writers. It is not particularly meaningful. They forget that the purpose of the process is to impregnate matter with spirit, to inspire.

To know plum blossoms,
one's own nose
and heart.
—Onitsura (1660–1738)

So to some, metaphor seems like a specialized field without much meaning to it, and it seems mechanical. But as we begin to examine language and study it, we cannot help but come to the observation sooner or later that the business of creating language is a metaphoric process, that the first time someone catches on to how to use a fabricated tool (a word) to get a grasp of a very slippery reality—he or she has made a tremendous advance in his or her thinking. It isn't long until these associations form webs and we have a whole metaphoric network system called language. It is a fabulous, fantastic achievement. In the midst of doing this, a person is taking part in an unbelievably complex process.

This process is always binary, it always goes in pairs, one by one. If you lay one instance next to another, it may not mean anything. But if you lay a similar one next to that bundle, eventually you have enough instances and enough experience of those instances to give them a title, say, *mother,* and that is what little kids do. As soon as they catch on to this process, they go wildly about their world using the process on everything:

- Daddy's outside shaving the windows.
- Where's the confederate sugar?
- If they can have a *Chrys*ler, let's get a *God*ler.
- Would you like a grilled cheese sandwich? Yes, and then let's make a boy-cheese sandwich—for Daddy.
- For heaven's snakes.
- I like those little red olives with the green around.
- My daddy got a lavender retriever yesterday.

Little children have a lively sense of language processes, and they eventually form these networks. They eventually create language. Children reach out and do this on their own, with very little help from adults. There is a genetic thrust in themselves. The probability of language lies within human beings and is somehow transmitted through them physiologically. If they are planted in a rich enough field, the process becomes triggered and they leap to the conclusion of language in order to generate this metaphoric process in themselves. They absolutely have to have it.

So all language is metaphor. We can grasp that. It is possible to know that about language, to know that it is the handle that we have on the world, that it is the way we get to know the world. Babies get to know their mothers through touch and contact, but they know all that and can hold it and contemplate it only through a mandala symbol, through something like the word *mommy* or *mother.* This sort of symbolizing process is what enables them to contemplate that experience out of its presence. That means one can go away someplace out of contact with the matter of

102

interest, sit down quietly and do something in the mind which would be impossible without some sort of symbol to hang on to.

In other words, this is a displacement process. That is the key to metaphoric processes. One thing is seen in terms of another. This is not direct contact with the physical object. It is something that takes place spiritually. Relationships are not physical. They are spiritual, always. You might say, "Well, certainly the person standing in front of me is no metaphor." But as William Gordon has suggested, "Perhaps the body itself is metaphoric." He is right. Nerve ending contact with reality *can* be recognized as metaphoric. If I put my hand on an object and touch it, you would say that this is just about as direct a contact with reality as I can get, but if you quietly realize that what happens is an immediate electrical and chemical impulse that shoots to my brain and mind, you see that it is not even physical by the time it gets to the nerve endings. I touch it. Right inside the epidermis is a translation, a metaphoric coding, and the code goes zipping off. What reaches my brain is not that outside thing but a symbol, a metaphor, for something out there. I touch my cheek and say, "It's warm, it's soft, it's me." Or when I view something, I will be told that that certainly is not metaphoric, but we know that viewing is only possible by elimination of matter. We brush stuff away. The human eye is designed not to let much in. It brushes away an infinite amount of information. My eye rejects the rest. What it does permit is called reality, but as you can see, I have already got a metaphor, even out there. When it gets back to the retina and to the back part of the eye, it is translated immediately into a code, a metaphor once more. What is in my brain is metaphoric. It is an encoding.

These images, translated into codes, hit my brain, and my mind thinks of them. That is what it has available to it. It has metaphors available to it. As you can see, this is a very lively process. But if I get accustomed to it, and if I permit it to become commonplace in my mind, I no longer feel myself as sharing in this activity. I feel as though it is happening to me and as though I am not *making* it happen. Little children know better. The fresh human being knows better. But you can see that if I feel as though metaphors are not my creations, I feel less active in this sharing.

We have been allowed to forget how we make metaphors and that we make them. We forget that metaphor is a fundamental part of our awareness, our perception, that it indeed is the world and that we make the world through this process. If we forget that, we grow very, very apathetic and dull. As "Simply Assisting God" from Piet Hein's *Grooks,* has it,

> I am a humble artist
> molding my earthly clod
> adding my labor to nature's
> simply assisting God.
> Not that my effort is needed;
> yet somehow, I understand,
> my maker has willed it that I too should have
> unmolded clay in my hand.

Unmolded clay in my hand. Or as the zen sculptor would say, "What would this marble in conjunction with me like to become?"

The whole process of analogy, the means whereby we mold clay, to use that metaphor, is similar to, even the same as, dialogue. Dialogue in its broadest sense is duality. Without it nothing happens. What happens in the atom is dialogue, what happens between print and reader, between plant and the sun. Dialogue is what causes matter to sizzle; it is what permits spirit to enter matter. When you solve a puzzle, for example, the point of fusion between spirit and matter, the contact between the desire and actuality of solving the puzzle, that flash right there is the sizzling of the universe. It is the point where spirit makes contact with matter. And that happens every time someone creates a metaphor. It happens every time. Obviously what has happened to human beings over our lives is that we have forgotten how metaphoric we really are. We forget that by our very nature, by the very nature of the universe, we are *poetic. It* is poetic. We may have thought we were nothing but clerks and recorders, but all the time we have been poets. We have to do this. It is our nature. We do it *anyway.* But if we are not aware that we are doing it, we get a sense of defeat and unimportance. This poem by Edward Lueders concerns our metaphoric birthright:

YOUR POEM, MAN . . .

unless there's one thing seen
suddenly against another—a parsnip
sprouting for a President, or
hailstones melting in an ashtray—
nothing really happens. It takes
surprise and wild connections,
doesn't it? A walrus chewing
on a ballpoint pen. Two blue tail-
lights on Tyrannosaurus Rex. Green
cheese teeth. Maybe what we wanted
least. Or most. Some unexpected
pleats. Words that never knew
each other till right now. Plug us
into the wrong socket and see
what blows—or what lights up.
Try
    untried
        circuitry,
new
     fuses.
Tell it like it never really was,
man,
and maybe we can see it
like it is.

104

Tell it like it never was, Man, and maybe we can see it like it is. Every analogy is always false, of course, because it takes two things that are not connected in nature and makes them connected. Through the fiction that is created, through that connecting which really doesn't work, we see these relationships. A man stands up in some forest, looks around, and wonders what he is doing here.

The function of all this is not to be clever or decorative or to produce a whole bunch of interesting metaphors in physical and verbal shapes (verbal shapes being physical, too, of course). The function isn't to make things. It is to realize the universe, to realize the world we live in, to make it real, to allow it to be alive before our eyes. In Lawrence Durrell's words, to see the cloth of gold under the sackcloth of "ordinary" reality. The way we do it is through the feel, through metaphor, through analogical processes.

WRAP SESSION

Try the following right-brained technique for reviewing chapter 2:

1. Think up one word or phrase that captures the essence of this chapter.
2. List everyone's on the chalkboard.
3. See if there is a consensus about which are right brained and which are left. If some are in doubt, explore each other's reasoning.
4. Pick out three or four and try to guess why each fits the chapter. Then see what the person who created it had in mind.
5. Pick out a few that most of you think work really well. What makes them so effective?

A SYNTHESIS

Pulling Yourself Together

As you know, much of this chapter is about what metaphor is and how you use metaphor in your thinking processes. Chapter 5 contains tips for combining the ways of thinking that are special to each side of your neocortex. But this chapter contains some tips, too. Metaphor, as you have seen, can be used deliberately to clarify or deepen your experience.

This is a good place to stop and pull together your reflections about chapter 2 in an extended entry in your learning log. First review the chapter quickly to refresh your memory. Take another look at the questions about meaning that begin the chapter. Though you should not have conclusive answers to any of them, you will probably have a much clearer sense of what is involved in the questions. In fact, if those questions have become matters of keen interest to you and remain so, long after you leave college, that would be as much as you or your teacher could reasonably hope. Ignorant people have no trouble settling such questions instantly.

Next, reread your learning log.

Then do your entry. About an hour and a half of writing and reflecting should give you a good grasp of the ideas that emerge in chapter 2 and their potential. Of course, any attractive tangents that come up should be pursued.

If you would like to make a more polished essay from your entry, you will have plenty of material to play with. But do be careful not to edit your own spirit out of your final version. You don't want to end up sounding like a textbook. Retain what is uniquely you, your own language, manner, and speech patterns, as much as possible. Just cut and paste, clean up spelling and punctuation, and cut out any clutter that is fogging up your ideas.

> When I'm writing and the words just seem to
> be flowing out of me, then there is a good
> melodious rhythm inside of me. When I
> reach a block, the music is turned off and
> the song is awkward.
>
> —Judy Young, Student

Home Cosmography

Direct your eye right inward, and you'll find
A thousand regions in your mind
Yet undiscovered. Travel them, and be
Expert in home-cosmography.
                          —Henry David Thoreau

3

HOW SYSTEMATIC THINKING IS PROGRAMMED

THIS IS JUST TO SAY

I have eaten
the plums
that were in
the icebox

and which
you were probably
saving
for breakfast

Forgive me
they were delicious
so sweet
and so cold
—William Carlos Williams

WAYS OF THINKING

REALITY
VERSUS
THAT-WHICH-IS

KOAN ONE

Logic has no meaning.

Chapter 3 is about left-brained thinking. Of course, it is impossible to think exclusively with your left brain, just as you cannot think with only your right hemisphere. We pretend we can separate them only long enough to get an idea of how each functions. Then we have to hurry and put all the parts back together again.

If we could separate the parts of our brains, let's see what we would have. Try out Koan One with other students. When I first encountered the idea that logic is meaningless, it seemed an outrageous thought. Now it seems perfectly sensible. Try it out in small groups as a means of getting started on how your left brain works. Remember, the way to get the most out of these thought experiments is to start by finding ways in which the koan is right.

Here is a hint—which may be only slightly less outrageous:

COROLLARY ONE

Information is purely formal and has no meaning.

(The phrase "purely formal" is your hint—such as it is.) While you are at it, see how many useful applications of the koan your groups can create. Once you catch on, the idea ought to make your thinking more interesting for you, more of a kitten-watching activity.

REFLECTION

As usual, I suggest taking time to do some reflecting in your learning log.

Reality *means "everything you can*
think about." This is not "that-which-is."
No idea can capture "truth" in the
sense of that-which-is.
　　　　　　—Physicist David Bohm

COMMENTARY

Don't read this section until you have done as
much as you can with Koan One on your own.

Proof: Are Cold Plums Nourishing?

If you want to check out your facts, you are supposed to keep your hands
off the investigation. You are not supposed to influence the results. The
"facts" should be untainted by what you wish they would add up to. You
want your systematic, step-by-step left brain to do the arithmetic with no
fudge factors and no doctored results.

The last thing you want is an emotional computer: "Gosh, the answer is
going to come out 4, but I know my controlling self would like it to come
out 5. What the heck. Let's make it 5." Your controlling self says, "Hold on
there, left brain. I'll be the judge of that. Give me 4, like you're supposed to,
and if I want to monkey with the results, I'll decide, not you." If the intellect, your left brain, starts "caring," it will be useless to you. Caring, you
can see, is associated with purpose—which is associated with meaning.
But that is not what the part of your brain that analyzes data is for. It is
designed to put facts with other facts and grind out the results so that you
can interpret them and decide what to do.

This means there are two parts to the process: (1) feeding data into your
left brain and (2) interpreting the printout—that is, data classification and
information processing. In actual practice, these two functions are inseparable. They slip back and forth so smoothly that it seems like just one
thing going on.

For example, it is not really possible to get hold of a pure fact. As you may
have realized while reading chapter 2, every word comes into our vocabulary *charged with feeling.* The metaphoric process is based on our interest,
curiosity, and wonder. "Aha" lies behind every new metaphor. After a
while, of course, we get used to the idea, and it seems commonplace, a
dead metaphor. *Fact* is simply another name for *dead metaphor.* But these
"facts" aren't dead; they are temporary placeholders. As one student put it,
"I'm not sure about all these scientific, 'proven' facts. I wonder if they are
all-the-way-known or just a rest from searching anymore."

Nevertheless, in the face of all this uncertainty, we still seek to prove, to
verify, to validate. How do we decide aspirin is really safe for humans? Is
this movie really well made? Is so-and-so really guilty?

The idea of formal logic is to have a system for checking things out. We
want a process for making sure we don't fool ourselves. A first step is to
make sure all the "facts" are dead, like mathematical numerals, 1, 2, 3. In a

logical proof, any fact that starts breathing has to be konked on the head. One definition of logic is "the theory of valid inference." If I am given certain information, what conclusions can I reasonably draw from it? What makes it a *reasonable* deduction? So logicians set up a procedure, very much as in geometry or poker. Certain rules must be agreed upon; certain limitations must be set. Since logic plays its game with words and sentences, we find it hard to separate the game of logic from ordinary conversation, in which the right brain is fully operable. But using logic is really a matter of knowing that it is a game and what the rules are. To play tennis, you agree to accept the rules, however artificially contrived. That is part of the fun.

So when we seek proof, information cannot be weighted down with desires, expectations, or special angles of seeing. As much as possible, it has to be raw data—meaningless, like a pile of gravel on a river bank. If you perceive the gravel as building material, you have shifted to interpreting.

That is why logic has no meaning. At least it tries hard not to. You and I don't want it to have meaning either. Stripping information of meaning is impossible, but if we know it is impossible, we stand a better chance of getting reasonable results. After all, we do not need proof so much as the chance to improve the odds.

But we do have to be careful to keep in mind that proof is only proof within a predetermined frame of reference. We turn the left brain loose on data, and it does a brilliant job of churning out "answers." But we must never be lulled into thinking that is the end of the story. "It is only with the heart that one can see clearly." Decisions must always be made with the whole mind, both one's nose and one's heart. "We must never let the intellect be master," wrote Einstein. "Imagination is more important than knowledge." Putting the intellect in charge is like turning loose a Rolls Royce on the highway without a driver.

Teacher Robert Kopfstein wrote, "Thinking is a series of approximations, making and testing comparisons—often by the billions." We should never confuse thinking with logic. "The brain works as flexibly as it does precisely because it does not find isolated right answers, but functions happily by sloppy approximations—provided it can get enough approximations." So thinking is a much, much broader process than inspecting results for flaws. We need to be good logicians but we must never let proving take the place of thinking. Computers are always right, but life isn't about being right.

Thinking is organic, cold plums in the icebox.

Knowledge doesn't care.
Wisdom does.

113

LOOKING FOR GOD'S FINGERPRINTS
Evidence and Proof

Someone has argued that you can understand more about the nature of truth by reading a short story than by studying a libraryful of logic books. There is no doubt a point of view from which that idea is right. Perhaps the same can be said of proof.

Following is a story about proof by Nobel Prize winner Isaac Bashevis Singer, in this case proof that there are or are not mysterious forces in the universe. After you finish the story, you will find some ideas for thinking about it and for tying it in with thoughts developing in Thinking about Thinking. *But first simply enjoy it. If you read a well-written story like an assignment, you will destroy it. In fact, to read anything with understanding, anything at all, you have to have a thoroughly good time. Otherwise your mind will reject it. That is why most textbooks work like sleeping pills. If you do engage your mind in the story, you will continue to ponder it for days, months, even years. Delicious, so sweet and so cold.*

WHY THE GEESE SHRIEKED
Isaac Bashevis Singer

In our home there was always talk about spirits of the dead that possess the bodies of the living, souls reincarnated as animals, houses inhabited by hobgoblins, cellars haunted by demons. My father spoke of these things, first of all because he was interested in them, and second because in a big city children so easily go astray. They go everywhere, see everything, read profane books. It is necessary to remind them from time to time that there are still mysterious forces at work in the world.

One day he told us a story that is found in one of the holy books. If I am not mistaken, the author of that book is Rabbi Eliyahu Graidiker, or one of the other Graidiker sages. The story was about a girl possessed by four demons. It was said that they could actually be seen crawling around in her intestines, blowing up her belly, wandering from one part of her body to another, slithering into her legs. The Rabbi of Graidik had exorcised the evil spirits with the blowing of the ram's horn, with incantations, and the incense of magic herbs.

When someone questioned these things, my father became very excited. He argued: "Was then the great Rabbi of Graidik, God forbid, a liar? Are all the rabbis, saints, and sages deceivers, while only atheists speak the truth? Woe is us! How can one be so blind?"

Suddenly the door opened, and a woman entered. She was carrying a basket in which there were two geese. The woman looked frightened. Her matron's wig was tilted to one side. She smiled nervously.

Father never looked at strange women, because it is forbidden by Jewish law, but Mother and we children saw immediately that something had greatly upset our unexpected visitor.

"What is it?" Father asked, at the same time turning his back so as not to look upon her.

"Rabbi, I have a very unusual problem."

"What is it? A woman's problem?"

Had the woman said yes, I would have been sent out of the room immediately. But she answered: "No, it's about these geese."

"What is the matter with them?"

"Dear Rabbi, the geese were slaughtered properly. Then I cut off their heads. I took out the intestines, the livers, all the other organs, but the geese keep shrieking in such a sorrowful voice. . . ."

Upon hearing these words, my father turned pale. A dreadful fear befell me, too. But my mother came from a family of rationalists and was by nature a skeptic.

"Slaughtered geese don't shriek," she said.

"You will hear for yourself," replied the woman.

She took one of the geese and placed it on the table. Then she took out the second goose. The geese were headless, disemboweled—in short, ordinary dead geese. A smile appeared on my mother's lips.

"And *these* geese shriek?"

"You will soon hear."

The woman took one goose and hurled it against the other. At once a shriek was heard. It is not easy to describe that sound. It was like the cackling of a goose, but in such a high, eerie pitch, with such groaning and quaking, that my limbs grew cold. I could actually feel the hairs of my earlocks pricking me. I wanted to run from the room. But where would I run? My throat constricted with fear. Then I, too, screamed and clung to my mother's skirt, like a child of three.

Father forgot that one must avert one's eyes from a woman. He ran to the table. He was no less frightened than I. His red beard trembled. In his blue eyes could be seen a mixture of fear and vindication. For my father this was a sign that not only to the Rabbi of Graidik, but to him, too, omens were sent from heaven. But perhaps this was a sign from the Evil One, from Satan himself?

"What do you say now?" asked the woman.

My mother was no longer smiling. In her eyes there was something like sadness, and also anger.

"I cannot understand what is going on here," she said, with a certain resentment.

"Do you want to hear it again?"

Again the woman threw one goose against the other. And again the dead geese gave forth an uncanny shriek—the shriek of dumb creatures slain by the slaughterer's knife, who yet retain a living force, who still have a reckoning to make with the living, an injustice to avenge. A chill crept over me. I felt as though someone had struck me with all his might.

My father's voice became hoarse. It was broken as though by sobs. "Well, can anyone still doubt that there *is* a Creator?" he asked.

"Rabbi, what shall I do and where shall I go?" The woman began to croon in a mournful singsong. "What has befallen me? Woe is me! What shall I do with them? Perhaps I should run to one of the Wonder Rabbis? Perhaps they were not slaughtered properly? I am afraid to take them home. I wanted to prepare them for the

Sabbath meal, and now, such a calamity! Holy Rabbi, what shall I do? Must I throw them out? Someone said that they must be wrapped in shrouds and buried in a grave. I am a poor woman. Two geese! They cost me a fortune!"

Father did not know what to answer. He glanced at his bookcase. If there was an answer anywhere, it must be there. Suddenly he looked angrily at my mother.

"And what do you say now, eh?"

Mother's face was growing sullen, smaller, sharper. In her eyes could be seen indignation and also something like shame.

"I want to hear it again."

Her words were half pleading, half commanding.

The woman hurled the geese against each other for the third time, and for the third time the shrieks were heard. It occurred to me that such must have been the voice of the sacrificial heifer.

"Woe, woe, and still they blaspheme. . . . It is written that the wicked do not repent even at the very gates of hell." Father had again begun to speak. "They behold the truth with their own eyes, and they continue to deny their Maker. They are dragged into the bottomless pit and they maintain that all is nature, or accident. . . ."

He looked at Mother as if to say: You take after *them*.

For a long time there was silence. Then the woman asked, "Well, did I just imagine it?"

Suddenly my mother laughed. There was something in her laughter that made us all tremble. I knew, by some sixth sense, that Mother was preparing to end the mighty drama that had been enacted before our eyes.

"Did you remove the windpipes?" my mother asked.

"The windpipes? No. . . ."

"Take them out," said my mother, " and the geese will stop shrieking."

My father became angry. "What are you babbling? What has this got to do with windpipes?"

Mother took hold of one of the geese, pushed her slender finger inside the body, and with all her might pulled out the thin tube that led from the neck to the lungs. Then she took the other goose and removed its windpipe also. I stood trembling, aghast at my mother's courage. Her hands had become bloodied. On her face could be seen the wrath of the rationalist whom someone has tried to frighten in broad daylight.

Father's face turned white, calm, a little disappointed. He knew what had happened here: logic, cold logic, was again tearing down faith, mocking it, holding it up to ridicule and scorn.

"Now, if you please, take one goose and hurl it against the other!" commanded my mother.

Everything hung in the balance. If the geese shrieked, Mother would have lost all: her rationalist's daring, her skepticism which she had inherited from her intellectual father. And I? Although I was afraid, I prayed inwardly that the geese *would* shriek, shriek so loud that people in the street would hear and come running.

But alas, the geese were silent, silent as only two dead geese without windpipes can be.

"Bring me a towel!" Mother turned to me.

I ran to get the towel. There were tears in my eyes. Mother wiped her hands on the towel like a surgeon after a difficult operation.

"That's all it was!" she announced victoriously.

"Rabbi, what do you say?" asked the woman.

Father began to cough, to mumble. He fanned himself with his skullcap.

"I have never before heard of such a thing," he said at last.

"Nor have I," echoed the woman.

"Nor have I," said my mother. "But there is always an explanation. Dead geese don't shriek."

"Can I go home now and cook them?" asked the woman.

"Go home and cook them for the Sabbath." Mother pronounced the decision. "Don't be afraid. They won't make a sound in your pot."

"What do you say, Rabbi?"

"Hmm . . . they are kosher," murmured Father. "They can be eaten." He was not really convinced, but he could not now pronounce the geese unclean.

Mother went back to the kitchen. I remained with my father. Suddenly he began to speak to me as though I were an adult. "Your mother takes after your grandfather, the Rabbi of Bilgoray. He is a great scholar, but a cold-blooded rationalist. People warned me before our betrothal. . . ."

And then Father threw up his hands, as if to say: It is too late now to call off the wedding.

LEFT-BRAINED VERSUS RIGHT-BRAINED PROOF

After they read "Why the Geese Shrieked," my students usually discuss it in small groups, some preferring the rabbi's view, others his wife's. It doesn't take long, of course, until they realize that neither side is complete. There is one person in the story who struggles to include both. You will never guess who that is. He examines both positions, the romantic, as it is sometimes labeled, and the rational or reasonable. The argument is not really settled, is it, when the story ends. On one level the mother wins. But does she? Does Singer really think that the rabbi loses by rejecting the "cold-blooded rationalists"? Is anything ever "all-the-way-known"?

Another way to approach this story is to see the two characters as representing essentially right-brained and left-brained thinking and perhaps the third character as including both. Come to think of it, what kind of thinking is represented by the woman who brings the geese to the rabbi? One of the four is a C student.

117

DIALOGUE AND REFLECTION

You will enrich this story if you discuss it in small groups and reflect on it in your learning log. Then reread it and see how much richer it is the second time. If you read it again a year later, you will find it will be even better. That is the secret of how to make events *mean*.

Basically what Mark does is throw
stuff around, then gather it up.
Save the good stuff and toss the rest.
Play again, gather the good
stuff and toss the rest. When all
that gathering and tossing is
finished, he roots through the garbage
and finds the jewels that make the
good stuff shine. The game is in shuffling
the garbage and the good stuff.
If you play your cards right, you
can shine in the end. Mark's manual is a box
full of gold. Just needs polish.

—Eileen Giaquinto, Student

COMMENTARY

Don't read this section until after you have
finished your entry in your learning log.

Spirit in Matter

The wife in "Why the Geese Shrieked" doesn't really *prove* anything by taking the windpipes out of the geese. She shows *how* but not *why*. The rabbi feels temporarily defeated. He too thinks his wife has banished the "mysterious forces" in this instance, even though he will obviously continue looking elsewhere. But he could have stood his ground. The shrieking geese may indeed have served to remind us of the ultimate wonder of matter. A falling petal could have, too. Science may take much of the mystery out of how things work, but it can only increase our wonder that they *do* work. Art puts spirit back into matter, and science need not be thought of as removing it. The wife's approach, taken far enough, will lead to the mysterious forces inside the atom. The rabbi's will sensitize the mind to the "soft sound of wind darting over the face of a pond." Scientists now sound more and more like Chief Seattle. Mystics more and more seek an intense vision of the facts. Laser thinking combines both. To think clearly, both are needed.

We cannot really say *what* caused the geese to shriek. The point is that we must always define the limits we want to place on "proof." How far do we want to go with it? How large a frame will suit our purpose? Why are we seeking this "proof"? What do we want from it? Perhaps the rabbi and his wife could have had a charming conversation if they had used Carl Rogers's suggestion that the wife's meaning of proof had to be clear to the rabbi—and to his wife's satisfaction—before he could make his own argument. After all, being the daughter of the great scholar the Rabbi of Bilgoray, she probably would have agreed that there was some sort of "Creator of the Universe." She may have been simply sifting the evidence from a different angle. Perhaps she would have felt less indignant if the rabbi's view had been made clear. The commonplace, after all, is "just a rest from searching anymore."

PROPAGANDA
The Solar Power Company

KOAN TWO

The sun is a billboard.

Our solar system as a big ad agency? Try that one out in your discussion group.

On Guard

When my students begin thinking about *manipulation, propaganda, prejudice* and *bias, hidden persuaders,* and *logical fallacies,* I like them to consider these concepts in their most general sense. It depletes our vital energy to have to be on guard all the time against unscrupulous con artists. Ads, ads, ads, propaganda, propaganda, propaganda, lies, lies, lies—how tedious, how tiring. How can we actualize ourselves if we have to be constantly on guard? Eternal vigilance is the price of freedom? The end of living and the beginning of survival. There must be some other way.

In fact, there is. There are always alternative possibilities. For example, consider the story of the young student who appeared at the gate of a monastery seeking to study zen.

"You are not ready," said the roshi. "But if you insist, you may work here as a servant until you are ready."

So the student went to work helping in the kitchen, sweeping the courtyard, trimming the candlewicks. But whenever he became absorbed, the roshi would sneak up with a bamboo flail and whack him on the head and shoulders. The student, of course, became extremely nervous and did everything he could to anticipate the roshi's next attack. The game went on for several weeks, but the student was never able to outwit the master. He became a nervous wreck.

Finally, one afternoon the roshi found the student trimming wicks in a back hallway. Again he crept up and whacked the student with the flail. But this time the student continued his work as if nothing had happened, neither flinching nor trying to ward off the blow. He was now ready to begin his studies.*

The sun as a big propaganda machine? Let's define our terms. *Propaganda,* we find, is from the same root that gives us *propagate.* Aha: To reproduce itself, to raise or to breed, to transmit by reproduction; then, by extension, to spread *ideas,* even to transmit or extend *light.* So: Any widespread, systematic, deliberate indoctrination or plan. (Deception or distortion are recent narrowings of the more general meaning.) Let all these meanings *together* be your frame of reference when you think about life beating us with its bamboo flail.

---

*One of my students said the zen student's brain was probably numb from all those blows.

DIALOGUE AND REFLECTION

With that background, begin exploring Koan Two with your group. You will have to redefine in a more general sense what an *advertisement* is, as well as a *billboard—manipulation, bias,* and *prejudice,* too.

See what ideas your group can generate to support the statement that the sun is a billboard. Find some positive implications. "There's a sun show every second." Find some ways to be eternally vigilant and to go about your business of actualizing yourself both at the same time.

Reflect on all this in your learning log.

COMMENTARY

Don't read this until you have finished your entry
in your learning log.

Baby Fat Is a Subliminal Ad

Let's see. The sun as an ad for itself, as propaganda for its own continued existence? And if it is propaganda, then does it have to be on purpose, deliberate? Yes. If I am on purpose, if I am deliberate, then my solar system has to be, too, since it is an extension of me and I of it, all things being connected. The sun has my number; the sun punches my buttons. And vice versa. We are trying to indoctrinate each other. I have a solar complex. Could this be love?

While on this subject, one student, John Shanahan, commented that the sun is the source of all information. Many students couldn't see that, so we took ten minutes out for those who could to explain it to the rest. That worked out fine. Students are good explainers. Out of the discussion came the idea that we (all organisms and all matter) are the sun's "children." We are little "suns," little furnaces. Matter has translated solar energy into a vast array of forms. We are all metaphors for the sun. We would all go poof were it not for the energy hologram of the solar system. It is a system. That is the key. It is on purpose and certainly widespread, isn't it?

As to its being manipulative, one student called the sun "the big pusher." We are addicted to it, hooked. Thus, we don't have to think of advertising, manipulation, prejudice, propaganda as negative terms. They can be seen as perfectly natural and normal aspects of a universe that intends itself. Philosopher Alan Watts argued that if we are intelligent—and he thought that was not too outrageous an idea—then the universe is intelligent. Whatever you find in a system represents the whole system. That is, a footprint isn't just a footprint; it is evidence of the person and the entire surrounding support system, which takes up the whole universe. Thus, manipulation ultimately is the universe manipulating itself. If you get conned, you did it to yourself. More on that in a few pages.

The point is that the healthy approach to propaganda and persuasive devices is to realize that in themselves they are neither good nor bad. Or, you can look at them as biologically normal interplay of the parts of the universal organism. There is a knack for playing the game wisely. You wouldn't accuse a baby of duplicity for being cuddly or for giggling when you tickle it, would you? But one could argue that the little con artists do this just so you will be willing to put up with their puking and dirty diapers, give them some of your food and maybe some breast milk. Advertising, broadly defined, is perfectly natural in a universe that intends itself. Certainly there will be a yin part to every yang, de-structuring, destruction. All things are connected, as you will see if you trace your belly button to its ultimate source. And as Robert Frost noted, a good thinker wants to get beyond pro and con:

> Having ideas that are neither pro nor con is the happy thing. Get up there high enough and the differences . . . become only the two legs of a body. . . . Democracy monarchy; puritanism paganism; form content; conservatism radicalism; systole diastole; rustic urbane; literary colloquial; work play. I should think too much of myself to let any teacher fool me into taking sides on any of those oppositions. . . . I have wanted to find ways to transcend the strife method. I have found some.

Looking at it broadly, we can see that flowers do advertise. Bees are the target group and apparently we humans. Urine scent on a post is an ad pitched to other dogs. Tracing them back to their sources, we can see that both are ads for the sun. After all, the sun's rays are the source of all that we can see or contemplate. Once a thing exists, it has to have its own bias— something to hold it together. Any baby through its genetic imprint, its DNA, has made infinite prejudgments about what is worth noticing, what colors of the spectrum to admit to the brain, what to watch out for, what to respond to. It is a totally prejudiced organism. You can play with whether the baby is a bigot or not. It is and it isn't. So *prejudice* in its extended sense is not a nasty word; it depends on what you do with it. I have always been prejudiced for me; a quartz crystal has a bias for itself, the atom for itself. Anything that exists is a machine full of bias. So let's stop maligning the ad agents—at least not on that basis. Bias is simply your frame of reference— or frame of preference, as one student wrote.

123

Billboards? If we accept that we do deliberately promote ourselves—we wouldn't think much of anyone who didn't—and accept that when we open our mouths our utterances are an ad for ourselves, and further, that we are totally prejudiced for our own metaphor, our blueprint, for the planet, then aren't we all, willy-nilly, Archie Bunkers? We all know someone who loves to rub our noses in the prejudice of any of our assumptions. We should thank these cynics. If I can't see these natural prejudgments in myself, then I am in trouble; I am indeed an Archie Bunker. I have to see that my assurance is blind ignorance. All I have to work with are approximations, a door ajar to all conclusions. In fact there can be no conclusions, ever, only working hypotheses. Working hypotheses.

We have to use propaganda. We have to promote ourselves. We have to take our share of the available food and shelter and sex. Otherwise we will perish. When we see flowers trying to manipulate us, when we see ad agents, realtors, politicians, prophets with designs on us, we don't have to feel paranoid. We use the same strategies, the same resources, ourselves. Bunkerism, bigotry, may simply be a good thing gone bad. It is a matter of balance, keeping the yin yang halves equal. For example, take a minute to find the normal and natural source of each of the Seven Deadly Sins:

Pride	Gluttony
Covetousness	Envy
Lust	Sloth - laziness
Anger	

You can see that with each one we simply get a little carried away. We forget why we are doing these things in the first place and we lose our way. We haven't been using our neocortex very long, so it is not surprising if we get confused and put the emphasis in the wrong place. We all want the best for ourselves, but we have problems defining "best."

TIME OUT

Assumptions

"What is the meaning of fate, Mulla?"
"Assumptions."
"In what way?"
"You assume things are going to go well, and they don't—that you call bad luck. You assume things are going to go badly and they don't—that you call good luck. You assume that certain things are going to happen or not happen—and you so lack intuition that you don't know what is going to happen. You assume that the future is unknown.
"When you are caught out—you call that Fate."
                                                      —Indries Shah

ADVERTISEMENTS
Where Have All the Poets Gone?

KOAN THREE

Magazines are the common people's
art galleries.

Bring a magazine to class. Beforehand, select one ad and become an art expert on it. You can use the same approach as you used for the mandalas you created and examined in chapter 1.

An ad is a mandala for the ad agency. What are the people like who created the one you selected?

First, see what is there physically on the page: use of space and color, arrangement of images, and so on. Is the ad right brained (metaphoric, spontaneous), left brained (logical, deliberate), or a combination?

Then, as much as you are able, see what you think are likely to be the agency's values, needs, aspirations. Their attitudes toward you? Philosophy of life? Should they seek professional help? Do you enjoy their art? Does the ad persuade you? What kinds of ads do persuade you?

DIALOGUE AND REFLECTION

In your small group show the others your ad and describe what you noticed. What else do they notice?

In your large group discuss ads in general, what they are supposed to do, and how successful they are at it. How would Sister Corita view them ("Fly the friendly skies")? Would you rather there were no ads? Are they fun? Are they good for your spirit? Would you reform them? Would that help?

Reflect on persuasion and ads in your learning log.

ADVERTISEMENTS, PART TWO
Are the Drinks Watered?

KOAN FOUR

The easiest person to con is the con artist.

Does conscious knowledge of what the hidden persuaders are protect us from buying a lemon? We will get to some antidotes to ad poison shortly, probably not the ones you might have expected, but first let's look at the ads you analyzed in your last investigation from another angle. You should have the magazine you used on hand for backup. The present investigation is aimed at bringing persuasive devices to your conscious awareness, if they are not already there. If you grew up with TV, you are already saturated with every device the marketing researchers have up their sleeves. Part of you, probably your right brain, knows very well what has been going on. Now let's bring it up on your computer screen.

Work in small groups on the following list of persuasive devices compressed and classified by linguist Karl Staubach of Diablo Valley College, Pleasant Hill, California. The brackets indicate my additions. Spend just enough time on each item to be sure that everyone in your group knows what it means. If at all possible cite at least one example from an ad to illustrate each persuasive device.

This should be a cheerful activity. I would not want you to have to memorize the devices or be tested on them—unless you plan to write ads some day.

PERSUASIVE DEVICES
USED IN
ADVERTISING AND PROPAGANDA

Traditional: The Big Lie, Card-Stacking, Name-Calling, Testimonial, Transfer, Plain Folks, Bandwagon, Something-for-Nothing, The Broom (generalities)

Appeals to Sex, Appetite, Snobbery, Pity, Patriotism, Competition, Wit

Exploitation of Children, Dumb Animals, Popular Movements, Ethnicity

Depth Approach: Preying on the Subconscious*

Imagery—Role Models, Heroes and Heroines, Secret Fears and Desires

Concerns—Family, Intimacy versus Isolation, Health versus Death, Success versus Failure, Fulfillment versus Inadequacy

Subliminals—Fast-Cutting, Superimposition, Embedding, Packaging

Legitimate [Considered Fair Practices]

Humor

Expertise

Class [Quality] (Artwork, Space, *No* Prices)

Bias Words (Mostly in Politics): Words and phrases are rated positive or negative relative to the idea being promoted, usually on a scale of plus twenty to minus twenty; the "pitch" is then carefully rewritten to give maximum scores to the promotion and minimum scores to any opposition.

DIALOGUE AND REFLECTION

When you have finished, speculate in your large group on the significance of your investigation and the possible use you could make of it. Then reflect in your learning log.

---

*Triggered by symbols and images of three types: physical, emotional, or intellectual; developed for marketing by "motivational research"; effective symbolic images are those already embedded in every citizen's subconscious through acculturation during childhood; similar images appear in dreams, myths, popular art, and literature.

COMMENTARY

Complete your entry in your learning log before
reading this section.

Antidote to Ads
Communication Is Perception

If you are like my students, the list of persuasive devices on the preceding
page holds few surprises for you. You either knew them consciously or
recognized them as soon as they were pointed out to you. But all these persuaders are one aspect of an infinite medium. The environment itself is
one all-inclusive ad.

The medium is the message? The medium is also the massage, as Marshall McLuhan observed. If you grew up in America, you have been
kneaded by this culture, this society, day and night all these years. It is the
atmosphere you live in, and we must include the land, too, in this persuasion, and the weather and the latitude and longitude. That is why I wanted
you to start big, with the sun itself. If you live in a medium, it will massage
you. You will feed back to it. The whole structure is one big ad, but it
is mutual. You influence your medium. Your behavior influences and
changes me.

There is so much going on that trying to protect ourselves seems futile.
In fact my students usually spend part of a class session demolishing conventional ideas of security and insurance. It is easy to demonstrate that
both are illusions. Even if we know the names of the obvious persuaders,
even when we can spot them quickly, what about such persuaders as
charm? A good con artist could get us to buy that clunk without using any
of the conventional devices. How about body language, the way the per-
suader crosses his or her legs, tone of voice, eye movement, interest in *you*,
time spent with you? Charm, Albert Camus once observed, is "getting the
answer yes without asking a clear question."

If such con artists are really artistic, you will want to give them things
without even being asked. Ultimately no persuasion is needed. "Greater
love hath no man than this, that he will give up his life for a friend." Such
artists will make you feel that they are your friend. The best artist will
actually *be* your friend and will cease to be a con artist.

If you follow this line of thought to its ultimate end, you *must* end up
treating everyone and everything as a friend, indeed as your other self
(alter ego), or you must treat everything outside your skin—even inside
your skin—as a threat, as a likely enemy. Most people tend to line up with
one or the other attitude. The ones who are suspicious end up testing even

their friends and of course always find their friends wanting. Since behavior can always be interpreted both ways, none of us can withstand such scrutiny.

The villain, your own sweet self. Here is a key to this problem of being duped. In his book *Management,* Peter F. Drucker points out that

Communication is perception.

It is the receiver who communicates. The receiver, you. The ad agency utters. But unless there is an intelligence that perceives, sees, that utterance, it is just meaningless noise. What we see, Drucker adds, is not logic; what we see is experience, our experience. We see right-brained configurations, patterns that we recognize. If there is no place in your data bank that fits the ad agent's configuration, nothing will happen inside you and you won't buy that sugar-free cola. You won't even notice that he said anything.

So here is the point:

You yourself do the selling, not the ad.

You will see only what your bias system is capable of seeing, only what is within your range of response. The message is that if we want to change the effect ads have on us, we have to change the frequency we are tuned to, find other, more healthful channels. Change your dial and you alter the game. It is what is inside, physically, emotionally, conceptually—all our habit structures—that counts.

The past few pages have been devoted to altering your perception of what an ad is (our environment), who is responsible for its effectiveness (the buyer), and what we expect from ads (data to help us actualize ourselves). A specific solution for a healthful relationship to ads follows the next investigation.

Oh, yes. The reason con artists are the easiest persons to con is that they want something for nothing themselves. That is virtually the definition of a con artist. The greed they expect to tap in you, shortcuts to wealth and happiness, is inside themselves. This means their mammalian desires will dominate their thinking when a pretty package comes their way. They are primed to have their buttons punched.

Computers are always right,
but life isn't about being right.
—Steve Chambers, Student

LOGICAL FALLACIES

It Won't Compute

What does it profit a man if he gain the whole world and lose his raccoon coat?
Thinking about Thinking endorses the idea that you know a lot more about what is
going on than you can put into words. As Julian Jaynes points out (chapter 2), the right
side of your bicameral brain doesn't have a voice. So you may well "know" that a sales
pitch or a campaign promise has flaws, but you may not be able to get that knowledge
into your conscious awareness—except through dreams and metaphors. Or you may
be able to say exactly where an argument breaks down and still buy that swampland.
And you may be right. There is much, much more than logic going on in any transac-
tion, as you will see in the story that follows.

Don't read "Love Is a Fallacy" as a lesson. If there are any lessons in it, they will
emerge because of your involvement, not because you force a lesson onto the story. A
good story lingers in your mind whether you want it to or not and alters your reality. In
fact, the way to study chemistry is to turn it into a good story.

LOVE IS A FALLACY

Max Shulman

Cool was I and logical. Keen, calculating, perspicacious, acute and astute—I was
all of these. My brain was as powerful as a dynamo, as precise as a chemist's
scales, as penetrating as a scalpel. And—think of it!—I was only eighteen.

It is not often that one so young has such a giant intellect. Take, for example,
Petey Burch, my roommate at the University of Minnesota. Same age, same background, but dumb as an ox. A nice enough fellow, you understand, but nothing
upstairs. Emotional type. Unstable. Impressionable. Worst of all, a faddist. Fads, I
submit, are the very negation of reason. To be swept up in every new craze that
comes along, to surrender yourself to idiocy just because everybody else is doing
it—this, to me, is the acme of mindlessness. Not, however, to Petey.

One afternoon I found Petey lying on his bed with an expression of such distress
on his face that I immediately diagnosed appendicitis. "Don't move," I said. "Don't
take a laxative. I'll get a doctor."

"Raccoon," he mumbled thickly.

"Raccoon?" I said, pausing in my flight.

"I want a raccoon coat," he wailed.

I perceived that his trouble was not physical, but mental. "Why do you want a raccoon coat?"

"I should have known it," he cried, pounding his temples. "I should have known
they'd come back when the Charleston came back. Like a fool I spent all my money
for textbooks, and now I can't get a raccoon coat."

"Can you mean," I said incredulously, "that people are actually wearing raccoon
coats again?"

131

"All the Big Men on Campus are wearing them. Where've you been?"

"In the library," I said, naming a place not frequented by Big Men on Campus.

He leaped from the bed and paced the room. "I've got to have a raccoon coat," he said passionately. "I've got to!"

"Petey, why? Look at it rationally. Raccoon coats are unsanitary. They shed. They smell bad. They weigh too much. They're unsightly. They—"

"You don't understand," he interrupted impatiently. "It's the thing to do. Don't you want to be in the swim?"

"No," I said truthfully.

"Well, I do," he declared. "I'd give anything for a raccoon coat. Anything!"

My brain, that precision instrument, slipped into high gear. "Anything?" I asked, looking at him narrowly.

"Anything," he affirmed in ringing tones.

I stroked my chin thoughtfully. It so happened that I knew where to get my hands on a raccoon coat. My father had had one in his undergraduate days; it lay now in a trunk in the attic back home. It also happened that Petey had something I wanted. He didn't *have* it exactly, but at least he had first rights on it. I refer to his girl, Polly Espy.

I had long coveted Polly Espy. Let me emphasize that my desire for this young woman was not emotional in nature. She was, to be sure, a girl who excited the emotions, but I was not one to let my heart rule my head. I wanted Polly for a shrewdly calculated, entirely cerebral reason.

I was a freshman in law school. In a few years I would be out in practice. I was well aware of the importance of the right kind of wife in furthering a lawyer's career. The successful lawyers I had observed were, almost without exception, married to beautiful, gracious, intelligent women. With one omission, Polly fitted these specifications perfectly.

Beautiful she was. She was not yet of pin-up proportions, but I felt sure that time would supply the lack. She already had the makings.

Gracious she was. By gracious I mean full of graces. She had an erectness of carriage, an ease of bearing, a poise that clearly indicated the best of breeding. At table her manners were exquisite. I had seen her at the Kozy Kampus Korner eating the specialty of the house—a sandwich that contained scraps of pot roast, gravy, chopped nuts, and a dipper of sauerkraut—without even getting her fingers moist.

Intelligent she was not. In fact, she veered in the opposite direction. But I believed that under my guidance she would smarten up. At any rate, it was worth a try. It is, after all, easier to make a beautiful dumb girl smart than to make an ugly smart girl beautiful.

"Petey," I said, "are you in love with Polly Espy?"

"I think she's a keen kid," he replied, "but I don't know if you'd call it love. Why?"

"Do you," I asked, "have any kind of formal arrangement with her? I mean are you going steady or anything like that?"

"No. We see each other quite a bit, but we both have other dates. Why?"

"Is there," I asked, "any other man for whom she has a particular fondness?"

"Not that I know of. Why?"

I nodded with satisfaction. "In other words, if you were out of the picture, the field would be open. Is that right?"

"I guess so. What are you getting at?"

"Nothing, nothing," I said innocently, and took my suitcase out of the closet.

"Where are you going?" asked Petey.

"Home for the weekend." I threw a few things into the bag.

"Listen," he said, clutching my arm eagerly, "while you're home, you couldn't get some money from your old man, could you, and lend it to me so I can buy a raccoon coat?"

"I may do better than that," I said with a mysterious wink and closed my bag and left.

"Look," I said to Petey when I got back Monday morning. I threw open the suitcase and revealed the huge, hairy, gamy object that my father had worn in his Stutz Bearcat in 1925.

"Holy Toledo!" said Petey reverently. He plunged his hands into the raccoon coat and then his face. "Holy Toledo!" he repeated fifteen or twenty times.

"Would you like it?" I asked.

"Oh yes!" he cried, clutching the greasy pelt to him. Then a canny look came into his eyes. "What do you want for it?"

"Your girl," I said, mincing no words.

"Polly?" he said in a horrified whisper. "You want Polly?"

"That's right."

He flung the coat from him. "Never," he said stoutly.

I shrugged. "Okay. If you don't want to be in the swim, I guess it's your business."

I sat down in a chair and pretended to read a book, but out of the corner of my eye I kept watching Petey. He was a torn man. First he looked at the coat with the expression of a waif at a bakery window. Then he turned away and set his jaw resolutely. Then he looked back at the coat, with even more longing in his face. Then he turned away, but with not so much resolution this time. Back and forth his head swiveled, desire waxing, resolution waning. Finally he didn't turn away at all; he just stood and stared with mad lust at the coat.

"It isn't as though I was in love with Polly," he said thickly. "Or going steady or anything like that."

"That's right," I murmured.

"What's Polly to me, or me to Polly?"

"Not a thing," said I.

"It's just been a casual kick—just a few laughs, that's all."

"Try on the coat," said I.

He complied. The coat bunched high over his ears and dropped all the way down to his shoe tops. He looked like a mound of dead raccoons. "Fits fine," he said happily.

I rose from my chair. "Is it a deal?" I asked, extending my hand.

He swallowed. "It's a deal," he said and shook my hand.

I had my first date with Polly the following evening. This was in the nature of a survey; I wanted to find out just how much work I had to do to get her mind up to the standard I required. I took her first to dinner. "Gee, that was a delish dinner," she said as we left the restaurant. Then I took her to a movie. "Gee, that was a marvy movie," she said as we left the theater. And then I took her home. "Gee, I had a sensaysh time," she said as she bade me good night.

I went back to my room with a heavy heart. I had gravely underestimated the size of my task. This girl's lack of information was terrifying. Nor would it be enough merely to supply her with information. First she had to be taught to *think*. This loomed as a project of no small dimensions, and at first I was tempted to give her back to Petey. But then I got to thinking about her abundant physical charms and about the way she entered a room and the way she handled a knife and fork, and I decided to make an effort.

I went about it, as in all things, systematically. I gave her a course in logic. It happened that I, as a law student, was taking a course in logic myself, so I had all the facts at my finger tips. "Polly," I said to her when I picked her up on our next date, "tonight we are going over to the Knoll and talk."

"Oo, terrif," she replied. One thing I will say for this girl: you would go far to find another so agreeable.

We went to the Knoll, the campus trysting place, and we sat down under an old oak, and she looked at me expectantly. "What are we going to talk about?" she asked.

"Logic."

She thought this over for a minute and decided she liked it. "Magnif," she said.

"Logic," I said, clearing my throat, "is the science of thinking. Before we can think correctly, we must first learn to recognize the common fallacies of logic. These we will take up tonight."

"Wow-dow!" she cried, clapping her hands delightedly.

I winced, but went bravely on. "First let us examine the fallacy called Dicto Simpliciter."

"By all means," she urged, batting her lashes eagerly.

"Dicto Simpliciter means an argument based on an unqualified generalization. For example: Exercise is good. Therefore everybody should exercise."

"I agree," said Polly earnestly. "I mean exercise is wonderful. I mean it builds the body and everything."

"Polly," I said gently, "the argument is a fallacy. *Exercise is good* is an unqualified generalization. For instance, if you have heart disease, exercise is bad, not good. Many people are ordered by their doctors *not* to exercise. You must *qualify* the generalization. You must say exercise is *usually* good, or exercise is good *for most people*. Otherwise you have committed a Dicto Simpliciter. Do you see?"

"No," she confessed. "But this is marvy. Do more! Do more!"

"It will be better if you stop tugging at my sleeve, " I told her, and when she desisted, I continued. "Next we take up a fallacy called Hasty Generalization. Listen carefully: You can't speak French. I can't speak French. Petey Burch can't speak French. I must therefore conclude that nobody at the University of Minnesota can speak French."

"Really?" said Polly, amazed. "*Nobody?*"

I hid my exasperation. "Polly, it's a fallacy. The generalization is reached too hastily. There are too few instances to support such a conclusion."

"Know any more fallacies?" she asked breathlessly. "This is more fun than dancing even."

I fought off a wave of despair. I was getting nowhere with this girl, absolutely nowhere. Still, I am nothing if not persistent. I continued. "Next comes Post Hoc. Listen to this: Let's not take Bill on our picnic. Every time we take him out with us, it rains."

"I know somebody just like that," she exclaimed. "A girl back home—Eula Becker, her name is. It never fails. Every single time we take her on a picnic—"

"Polly," I said sharply, "it's a fallacy. Eula Becker doesn't *cause* the rain. She had no connection with the rain. You are guilty of Post Hoc if you blame Eula Becker."

"I'll never do it again," she promised contritely. "Are you mad at me?"

I sighed deeply. "No, Polly, I'm not mad."

"Then tell me some more fallacies."

"All right. Let's try Contradictory Premises."

"Yes, let's," she chirped, blinking her eyes happily.

I frowned, but plunged ahead. "Here's an example of Contradictory Premises: If God can do anything, can He make a stone so heavy that He won't be able to lift it?"

"Of course," she replied promptly.

"But if He can do anything, He can lift the stone," I pointed out.

"Yeah," she said thoughtfully. "Well, then I guess He can't make the stone."

"But He can do anything," I reminded her.

She scratched her pretty, empty head. "I'm all confused," she admitted.

"Of course you are. Because when the premises of an argument contradict each other, there can be no argument. If there is an irresistible force, there can be no immovable object. If there is an immovable object, there can be no irresistible force. Get it?"

"Tell me some more of this keen stuff," she said eagerly.

I consulted my watch. "I think we'd better call it a night. I'll take you home now, and you go over all the things you've learned. We'll have another session tomorrow night."

I deposited her at the girls' dormitory, where she assured me that she had had a perfectly terrif evening, and I went glumly home to my room. Petey lay snoring in his bed, the raccoon coat huddled like a great hairy beast at his feet. For a moment I considered waking him and telling him that he could have his girl back. It seemed clear that my project was doomed to failure. The girl simply had a logic-proof head.

But then I reconsidered. I had wasted one evening; I might as well waste another. Who knew? Maybe somewhere in the extinct crater of her mind, a few embers still smoldered. Maybe somehow I could fan them into flame. Admittedly it was not a prospect fraught with hope, but I decided to give it one more try.

Seated under the oak the next evening I said, "Our first fallacy tonight is called Ad Misericordiam."

She quivered with delight.

"Listen closely," I said. "A man applies for a job. When the boss asks him what his qualifications are, he replies that he has a wife and six children at home, the wife is a helpless cripple, the children have nothing to eat, no clothes to wear, no shoes on their feet, there are no beds in the house, no coal in the cellar, and winter is coming."

A tear rolled down each of Polly's pink cheeks. "Oh, this is awful, awful," she sobbed.

"Yes, it's awful," I agreed, "but it's no argument. The man never answered the boss's question about his qualifications. Instead he appealed to the boss's sympathy. He committed the fallacy of Ad Misericordiam. Do you understand?"

"Have you got a handkerchief?" she blubbered.

I handed her a handkerchief and tried to keep from screaming while she wiped her eyes. "Next," I said in a carefully controlled tone, "we will discuss False Analogy. Here is an example: Students should be allowed to look at their textbooks during examinations. After all, surgeons have X-rays to guide them during an operation, lawyers have briefs to guide them during a trial, carpenters have blueprints to guide them when they are building a house. Why, then, shouldn't students be allowed to look at their textbooks during an examination?"

"There now," she said enthusiastically, "is the most marvy idea I've heard in years."

"Polly," I said testily, "the argument is all wrong. Doctors, lawyers, and carpenters aren't taking a test to see how much they have learned, but students are. The situations are altogether different, and you can't make an analogy between them."

"I still think it's a good idea," said Polly.

"Nuts," I muttered. Doggedly I pressed on. "Next we'll try Hypothesis Contrary to Fact."

"Sounds yummy," was Polly's reaction.

"Listen: If Madame Curie had not happened to leave a photographic plate in a drawer with a chunk of pitchblende, the world today would not know about radium."

"True, true," said Polly, nodding her head. "Did you see the movie? Oh, it just knocked me out. That Walter Pidgeon is so dreamy. I mean he fractures me."

"If you can forget Mr. Pidgeon for a moment," I said coldly, "I would like to point out that the statement is a fallacy. Maybe Madame Curie would have discovered radium at some later date. Maybe somebody else would have discovered it. Maybe any number of things would have happened. You can't start with a hypothesis that is not true and then draw any supportable conclusions from it."

"They ought to put Walter Pidgeon in more pictures," said Polly. "I hardly ever see him any more."

One more chance, I decided. But just one more. There is a limit to what flesh and blood can bear. "The next fallacy is called Poisoning the Well."

"How cute!" she gurgled.

"Two men are having a debate. The first one gets up and says, 'My opponent is a notorious liar. You can't believe a word that he is going to say.' . . . Now, Polly, think. Think hard. What's wrong?"

I watched her closely as she knit her creamy brow in concentration. Suddenly a glimmer of intelligence—the first I had seen—came into her eyes. "It's not fair," she said with indignation. "It's not a bit fair. What chance has the second man got if the first man calls him a liar before he even begins talking?"

"Right!" I cried exultantly. "One hundred percent right. It's not fair. The first man has *poisoned the well* before anybody could drink from it. He has hamstrung his opponent before he could even start. . . . Polly, I'm proud of you."

"Pshaw," she murmured, blushing with pleasure.

"You see, my dear, these things aren't so hard. All you have to do is concentrate. Think—examine—evaluate. Come now, let's review everything we have learned."

"Fire away," she said with an airy wave of her hand.

Heartened by the knowledge that Polly was not altogether a cretin, I began a long, patient review of all I had told her. Over and over and over again I cited instances, pointed out flaws, kept hammering away without letup. It was like digging a tunnel. At first everything was work, sweat, and darkness. I had no idea when I would reach the light, or even *if* I would. But I persisted. I pounded and clawed and scraped, and finally I was rewarded. I saw a chink of light. And then the chink got bigger and the sun came pouring in and all was bright.

Five grueling nights this took, but it was worth it. I had made a logician out of Polly; I had taught her to think. My job was done. She was worthy of me at last. She was a fit wife for me, a proper hostess for my many mansions, a suitable mother for my well-heeled children.

It must not be thought that I was without love for this girl. Quite the contrary. Just as Pygmalion loved the perfect woman he had fashioned, so I loved mine. I determined to acquaint her with my feelings at our very next meeting. The time had come to change our relationship from academic to romantic.

"Polly," I said when next we sat beneath our oak, "tonight we will not discuss fallacies."

"Aw, gee," she said, disappointed.

"My dear," I said, favoring her with a smile, "we have now spent five evenings together. We have gotten along splendidly. It is clear that we are well matched."

"Hasty Generalization," said Polly brightly.

"I beg your pardon," said I.

"Hasty Generalization," she repeated. "How can you say that we are well matched on the basis of only five dates?"

I chuckled with amusement. The dear child had learned her lessons well. "My dear," I said, patting her hand in a tolerant manner, "five dates is plenty. After all, you don't have to eat a whole cake to know that it's good."

"False Analogy," said Polly promptly. "I'm not a cake. I'm a girl."

I chuckled with somewhat less amusement. The dear child had learned her lessons perhaps too well. I decided to change tactics. Obviously the best approach was a simple, strong, direct declaration of love. I paused for a moment while my massive brain chose the proper words. Then I began:

"Polly, I love you. You are the whole world to me, and the moon and the stars and the constellations of outer space. Please, my darling, say that you will go steady with me, for if you will not, life will be meaningless. I will languish. I will refuse my meals. I will wander the face of the earth, a shambling, hollow-eyed hulk."

There, I thought, folding my arms, that ought to do it.

"Ad Misericordiam," said Polly.

I ground my teeth. I was not Pygmalion; I was Frankenstein, and my monster had me by the throat. Frantically I fought back the tide of panic surging through me. At all costs I had to keep cool.

"Well, Polly," I said, forcing a smile, "you certainly have learned your fallacies."

"You're darn right," she said with a vigorous nod.

"And who taught them to you, Polly?"

"You did."

"That's right. So you do owe me something, don't you, my dear? If I hadn't come along you never would have learned about fallacies."

"Hypothesis Contrary to Fact," she said instantly.

I dashed perspiration from my brow. "Polly," I croaked, "you mustn't take all these things so literally. I mean this is just classroom stuff. You know that the things you learn in school don't have anything to do with life."

"Dicto Simpliciter," she said, wagging her finger at me playfully.

That did it. I leaped to my feet, bellowing like a bull. "Will you or will you not go steady with me?"

"I will not," she replied.

"Why not?" I demanded.

"Because this afternoon I promised Petey Burch that I would go steady with him."

I reeled back, overcome with the infamy of it. After he promised, after he made a deal, after he shook my hand! "The rat!" I shrieked, kicking up great chunks of turf. "You can't go with him, Polly. He's a liar. He's a cheat. He's a rat."

"Poisoning the Well," said Polly, "and stop shouting. I think shouting must be a fallacy too."

With an immense effort of will, I modulated my voice. "All right," I said. "You're a logician. Let's look at this thing logically. How could you choose Petey Burch over me? Look at me—a brilliant student, a tremendous intellectual, a man with an assured future. Look at Petey—a knothead, a jitterbug, a guy who'll never know where his next meal is coming from. Can you give me one logical reason why you should go steady with Petey Burch?"

"I certainly can," declared Polly. "He's got a raccoon coat."

DIALOGUE AND REFLECTION

Discuss "Love Is a Fallacy" in small groups. In the context of a critical thinking course, my students usually want to talk about the role of logic in ordinary life, the importance of rational decisions. Can we apply rules of logic in friendship, love, choice of work, and so on? How does it fit in? When?

But go in whatever direction interests your group. Then pool your thoughts in your large group, and later reflect in your learning log.

COMMENTARY

Don't read this until you have finished your entry
in your log.

TEGWAR: A Vaccine Against Ads

In Mark Harris's *Bang the Drum Slowly,* a couple of professional ball players
pass the time playing a card game called TEGWAR in the lobby of their
hotel. People gather around to watch. They get curious and want to join
in. Although they have a hard time figuring out the rules—which seem
to keep changing all the time—they never think to ask what TEGWAR
means. It means "The Exciting Game Without Any Rules." In Harris's
book TEGWAR comes to stand for the life game, which apparently did not
come with a manual.

From some viewpoints, it did come with a rule book. When someone
asked Louis Armstrong to explain jazz he said: "If you have to ask, don't
mess with it." The hustler gets conned because he thinks life can be lived
by sleight of hand. Careful people think the way to play the game is to take
out insurance. Others turn to packaged formulas, doctrines, strategies.
It appears that all such approaches are doomed.* It isn't in any book.
Momentary give-and-take is too swift for deliberation. We cannot dance
with the left brain. TEGWAR is riding a bicycle. Quantum physicist
Richard Feynman says, "You see, one thing is, I can live with doubt and
uncertainty and not knowing. I think it's much more interesting to live not
knowing than to have answers which might be wrong. I have approximate
answers and possible beliefs and different degrees of certainty about different things." Someone else said that an artist is not someone who
answers life's questions but someone who accepts them. One way to play
TEGWAR is to accept TEGWAR.

But we cannot say intellectually, "I will accept life's conditions, whatever
they are," and that's that. We cannot gain balance from a book, but we can
set up situations in which "going with the flow" is more likely. We can see,
as numerous anecdotes in *Thinking about Thinking* demonstrate, that
autonomy and spontaneity involve an integrated organism: lymph nodes,
sensors, reptile, mammal, and new brains all working in harmony, right
and left hemispheres in a user-friendly atmosphere, the organism in tune
with its support system, the universe. This would be playing life's game,
becoming one with it, so that ultimately, as in William Butler Yeats's
phrase, we cannot "know the dancer from the dance."

---

*Unless you are surprised by joy. You may get so good at sleight of hand that it ceases being
sleight of hand.

Thus, the con artist is not "out there." The con artist is within. Happiness cannot be pursued directly; it can only be glimpsed out of the corner of the eye, when we are absorbed in other things. When we allow ourselves to become so involved in our work, any work, that our spirit is in all that we do, we have gotten beyond what Robert Frost called the strife method.

You have observed such states of being in your own life. As a child you became so absorbed in play that you lost all sense of time and space. As an adult you have experienced it while you were fixing a car or riding a motorcycle or dancing—just the right mix of body and spirit so that you suspended the external world and entered totally into that moment. Peaks of sexual feeling are another example. When you are in such an altered state of consciousness, persuasive devices don't stand a chance. So one way to protect ourselves from unscrupulous ad agents and politicians is to choose another game, to choose not to play the con game, to turn to TEGWAR instead. After all, it's the only real game in town, all the rest being cheap substitutes.

In his book *Working*, Studs Terkle interviewed hundreds of people in the "work force." Their biggest complaint? Their jobs weren't big enough to fit their spirits. But most jobs can be big enough, for we do see weavers, assembly–line workers, garbage collectors, who have allowed themselves to enter into their work and become one with it. They play with a full deck. As we all know only too well, anything less is agony.

Consider the idea, then, that the way to play TEGWAR is, in the words of Don Juan, to choose a path with a heart:

> A diablero is a diablero, and a warrior is a warrior. Or a man can be both. There are enough people who are both. But a man who only traverses the paths of life is everything. Today I am neither a warrior nor a diablero. For me there is only the traveling on the paths that have a heart, on any path that may have a heart. There I travel, and the only worthwhile challenge for me is to traverse its full length. And there I travel—looking, looking, breathlessly.*

---

*Carlos Castaneda, *The Teachings of Don Juan* (Berkeley: University of California Press, 1968).

PATTERN RECOGNITION
Unmolded Clay

Try this. Pace your work to be finished, assembled, and hung on a wall within one class session.

1. Each person take one 8½-inch square of white or yellow paper and some Cray-Pas colors.
2. Each person enlarge one square from Charles Demuth's painting (inner fold of back cover) to fill an 8½-inch square. Use up all the little squares.
3. Piece the large squares together to form a picture. Turn the whole thing over and tape all adjoining edges.
4. Hang your mural on a wall, stand back, and make whatever observations occur to you. There are additional suggestions for discussion in the Commentary that follows, but don't refer to them until you have had a chance to see what you come up with on your own.

DIALOGUE AND REFLECTION
The Creation of Meaning

Traditional schooling emphasizes data classification. Educational theorists recommend plenty of experience in pattern recognition as well.

In your small groups consider which aspects of your project seem to be left brained and which seem to be right brained. Or do they flip back and forth as you work?

Consider also the role of precision and what happens to the whole picture if a few pieces are not carefully executed. Does the big picture still "make sense"? What if a lot are sloppy?

If the project were a metaphor for life itself and the role of an individual among his or her fellow creatures and the value of others to an individual, what would some messages be?

As a metaphor for the roles of the two hemispheres of your neocortex, what are some messages?

As you worked, was there any evidence of your reptilian and mammalian brains participating?

Reflect on the significance of this project in your learning log.

COMMENTARY

Complete an entry in your learning log before
reading this.

A Submerged Sunrise of Wonder

My students are always enthusiastic about doing this project. They like making the squares and are pleased with the resulting mural even when a few squares don't come out accurately. The students draw closer together and value each other's contributions to the project and to the discussion. There is a warmer feeling and a mutuality that develops, a good learning and growing atmosphere. If only for these reasons, the project would be valuable in any class on any subject. Education is enhanced when the setting is a warm and friendly place.

But there is more to chew on. For one thing it is clear that we can get a pretty good picture of the picture—what the picture could be—even when several squares are crummy. Some students are color-blind. Many have had unmolded clay in their hands only rarely in their academic careers and are quite inexperienced. Some students don't realize how important their contribution will be to the whole picture and don't do their best work. Then, too, there is a problem of time. In life there is always a problem of time. The project deliberately limits the time so that everyone will be on the same footing. We want it to be a playful atmosphere. Even so, some students cannot be persuaded to hurry. The way each approaches the task is a statement about his or her philosophy of what life is all about.

Nevertheless, with all the inevitable shortcomings and limitations, a picture does emerge, and the mind stitches over the rough spots to produce an idea of what the picture could be, indeed is. The idea of reality in every mind is more complete than is the physical representation. Could that be what Plato meant?

Each of us does contribute to the idea of what is going on on this planet in his or her own way with his or her own skills and commitment. Each accurate square is a plus. Thank you, Albert; thank you, Henry; thank you, Imogen. We tinker with our own part, step back and look at the whole picture, and go back and tinker some more. Dialogue helps us fix up the squares that are off the mark. Clearly the group as a whole and the unique individual are equally vital, one dancer and dance. I may not even have an inkling of what the big picture may finally be, but I am contributing to it and must fine-tune my own square with precision and care.

This project puts competition in a new light, too. One can only wish one's fellow participants well. Your sloppy work diminishes me. When you do well, I benefit. If I help you do your best, I help myself. That goes for my relationship with all other creatures and things, too. Healthy self-interest. Competition doesn't have to be against others; it can be thought of as a means of getting everyone closer to an accurate composite picture, closer to recognizing the pattern. In Special Olympics competition it is touching to see participants encouraging, even assisting, each other to a goal. Constructive competition. Classrooms must be like that. Your success, your unique ideas, are to my benefit. We need all views for a successful project.

We can also see as we reflect on this project that we can get a good picture of the whole image even with incomplete or missing or poorly executed data. That should be encouraging. Since an individual's lifetime is a grain of sand, it would be depressing in the extreme to think that therefore the pursuit of enlightenment, of clarity, is hopeless. The mural suggests that it is not hopeless. It depends on our willingness to take flying leaps in the dark. John Keats may have had this idea in mind when he wrote the following in a letter to his friend Reynolds:

> Now it appears to me that almost any Man may like the spider spin from his own inwards his own airy Citadel—the points of leaves and twigs on which the spider begins her work are few, and she fills the air with a beautiful circuiting. Man should be content with a few points to tip with the fine Web of his Soul, and weave a tapestry empyrean—full of symbols for his spiritual eye, of softness for his spiritual touch, of space for his wandering, of distinctness for his luxury.

That can translate into brain metaphor. The thrust for meaning comes from within, from our own guts or, we could say, the feeling centers of our mammalian brain. Our cold-blooded persistence against seemingly impossible odds is reptilian, or we could call it our genetic programming, our DNA. Our neocortex, when the picture emerges—as a result of oh, so careful left-brained precision and oh, so playful right-brained hunches—is shot full of brilliant light, perhaps enough to see by even in the dark.

At the back of the brain there is a forgotten blaze, or a burst of astonishment at our own existence. The object of an artistic and spiritual life is to dig for this submerged sunrise of wonder.
—G. K. Chesterton

143

VALID CONCLUSIONS
Capturing Snowflakes

In chapter 1 three sets of statements were given for you to examine for faulty reasoning. Without training, can you detect flaws in arguments? If you have enough time, can you figure out whether a conclusion is justified?

Several times in *Thinking about Thinking* the argument has been given that *no conclusion is ever justified;* it is only a rest from thinking anymore. There is always something more to be said or some other angle of perception. The uncertainty principle is developed further in chapter 4.

Nevertheless, within a framework in which the made-up boundaries are set in advance and accepted by the game players, conclusions can be drawn, as in poker and hopscotch.

John Locke, in his *Essay Concerning Human Understanding*, appears to have thought that we do not have to be taught how to be rational thinkers: "But God has not been so sparing to men to make them barely two-legged creatures, and left it to Aristotle to make them rational." Following are a few syllogisms for you to try. See if Locke and this book are right in thinking that with enough time you can indeed figure out whether the conclusions in these groups are justified. A technical definition of *syllogism* will be supplied later, but you won't need it for this exercise.

Work in groups of three or four.

Test each conclusion. If you were a computer, would it compute?

As you think your way through, look over your own shoulder to watch the process you use. Make sure everyone in your group understands the reasoning. How you think your way to your judgment is what you want to explore.

While you are kitten-watching, see if this theory holds true: *You know your conclusion is correct before you find the words to prove it.*

Example 1.

        All CPAs are careful planners.
        Some embezzlers are careful planners.
        Therefore, some embezzlers are CPAs.

The first statement says all CPAs are careful planners, but it does not work the other way around. It does not say that all careful planners are CPAs. Homemakers could be careful planners; students could be careful planners. There is no necessary connection between embezzlers who are careful planners and CPAs, but that issue is not at all connected with the first two statements. So any well-built computer would reject it. In this logic game, the rules say that you cannot go outside the data bank for additional information. But since you are smarter than any computer, did you sense your answer before the words came? Did you feel something was fishy and then see what it was?

Example 2.
> All careful planners are CPAs.
> Some embezzlers are careful planners.
> Therefore, some embezzlers are CPAs.

If you plan carefully, you are indeed a CPA. So the conclusion does work. But any student or homemaker who is a careful planner would have to be a CPA, too, according to this premise. Never mind that your experience tells you that the first premise (statement) is a bald-faced lie. The computer doesn't care whether it is a lie or not. This is the garbage-in, garbage-out principle of computer programming. Once the stuff gets into the program, the computer will take it exactly as stated and will draw only those conclusions that follow from the combination of the statements. For example, if you ask a mindless computer to interpret the statement, "I saw the man in the park with a telescope," one of the interpretations it would have to offer is that you are using a telescope to cut him in two. You must think in exactly this manner when you play the syllogism game. It seems almost reptilian, doesn't it?

Now, try a few syllogisms in your small groups. Computers are mindless, and logic is mindless. But that is exactly what they are designed to be. After having so much fun thinking about thinking, my students at first resist narrowing their options so drastically. But if you think about logic as if you were writing a computer program, you will see that it can be a stimulating challenge to set up a series of statements that lock into place like a mathematical equation. When you use a computer program, this experience will help you appreciate why it is so important to punch in precise commands.

Don't forget to observe what flip-flops your mind has to go through to play this game. What do you have to set aside, what part of your head hurts the most? One student said he felt like he had pulled a muscle in his brain.

A. Every virtue is praiseworthy.
   Kindness is a virtue.
   Therefore, kindness is praiseworthy.

B. Some involuntary acts work out for the best.
   Some presidential acts do not work out for the best.
   Therefore, some presidential acts are not involuntary.

C. All chickens are fowls.
   All Rhode Island Reds are fowls.
   Therefore, all Rhode Island Reds are chickens.

D. No person who assigns overtime is nice.
   Some bosses do not assign overtime.
   Therefore, some bosses are nice.

DIALOGUE AND REFLECTION

After you finish your analysis, discuss its implications and later reflect on the experience in your learning log. Do pursue any intriguing tangents.

COMMENTARY

Read this only after you have finished your
reflections in your learning log.

The Logic of English Sentences

If you watched your mind at work as you looked for flaws in the four syllogisms, you saw that you were really doing sentence analysis. Logic is based on sentence structure. You could not speak English if you didn't understand how English sentences are put together. Your experiment with nonsense sentences in chapter 1 showed that. So of course you are programmed to recognize what follows and what doesn't follow in a series of statements. Common sense.

Well, not so much common sense as common programming. Locke was right; it wasn't Aristotle who gave us logic. It was language itself.* They are the same thing, a program for processing data (called language) that is located in Broca's and Wernicke's areas of your left brain. As you reasoned your way along, you could see you were using tests that were already in your mind that might be called your "validity-checking program." You know by the rules of English sentence structure that though all chickens are fowls, not all fowls are necessarily chickens. You are programmed to know that the reverse won't compute. It would take some time to get that

---

*By the way, English logic is not the same as Chinese logic. Different language systems produce different structures for testing truth.

programmed into a computer, but you had that all sorted out by the time you hit first grade, not in the conscious area of your mind, of course. And even though you may be certain that all Rhode Island Reds are indeed chickens, you are preprogrammed to know that you didn't get that notion from the premises in the syllogism. English sentences don't add up that way, and you know it. Even if you don't always look that closely at an argument, nevertheless the fact that it is indeed an error of logical deduction is built right into the English system of language.

You may not consciously know the rules by which you reason, but you certainly are an expert logic user, logic and language being identical. If your brain is functioning normally, you know as part of your programming how English sentences are put together, and you know how the parts must interconnect. You know how sentences add up, also. Since you use language for all sorts of purposes, you may be quite imprecise in your statements much of the time. That could be perfectly justifiable. Among other things, language is a tool. A rake doesn't always have to be used for raking. If you are a sculptor, you may not need to use language with conscious precision very often. You may not often need to validate your arguments. That doesn't mean you can't. By definition, as a language user, you can and do. Your emphasis may simply be elsewhere. You are focusing on other things. Since you have other fish to fry, you may not care if the spoked hubs on your Lincoln are artificial or not.

A computer user doesn't have to be a trained programmer, nor does a user of language have to study English sentence structure. Some of us like it, and we become linguists. Some of us like to study logical categories and the rules—which are built right into sentences—by which we reason our way to conclusions, and we become professional logicians. Neither logicians nor linguists can claim that their interest makes them better thinkers or better language users. They could put that argument into a syllogistic form and immediately see the error.

But any attention we give to how our minds work can be enlightening and can help us piece together our picture of reality. Attention to music theory, the body's immune system, mathematical equations, and Scrabble can be just as enlightening: We need what William Carlos Williams called *an intense vision of the facts.* We also need to reflect on those facts and give them general meaning.

SYLLOGISMS
The Underlying Rules for Classifying
Cold Plums

In the next few pages is a brief analysis of standard syllogistic argument and the four rules that must apply in order for the conclusion to be valid. Since most readers will not specialize in logic, it is unnecessary to memorize the definitions and rules. It is interesting, though, to take time to see that the reasoning you had to use to check the arguments in the four syllogisms does fall into precise categories and can indeed be reduced to a few standard formulas.

While we may blind ourselves to the flaws in tricky ads and unscrupulous political arguments, we can spot faulty arguments when we take the time. The tests are built right into English sentence structure. *All* and *every, never* and *no* are inclusive or exclusive universals. *Some* is noninclusive, and so on. Because we are experts at using language, we can tell, given enough time, when an argument goes in circles.

But if you were going to spend much time on testing arguments for truth or validity, you would soon figure out some shortcuts. Logicians have done this, for example, in their analysis of syllogistic arguments. They have found that once an argument is set up in a standard form, then they can apply *four* tests to ascertain the validity of a conclusion. The rules can be and have been reduced to formulas that in the most concise form look very much like math.

Indeed, math is a good comparison. Arithmetic, for example, is nothing more than common sentence structure. You can translate any statement in arithmetic back to ordinary English. The same is true of algebra or calculus. The symbols used are for speed and convenience, but they all stand for linguistic concepts. As Einstein, among others, has said, "Most of the fundamental ideas of science are essentially simple, and may, as a rule, be expressed in a language comprehensible to everyone."

In-Class Workshop

With the foregoing in mind, work your way through the following analysis. Work with one or two others and make sure each step is clear to everyone before going to the next. Make sure you understand each point, but do not try to master or memorize it. The object here is to bring to your conscious awareness the steps you had to take out-of-awareness when you checked the conclusions to the syllogisms. So do the next few pages as an in-class workshop. I would not like you to have to be tested on the definitions and rules. A general awareness will be fine. Allow two class sessions for workshop and discussion.

Description of a Syllogism

A syllogism is a deductive argument. It consists of *three statements.*
The statements are *unconditional.* No waffling.
Two of the statements *serve as the basis of the argument.* They are called *premises.*
The third statement serves as the conclusion.

Conditions that must be met

To be a true syllogism, an argument must meet *two other conditions.*

1. *There must be exactly three terms.*
    The *terms* are the classes to be lumped or separated:
    All [CPAs] are [careful planners.]

2. *Each term must appear twice but never twice in the same statement.*

Names of the terms: major, minor, middle

Each of the three terms of a syllogism has been given a name. Thus,

> Every virtue is praiseworthy.
> Kindness is a virtue.
> Therefore, kindness is praiseworthy.

The *subject of the conclusion,* kindness, is the *minor term.* The *major term,* praiseworthy, appears in the *predicate of the conclusion.*
The remaining term, virtue, is called the *middle term. The middle term appears in each premise* (the first two statements).

Names of the premises: major premise, minor premise

The premise that contains the predicate of the conclusion is called the *major premise.*
The other premise, containing the minor term, is called the *minor premise.*

Practice

Label the *terms* and *premises* in the following syllogism. Work with one or two other students. Make sure everyone understands *major, minor,* and *middle* terms and *major* and *minor* premises. Don't bother to memorize these labels. If you need to refresh your memory, you can refer to this section.

All thinkers are rational.
Some English teachers are not rational.
Therefore, some English teachers are not thinkers.

The Four Tests for Validity

Once set in syllogistic form, arguments, logicians have found, can be checked by using four tests that will always work. If the syllogism fails any of the four tests, it is invalid.

Test 1. *Distribution of the middle term.* The middle term has to fit all members of the class referred to by one of the other two terms. When it does, it is said to be *distributed,* "spread out over."
Thus, in the statement "All hallways are lighted," the subject, hallways, is *distributed* because it includes all the members of the class called hallways. But the predicate term, lighted, is *not distributed* because it says nothing about all members of the class of lighted things.

Practice

Work with one or two others to see if the middle term, lovable, is distributed in this syllogism. Make sure everyone understands before you go on. Don't try to memorize; work on understanding.

> All dogs are lovable.
> All poodles are lovable
> Therefore, all poodles are dogs.

Try another. See if the middle term, persons who assign overtime, is distributed in this syllogism.

> No person who assigns overtime is nice.
> Some bosses do not assign overtime.
> Therefore, some bosses are nice.

Thus, *the subject of a universal statement (All cats are dumb) is distributed. The predicate of a negative statement (No snowflakes are ugly) is distributed.* No other terms are distributed.

Tests 2, 3, and 4. The remaining tests are self-explanatory. So all four are listed next along with a few syllogisms for you to practice on. It is more fun to work them out with a couple of other students. Treat the investigation as a workshop. Keep one book open to the descriptions and explanations while you work. Remember, you are working for understanding, not mastery.

Tests for Validity

Test 1. *The middle term has to be distributed at least once.*

Test 2. *At least one term has to be affirmative.*

Test 3. *If there is a negative premise, there has to be a negative conclusion. And vice versa: If the conclusion is negative, there has to be a negative premise too.*

Test 4. *Any term distributed in the conclusion has to be distributed in a premise too.*

Practice

Work with one or two others. See if each argument is a syllogism. If so, see if it is valid. If you decide an argument is not valid, what rule is violated? Make sure everyone in your group understands the reasoning.

1. No act that causes death is acceptable.
   Drunk driving is an act that causes death.
   Therefore, no drunk driving is acceptable.

2. All daisies have petals.
   All daisies are sun-loving flowers.
   Therefore, all sun-loving flowers have petals.

3. All Finns are skaters.
   Some skaters are not graceful
   Therefore, some Finns are not graceful.

4. All readers of *Rolling Stone* are young.
   Some students do not read *Rolling Stone.*
   Therefore, some students are not young.

5. All readers of *People* are moderates.
   Forty percent of our students read *People.*
   Therefore, forty percent of our students are moderates.

6. Some swimmers are self-taught.
   All swimmers are water lovers.
   Therefore, some water lovers are self-taught.

7. All producers are middle-aged.
   No middle-aged person is lazy.
   Therefore, no one who is lazy is a producer.

DIALOGUE AND REFLECTION

In your small-group discussions first try to see the systematic analysis of argument from a logician's point of view. In other words, what is so good about it? What do logicians see in it? List the best of your observations.

Then list your concerns. What problems are there in this sort of discipline for you? Resolve these if you can.

In your large group, pool your findings. Later reflect in your log on the whole experience and its connection with ideas in *Thinking about Thinking*.

> *The true intellectual is someone*
> *who thinks about what he is*
> *thinking about.*
> —Christine McEllerhan, Student

COMMENTARY

Make an entry in your learning log before reading
this section.

A Slow Walk Through Logic
Taking Care

If I lean toward spontaneous, right-brained thinking, syllogistic argument is likely to feel foreign to me. But as my five-year-old niece said to her seven-year-old sister, "You'd better learn your numbers, Mary. If you don't, somebody might cheat you." If you are outwardly serious, then you had better have an inner humor. And if you are humorous on the outside, then you had better be dead serious within. I would hate to be just one. It is fine to lean one way if there is a strong hold on the other.

When we are good at something, we tend to go with it, but that can get us in a jam. A poet who thinks sloppily gives poetry a bad name. A technician who is naive enough to believe it is all done by the numbers quite literally is not all there.

On the other hand it is lucky for all of us that each person puts a unique curve on the thinking process. It is excellent that there are extremely spontaneous and extremely deliberative thinkers and infinite variations of

152

the two. Look at the mutual-aid picture you and your classmates put together; look at a whole classroom of mandalas.

There is no need to take sides—unless we take both sides. There is much math in a Bach fugue or a Frost poem. There is sheer poetry in the mind of a Richard Feynman. Yes, poets need to be logicians, not for the sake of being well-rounded, but to make their poems accurate, to make the physical fit what their spirits have seen. Careful use of language is a step toward enlightenment.

If only the taste of careful use of language emerges from work with syllogisms, the time is well spent. Eventually every important symbol in your wordbag will have to be redefined by you. When you use other people's definitions, you are other-directed. "I must create my own system," wrote William Blake, "or be enslaved by another man's." We really don't have a choice. The problem of definition tyranny, a problem every human being must resolve, is one of the topics taken up by Neil Postman in the transcript of his speech that appears later in this chapter.

> Common sense is merely
> another name for dead metaphors.
> —Charlie Kyle, Student

TIME OUT

KOAN

What would happen to humor if we
all defined our terms?

THE FAR SIDE   By GARY LARSON

Circa 1500 A.D.: Horses are introduced to America.

NURTURING THE MIND
Questions, Metaphors, Definitions, and Style

One concern of my students about deductive and inductive reasoning is having to accept statements as "proved" when they are anything but proved. Premises and their underlying assumptions are the problem. For you cannot go on with the argument if you cannot agree on the basic stuff. "We hold these truths to be self-evident"? Who is "we," what do you mean by "truth," are these words really self-evident? "All men are created equal"? What do you mean by "equal"? By "men" do you mean all people, women and children too? Created by whom? Or doesn't that matter? What do you mean by your statement?

Questioning assumptions and premises can be a genuine concern. A + B = C? C. G. Jung found that impossible to accept. A is one separate thing, B is another, and the two together are certainly not C. C is something else altogether. Jung's mind wouldn't accept such lumping, and he hated math. Nevertheless, his viewpoint can help us to see math better. When the questioning is genuine, it should be welcomed.

We all know obnoxious bores, though, who have learned just enough of logic to ask such questions mechanically. They do more to destroy good dialogue than to enhance it. The same can be said for would-be poets who know just enough of metaphor to throw language around like confetti. That is a good way to obscure light, too.

These problems and others are addressed by Neil Postman in the transcript that follows of a talk he gave to English teachers one Thanksgiving in San Francisco. As Postman makes clear, scientists must realize that every theory is a metaphor. If they do not realize that, they are blind to the bedrock of their discipline and will box themselves in in such a way that their thinking will be narrow. But poets must realize that their poems rely on definition. One must be brutally certain of what one means by each word set on paper. To read economics successfully, a student has to know how to recognize style, for as Postman points out, style is indeed the message of every discipline. The medium is the message.

Do spend some time on Postman's speech. Browse through it a few times. You will see that he illuminates four topics important to anyone on a path with a heart:

- *The art of asking questions*
- *The art of discovering the inherent metaphor in any area of knowledge*
- *The art of learning what a definition is and how a definition is arrived at*
- *The art of identifying the style of an academic subject*

As you will see, even though this speech was made to English teachers, there are valuable nuggets in it for everyone. So get out your metal detectors. Use the BFAR method described near the beginning of chapter 2.

TEACHING INTO THE FUTURE

Dr. Neil Postman

[Even though Postman's introduction is directed specifically to English teachers, students should find it interesting to see what teachers talk about at their conferences—and then reflect on whether any of that gets translated into classroom practices.]

This morning I want to put forward some ideas about how in the future English teachers might exert a more useful influence than they presently do on the nurturing of student intelligence. I would like to propose an enlarged conception of what it means to teach language, and I suppose I should begin by telling you what I do not mean, this morning at least, by language education. I am not referring to all of the issues that are usually called forth by such phrases as "Black English," "students' rights to their own language," or "sexist" language. These issues are certainly not trivial, and sometime in the years ahead we shall have to resolve them. I must confess that at the moment I am somewhat confused about what positions an enlightened English teacher is supposed to take in respect to these issues. For example, as far as I can make out, at the present time a student is to be granted the right to say *I ain't got none* but not the right to say *chairman*. I shall let this one alone today except to remark that I trust that our future as English teachers will not become obsessed with the politics of language. In any case, what I wish to discuss this morning is not language in a social or political context but language in a *knowledge* context.

THE LANGUAGE OF SUBJECTS

I want to suggest a reversal of the old saw that every teacher must be an English teacher, which is a splendid but, I fear, a far-fetched idea, and suggest instead that every English teacher must be a teacher of all subjects, which is a far-fetching but, I believe, practical idea. Here's what I mean:

Every subject in the school curriculum is, of course, language. Knowledge of a subject means knowledge of the language of that subject, which includes not only what its words mean but, far more important, how its words mean. As one learns the language of a subject, one is also learning what the subject is. If you eliminate all the words of a subject, you have eliminated the subject. Biology, for instance, is not plants and animals. It is language about plants and animals. History is not events or past events. It is language describing and interpreting events. Astronomy is not planets and stars. It is a way of talking about planets and stars. What I am getting at is this: There are two levels of knowing a subject. There is the student who knows what the definition of a noun or a chromosome or a molecule is. Then there is the student who shares that knowledge but who also knows how the definition

NOTE: *This transcript is from a speech given at the annual convention of the National Council of Teachers of English in San Francisco, November 24, 1981. Subheads and bracketed commentary have been inserted by the author of this book.*

was arrived at and what a definition is. There's the student who can answer a question. Then there is the student who also knows what are the biases and assumptions of the question. There is the student who can give you the facts. Then there is the student who also knows what is meant by a fact and how that is different from an inference and a theory. [*Which kind of student has more fun?*] It will be obvious to you that in all these cases it is the second student who has a serious education, the first, a frivolous one. And it must be obvious as well what all this has to do with the English teacher.

[*One way to check our understanding is to rephrase the speaker's or writer's words. Let's rephrase some of Postman's ideas to this point: When I study a new subject, my studying boils down to putting some new twists on language. Right so far? If I think I am studying trees when actually I am studying words and sentences, I am bound to screw up on tests. The way people talk about trees has a feel to it that is as important as what they are saying. (Study the medium.) If I am full of definitions but do not have the feel of those definitions, I have a superficial schooling. I need to know more about how definitions get created and by whom and what sorts of feelings lie behind questions. The facts are always just the beginning.*]

THE ART OF QUESTION ASKING

Since every subject is generated by questions, since every subject is built on metaphors, since every subject relies on definitions, and since every subject is characterized by a distinct literary style, no member of any faculty is better suited than is the English teacher to help students learn how to approach the world of systematic knowledge. If we have not lost our zest for the idea that we must teach our students how to learn, then the English teacher by training and interest is well positioned to give leadership to school faculties. Our business, after all, is to teach about sentences, about words, about metaphors, about tone, about style, about definitions. In short, about what the school curriculum is about.

Let me suggest then what a language education of the future might deal with, beginning with questions. It is sometimes overlooked even by English teachers that questions are language. To put it simply, a question is a sentence. Badly formed it produces no knowledge and no understanding. Aptly formed it leads to new facts, new perspectives, new ideas. As Francis Bacon put it more than 350 years ago, "There arises from a bad and unapt formation of words a wonderful obstruction of the mind." In other words, stupidity. If we need a slogan, by the way, to guide our path in the future, let us then "go back to Bacon" and make the study of the art and science of question asking one of the central disciplines in language education.

I don't have the time here to specify most of the things that we would include in such a study, but I want to mention two concepts about questions that I think go to the heart of the matter. The first is suggested by a charming story attributed to psychologist Gordon Allport. It seems that two priests were engaged in a dispute on whether or not it is permissible to pray and smoke at the same time. One believed that it is, the other that it is not. And being unable to resolve the matter, each decided to write to the Pope for a definitive answer. After doing so, they met again to share their results and were astonished to discover that the Pope had agreed with each of them. "How did you pose the question?" asked the first. The other replied, "I asked if it is permissible to smoke while praying. His Holiness said that it is not, since praying is a very serious business, and how did you phrase the question?" The first replied, "I asked if it is permissible to pray while smoking, and His Holiness said that it is, since it is always appropriate to pray."

Now the point, of course, is that the form in which a question is asked will control what kind of answer one gets, and that every question, therefore, has a fact or bias imbedded in it. As has been aptly said, "We see nature only through the questions we put to it." To which I would add, we see *everything* only through the questions we ask. A question is a structure for thought, which is what Plato meant when he remarked that "when the mind is thinking it is talking to itself." That is why I think that language education must include the most serious exploration of the structure of questions, their assumptions, their limitations, their levels of abstraction, and the sources of authority to which they appeal. Now this is something that should not be inordinately difficult for English teachers to do. The next idea however will require a little learning on our part.

[*Ask a stupid question, you get a stupid answer. Garbage in, garbage out. There is no such thing as an innocent question. The next time you ask a question, notice what your own needs are that prompt you to ask the question in that way. A shortcut to remembering Postman's observations is to remember the anecdote about praying and smoking. Most of Postman's ideas are implicit in it.*]

Although there is essential general knowledge to be taught about questions, each subject in a school curriculum has its own particular rules about questions. The questions that are appropriate in history differ in their form and meaning from those that are appropriate in biology or mathematics or literature. The reason for this is that each subject has a unique vocabulary which reflects its own assumptions about what constitutes knowledge. The "facts" of mathematics are not anything like what is meant by the "facts" of history. A biological "truth" is something quite different from "truth" in a literary work. A "correct" answer in physics is different from a "correct" answer in economics. Thus, through explorations of how questions are asked in different subjects, our students may learn about the various uses of our culture's most important words. Our students can begin to learn something about what may be called the dialects of knowledge. (Let me add here that with all the talk one hears about how English teachers must increase their knowledge of and sensitivity to different ethnic and regional dialects, one hears nothing about their educating themselves in respect to the specialized modes of discourse we call subjects. I would venture the opinion that we would advance the intelligence of all of our students much further by familiarizing ourselves with the dialects of knowledge than with any other.)

[*The word* dialect *refers to the way a group of people within a larger language community use that language, their special touches. A dialect is like an accent but more inclusive; it includes things like sentence structure variations, vocabulary choices, cadence, emphasis, pronunciation. In school subjects, history is one dialect, physics is another, literature another.*]

ORGANS OF PERCEPTION

In this connection, I might observe that very few modern writers on education show any awareness of the metaphors that control beliefs. This in contrast to such venerable educationists as Plato, Cicero, Comenius, Locke, and Rousseau, who never failed to make their metaphors explicit. "Plants are improved by cultivation," Rousseau wrote in *Emile,* "and man by education." And his entire philosophy is made to rest upon comparison of plants and children. Even in such ancient texts as the *Mishnah,* we find that there are four kinds of students: the sponge, the funnel, the strainer, and the sieve. It will surprise you to know which one is preferred. The sponge, we are told, absorbs all; the funnel receives at one end and spills out at the other; the strainer lets the wine flow through and retains the dregs; but the sieve, that is the best, for it lets out the flour dust and retains the fine flour. The difference in education philosophy between Rousseau and the compilers of the *Mishnah* is precisely reflected through the difference in a wild plant and a sieve. [*Aha! A tip for reading any book: Extract its metaphors.*]

So in teaching about dialects of knowledge, we must explore the uses of metaphor, not as ornaments to poetic expression, which is our tradition, but as the backbones of the subjects our students are required to comprehend. [*The metaphors we use to examine the world are like hands and nostrils, not rouge and eye shadow.*]

To this must be added all the issues involved in what may be called "definition." There is no more depressing symptom of a frivolous education than to hear a student ask for *the* definition of a term, since the question so often implies a lack of understanding of what a definition is and where definitions come from.

DEFINITION TYRANNY

Definitions, like questions and metaphors, are instruments for thinking. Their authority rests entirely on their usefulness. We use definitions in order to delineate problems we wish to investigate or to further interests we wish to promote. We invent definitions and distort them as suits our purposes. And yet one gets the impression that students and not a few teachers believe that God has provided us with definitions from which we depart at the risk of losing our immortal souls. This is the definition I have elsewhere called "definition tyranny," which may be defined by me, not God, as the process of accepting without reflection someone else's definition of a word, problem, or situation.

[Definition tyranny. *That is worth repeating: The process of accepting* without reflection *someone else's definition of a word, problem, or situation. One student reflected on definition tyranny and realized that she herself had become her own tyrant. That is, she had decided on numerous things earlier and then felt stuck with her conclusions. "Hey," she wrote, "I just gave myself the right to stop definition tyranny of myself."*]

I can think of no better method of freeing students from this "wonderful obstruction to the mind" than to provide them with alternative definitions of every important concept or term with which they must deal in a given subject. Whether it be

159

molecules, facts, law, art, whatever, it is essential to students to understand that definitions are hypotheses and that embedded in them are particular philosophical,
sociological, or even epistemological points of view.

[*Epistemology, from* episteme, *"knowledge," and* ology, *"the study of."
Thus, the theory or study of what knowledge is and what its limits are.*]

THE DIALECTS OF KNOWLEDGE

These dialects of knowledge include, of course, what we are accustomed to calling
metaphors. Unfortunately for our children, English teachers are just about the only
people on school faculties who know anything about metaphors. And even we frequently confine our understanding to the teaching of poetry. But every discipline in
the school curriculum is based on powerful metaphors which give direction and
organization to the way we will do our thinking: In history, economics, physics,
biology, or linguistics, metaphors, like questions, function as organs of perception.
Through our metaphors we see the world as one thing or another. Is light a wave or
a particle? Are molecules like billiard balls or force fields? Is language like a tree or
a river or the ever-shifting winds? Is history unfolding according to some instructions of nature or according to a divine plan? Are our genes like information codes?
Is a literary work like an architect's blueprint or a mystery to be solved? It is questions like these that preoccupy scholars in every field because they are basic questions, which is to say that you cannot understand what a subject is without some
understanding of the metaphors which are its foundation.

This, by the way, is certainly as true of the subject of education as any other. Any
proposal you will hear at this conference, including my own, will be rooted in some
metaphor of the mind or of learning or of school or of children. And every dispute
you witness at the conference is about the aptness of one metaphor against
another. For there can be no conversation about education that will extend beyond
two or three sentences before a metaphor is invoked which provides structure,
authority, or explanation for certain beliefs.

[*Reflect on the idea that a metaphor is a tool or device for seeing. A question
is an instrument for taking a look at things. With either one you can move the
world.*]

In this connection, I want to tell you of a student who some years ago applied for
admission to Columbia University and was rejected. He wrote the following letter to
the chief admissions officer:

Dear Sir,

Thank you for informing me so promptly about your decision. Unfortunately,
yours was the fourth college rejection I have received and this is one over my
limit. Therefore, I must reject your rejection and will present myself for classes
on September 17th.

I am pleased to tell you that the decision in this man's case was reversed, but
even had it not been, we wouldn't need to worry about him. This is a student who

will not accept without critical reflection the definitions of others. He will make a good scholar.

[*There is no such thing as* the *definition of a word. You need to know whose definition it is and what his or her purposes in defining it that way are. In other words, what lies behind the definition? Definitions are inventions for tinkering with the perceived world. Every educated person writes his or her own dictionary.*]

STYLE AND TONE OF SCHOOL SUBJECTS

In addition to the study of definitions, we must obviously give considerable attention to the style and tone of the language of a given subject. Each subject is a manner of speaking and writing. There is a rhetoric of knowledge, a characteristic way in which arguments, proofs, speculations, experiments, polemics, even humor, are expressed. One might even say that speaking or writing a subject is a performing art. And each subject requires a somewhat different performance from every other. Historians, for example, do not speak or write history in the same way that biologists speak or write biology. The differences have as much to do with the kind of material they are dealing with, the degree of precision their generalizations permit, the types of facts they martial, the traditions of their subjects, and the purposes for which they are making their inquiries. The rhetoric of knowledge is not an easy matter to go into, but it is worth remembering, I think, that some scholars have exerted as much influence through their manner as their matter. One thinks of Veblen in sociology, Freud in psychology, Galbraith in economics, Sapir in linguistics. The point is that *knowledge is a form of literature.* And the various styles of knowledge ought to be studied and discussed as a part of any field called language education. I will grant that the language found in the typical school textbook tends to obscure this entire area. Textbook language is apt to be the same from subject to subject and creates the impression that systematic knowledge is always expressed in a dull, uninspired monotone. I have seen recipes on the backs of cereal boxes written with more verve and personality than textbook descriptions of the causes of the Civil War. Of the language of grammar books I will not even speak, for to borrow from Shakespeare, "It is unfit for a Christian ear to endure."

[Knowledge is a form of literature. *Keep this metaphor in mind when you undertake to master a new school subject. Read art history as you would a good short story or a novel: plot, setting, tone, style, theme, metaphors, and so on. You will catch on much more quickly than if you just memorize the so-called facts.*]

But the problem is not insurmountable. Teachers who are willing to take the time and trouble can find materials which convey ideas in a form characteristic of different disciplines. As a matter of fact, I took the trouble myself to do this for English teachers many years ago in a textbook called *The Languages of Discovery.*

It was my hope then that English teachers might be willing to redefine what was meant by the study of language, conceiving of it as a formal matter of education, wherein students learn to talk about talk, and particularly how to talk about the kind of talk that is called knowledge. But I misjudged the situation. Of all the books I have done, this is one that was the least well received, the most decisively ignored. I bring the idea before you again, because I sincerely believe that there is no more honorable role for us in the years ahead than that we should take command in this way of our children's education. In my most recent book, *Teaching as a Conserving Activity*, I propose that all teachers teach their subjects as human situations whose language is at all times problematic. But I don't have much hope that this appeal will strike home. There is only one group of teachers, English teachers, with the background to get into this, indeed who have the mandate to do it; for the task of making our students literate has fallen largely to us.

[*Subjects, fields of study, are created by human beings. Explore them as things human beings have thought up, not God. They are points of view about how the world works, what it is like. In other words, metaphors.*]

What does literacy mean? As Wendell Johnson once remarked, "You cannot write writing, neither can you read reading or speak speaking. You must write about something, just as you must read and speak about something." Now that "something," at least in an academic context, is some aspect of human knowledge which has been given expression in a particular kind of language. Thus, all reading and writing in truth is reading and writing in a content area. To read the phrase "the law of diminishing returns" requires that you know how the word "law" is used in economics, for it does not mean what it does in the phrase "the law of inertia" or "Grimm's law" or "law of the land" or "the law of the survival of the fittest." To the question "What does law mean?" the answer must always be, "In what context?" In fact, to the question "How well does one read?" we must give the same reply. No one is a good reader, period. There are those who read the physical sciences well, but not history. And there are those who read political science well, but not poetry. I cannot accept that English teachers are content to restrict their concept of literacy to poetry and fiction. By teaching our students about the rhetoric of subjects, about the meanings of facts and assumptions in subjects, about how definitions, metaphors, and questions are formed in different subjects, we will be teaching how to read, write, speak and listen.

[*To become a good reader in a new subject, act as if you have just moved from Atlanta to Boston. Use the same strategies in reading as you would in learning to cope with a new dialect.*]

So this is the picture of our future I hope you will consider: The English curriculum as education about education, the content of English as the exploration of the language of learning.

I do not regard this proposal as grandiose or fanciful in any way, but, on the contrary, a practical means by which we may have direct access to the intellectual development of our children. Such access is what Charles Weingartner and I meant twelve years ago by the phrase "teaching as a subversive activity." It is also what I mean today by teaching as a "conserving activity."

DIALOGUE AND REFLECTION
Talk about Talk

Once you feel you understand Postman's argument, go back over the transcript and pick out a few intriguing ideas to explore in your small groups. Of course, Postman's main idea is that English teachers ought to show students how to master other subjects. English should be "talk about talk."

You can study English in a social context and notice which social class or classes say, "I ain't got none." Or you can examine it from a political standpoint and notice sexism in language. But Postman argues that we can go much deeper and look at language in a knowledge context that cuts across all subjects.

The object of your dialogue is to get Postman's ideas worked into your nervous system so that new views can be added to what you already know. The anecdote about praying and smoking, for example, will always stick in some minds as a reminder of the art of question asking, as it certainly will in the mind of the student who commented, "Hey, is it all right to pray while fornicating?"

What about the difference between a frivolous and a serious education? Which are you getting? Which do you prefer? What about the idea that how a word means is far more influential than what it means? What about definition tyranny? And so on.

Devote one class session to discussion of Postman's ideas, allowing about fifteen minutes for your large group to pool your key observations.

Then make an entry in your learning log. Find some connections with ideas from chapters 1 and 2. Consider how your own education might change if Postman's suggestions were followed. Would it be more stimulating? How about applying his ideas yourself? Would you like college better?

Don't try to write like people you admire.
Write like people you enjoy. You.

COMMENTARY

Read this section only after you have made an
entry in your learning log.

A Few Points to Tip with the Fine Web
of the Soul

All materials in *Thinking about Thinking,* including "Teaching into the Future," are selected for newness and freshness for its readers. Knowing about question asking opens the mind to possibilities; not knowing keeps it closed. That goes for definition tyranny, too. Few people realize there is no such thing as *the* definition of a word or even realize how definitions come into being in the first place. Is that a matter of consequence? Yes. The same goes for knowing about the sources of assumptions and premises and the sources of whole blocks of knowledge such as history, biology, algebra, and dental hygiene.

Postman's lecture is in itself a version, a picture generated by his mind, that he then superimposes on the perceived world. His data—or more accurately, *similar* data—are available to others, too, but he shapes the picture his way. His word painting is the Postman metaphor. Each of us has or is one metaphor; we work on it all our lives. And Postman's manner indeed influences the matter. *How* he means—his style, his selection of examples, his tone of voice, his accent, even the way he stands at the podium—is the Postman message.

We are all like that. Postman is a walking viewpoint. So am I. So are you. After reading Postman, will I become a Postman clone? What usually happens is that if someone has been stimulating, for a while we will be intensely conscious of his or her ideas and will notice them in action as we walk around the planet. Then, of course, his or her influence will settle down and fit into the general background out of which we approach new events, much like eating and digesting a steak.

But this process cannot be forced. In the art of questioning questions or of critical analysis of the literature of biology, I would take others only as far as they would go willingly. There is a natural way to proceed: See as sharply and attentively as possible, and then let the mind do its sorting and classifying. Let it generate its own pattern. The process takes time. Meanwhile we wash our socks, wait on tables, and chat with friends. Sometimes we go back and look at the painting or listen to the song again. Sometimes we sit. If not distracted, the mind continues working toward synthesis. It will flesh out what it can from what food has been made available to it.

Choosing a path with a heart ensures a supply of nourishing ideas. Too heady a diet can overload the mind. The system needs roughage too.

It is good to look closely at the Postman mandala. It is good to discuss and reflect on his ideas and to notice how they affect our understanding of propaganda, syllogisms, raccoon coats, and shrieking geese. More important, it is vital to realize that my world is shaped by the questions I ask of it. Ask a different kind of question and I get a different kind of answer. My questions, my definitions, all help cleanse "the doors of perception," as William Blake put it, so that we can see "everything as it is, infinite."

> *A dictionary is a book of common feelings.*
> —Frances Hagen, Student

STATISTICS
The Illusion of Certainty

The following section concerns the danger of relying on statistics. You can prove anything with statistics, goes the old saying—or seem to, anyway. Earlier in *Thinking about Thinking* it was shown how hard it is to prove anything—beginning with the problem of agreeing on what the word *prove* means. In chapter 4 quantum physicist Richard Feynman remarks on how difficult it is to know something, there being so much that we don't know.

Nevertheless Americans do love statistics. Newspaper stories and ads are loaded with percentages. Parents accept unquestioningly the scores of their children on scholastic aptitude tests and IQ tests. Being classified as a numbskull can follow a person throughout life; even the victim believes the statistics. After all, wasn't it done scientifically? In the case of scholastic aptitude and IQ, the answer is a resounding No. Does wearing tight-fitting jockey shorts cause sterility in males? Sure, as tests with laboratory rats amply show.

Am I working up to my potential? Am I reading at grade level? I got 99 on my history exam: I'm a brilliant historian? Scores on national scholastic tests are dropping: Schools are doing a bum job? There isn't room in this book to develop the case against mindless acceptance of statistics, but I do want to include enough examples to get you started thinking about the foolishness of it, if you haven't already realized that. If you have, do share your findings with other students as you go through the examples that follow.

I hope you do realize that there is no such thing as an Intelligence Quotient in nature. People like Alfred Binet, Lewis Terman, and Arthur Otis thought them up. It is enlightening to read about the biases that influence the kinds of items that find their way into such tests, not the least of which is the assumption that a short answer chosen from three others under the stress of limited time is a fair measure of how a human mind functions. Even worse is the stupid and ignorant use to which these tests have been put by psychometricians, school districts, and college admissions offices.*

Some Fishy Statistics

Following are some samples for you to work on in your discussion group. Make sure everyone in your group understands how the figures have gone wrong before you go on to the next one. Wait until you finish your own investigation of an item before reading the comments about it on the pages that follow.

1. **On the average.** Think up four or five possible problems with this statistic: The average 1964 graduate of Desert University earns $40,730 a year.

2. **Playing Around with Graphs.** Each graph below shows the amount of increase in inflation month by month for one year. Which year had the larger increase, A or B? (Trick question)

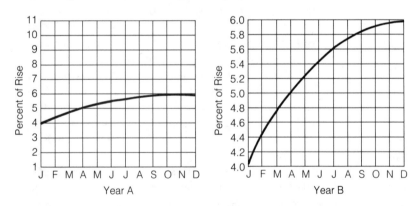

After you figure out your answer, find two or three other problems in reading these graphs.

3. **Scoring.** Your score on that standardized test of scholastic aptitude that you took to get into college was 550. Your friend's score was only 500. So you should get the higher priority. True or false?

---

*A full discussion and analysis of the testing mania is contained in the collection of articles edited by Paul L. Houts in *The Myth of Measurability* (New York: Hart Publishing Co., 1977).

4. **Smoke Screens.** Studies show that the more people smoke, the less active their sex lives. So for heaven's sake, give up smoking. True or false?

5. **Precision.** See if there are any problems with this statement: A poll of the 1251 students at Valley View High School shows students spend 1.216 hours a day on homework.

COMMENTARY

You can read these comments after you have done your own investigating.

Some Comments on the Samples

1.   One obvious concern is what the word *average* means here. Remember, a word never, ever means just one thing. For example, let's say you have three employees. Two make $10,000 a year and one makes $70,000. You could add up the salaries and divide by three: 10,000 + 10,000 + 70,000 is 90,000. Divide that by 3 and you get an average of 30,000. That is one kind of average, but it isn't very satisfying, is it? An average arrived at by this method is technically termed a *mean*, but such a figure isn't much good for talking about salaries. If the average is a mean average, we have learned nothing useful about the earnings of Desert University graduates.

Other problems with the $40,730 figure? How reliable are the surveyors? Do they have an axe to grind? How "clean" are the figures? That is, how were they gathered? Is every graduate included? Are any groups left out? If a questionnaire was sent, can you count on answers being truthful? As you know, even the way the questions are worded can influence responses. Typos and arithmetic errors can botch the results, too.

In the Desert University example, I did use a mean average. I pretended that we did hear from all 500 graduates and that we were able to verify everyone's income. I fixed it so that 450 earned $30,000 or less. I let 275 earn $30,000. I gave 125 grads $15,000 a year, and 50 others got only $8,000. I gave 49 grads $160,000 and one Silicon Valley entrepreneur $2 million. You can see that the *mean* of $40,730 is extremely misleading about the actual incomes of the 1964 grads. In fact, 450 earned considerably less than that.

Another way I could have done my figuring would have been to spread the incomes out from lowest to highest and count my way to the middle, in this case to the 250th graduate. His or her income would be the *median* income, the middle income. I might then have said that the "average" graduate earns $30.000. But that would not be a very complete picture. One figure that might be useful would be the *mode,* the income that the largest number of graduates got. In this case, it is indeed $30,000 because 275 did get that amount. But what about the 175 who got far less and the 50 who earned far more?

It would all depend on what the reader wants to know, wouldn't it? The point is that neither the mean, the median, nor the mode is useful all by itself. *Information is meaningless.* The value of the statistic depends entirely on what particular human beings want from it.

2.   That's right, there is no difference. If you want to make inflation look staggering, just spread out the vertical parts of the graph. The graph on the right spreads the curve over ten squares instead of two.

Which graph would the political party out of power be inclined to use?

Whether the rate of increase is significant will also depend on other factors. For example, how does that compare with other years? What information was used to determine the percentage? Are any significant groups of figures left out that were used in previous calculations? Who did the study? Are they reliable? What is the margin of error? And so on.

The point? You can make a graph show just about anything you want it to.

3.   The figures have a satisfying appearance of precision, but even the test maker has to admit the scores are not all that precise. When you reflect on a number representing how apt you are at anything, the idea soon looks ludicrous. But since everyone seems bent on reducing a complex organism to a number, we may as well point out admitted limitations. The typical college entrance test comes with a booklet that warns users that your true error-free score could be anywhere within a 100-point range. A variance of 50 points in either direction would not be considered significant. So we cannot tell from the test whether you or your friend did better. Better on the test, that is. Studies show no relationship between subject mastery and test scores and no relationship between scores and future success.

Any college using absolute cutoff figures is ignorant of the meaning of test scores. It could choose students equally well simply by tossing a coin.

Anyone using or interpreting test scores should spend a couple of hours at least learning the technical meanings of *validity, reliability, objectivity,* and *standardization* and about how tests are constructed. A test could be faultless technically on all four counts and still provide no useful information about your capacity to think well in college. (In fact, under the right circumstances, I have seen virtually every configuration of student behavior imaginable succeed in college. Furthermore, tests devised by teachers are even less likely to reveal your grasp of a subject, there being no relationship between test-taking skill and subject mastery.

The point? All statistics must be viewed in a context of meaning. At best, the score you get on any test at all must be considered only a starting point.

4.   The implication is that smoking has caused the diminished sex life. But it could just as easily be that diminished sex life causes people to smoke more. The cause-and-effect relationship has not been established. There may not be any direct relationship at all. There could be other factors involved that the investigator didn't consider. Perhaps it is the personality type rather than the smoking that is causing the difference in sex life. Got that?

5.   The figure looks precise and scientific, but you can bet not one student would have given a response carried out to three decimal places. Anyway, no students could produce such a precise accounting of their time even if they wanted to. All 1251 figures provided would have to have been approximate. Also, there is no way to confirm that the students did indeed spend exactly the amount of time on homework that they stated. A statement such as "Students report spending a little more than an hour a day on homework" would reflect the situation more accurately.

The point? You cannot get a statistic more precise than the data used to produce it.

DIALOGUE AND REFLECTION

Now take some time to see what you think about living life by the number. In your large group consider the limits of statistics and their role in one's thinking. Consider the positive side, too. Get beyond pro and con, if you can.

Then pull your thoughts together in your learning log.

> *What is the difference between assertive thinking and passive reasoning?*
>
> *A computer can do the latter but not the former.*

169

COMMENTARY

Don't read this section until you complete an entry
in your learning log.

The Care and Feeding of Statistics

The riddle goes, What is the purpose of thinking? The answer, To stop thinking. It sounds cynical, but that is what happens, isn't it? When you get an itch, you scratch it until the itch goes away. We like things settled. So we use statistics as a back scratcher. Robert Frost said it is just as good to misunderstand a thing as to understand it. Both reduce the amount of botheration we have to put up with in life. It feels good to get things squared away. Since statistics seem to do that for us, naturally we rush to embrace them. It is biological, the side of our organism that wants to rest, to lie down and go to sleep.

But that is only half of the yin yang of life. The other side loves to mix it up, to get into hot water, to see what is over the hill or inside the black box. When we find ourselves caught up in a problem, really involved, the thought of rest never enters our minds. The whole being is at its liveliest.

So a statistic doesn't have to be a tranquilizer. The problem of being deceived by numbers evaporates the minute we quit using them to replace thinking. The same error has been made concerning the left brain in general. "If you use only your left brain," wrote student Alex Solario, "you are other-directed." Facts are definition tyranny only if we let them. They are food for thought, not thought itself.

IQs and aptitude scores can never replace thoughtful response to living, life-loving organisms. Another student, Moyra Price, wrote, "Math is definition tyranny." For most people it is, but it doesn't have to be. The same goes for statistics we read in the paper. Statistics tyranny is simple enough to counteract: Use statistics in ways that make you feel alive. Accepting ideas without reflection pollutes the mind. The key is to use them mindfully instead of mindlessly. They are not conclusions; they are starting points.

We now live in an information-rich environment. No one knows what portion of the available statistics is pure. I would guess hardly any. But if you seek clarity, your passion will override petty details. All thinkers start with a handful of gunk out of which magnificent ideas emerge with astonishing frequency. You are in excellent company.

TIME OUT

KOAN

Statistics are captured snowflakes.

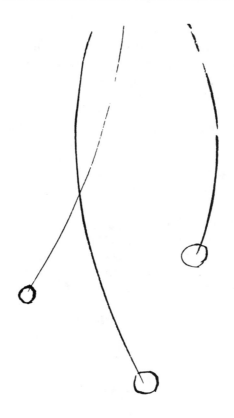

captured
snowflakes
suffering

A SYNTHESIS

Pattern Recognition

As you know, this chapter is about facts and figures and about proof. It includes such topics as bias and question asking, advertising, propaganda, logical fallacies, and systematic reasoning. And there are shrieking geese, plums, praying smokers, jockey shorts, and a path with a heart. Whether you like it or not, if you have gone through the whole chapter thoughtfully, the picture of reality on your mental scanner has been influenced. So in your learning log take some time to see what your mind has been creating for you during this time.

First review this chapter and your learning log entries. Go over your syntheses for chapters 1 and 2.

Then do your synthesis. Spend approximately an hour and a half writing and reflecting. Give your data as much significance as you can and create as many connections among the ideas as possible.

Here is a different approach to reflective writing that Henrietta Hagan discovered in another student's log:

"You write to your other self, and between the two of you you *work over* an idea, brushing away the fuzz (mess) so a clearer profile remains. Also you keep in touch with yourself continually this way."

"Yes," the student wrote back, "I do write as if I'm two people talking back and forth and I work at it to solve some problem I set for myself."

Whatever your approach, taking time to reflect on your journey is tremendously enriching, as you have no doubt observed as you developed a habit of writing in your learning log.

A Reason for Writing

No word that is not flesh, he said,
Can hold my wavering ear; but when
That golden physical flesh is clear,
I dance in a glory like your glory
With a force to stir the dead.

No word that is not thought, he said,
Can hook my slippery mind; but when
That silver accurate thought I find,
I dance in a glory like your glory
With a force to stir the dead.

Words both flesh and thought, he said,
Hold and hook my heart; and when
The gold, the silver, shudder apart,
Still in glory like your glory
I'll dance to stir the dead.

—Theodore Spencer

4

CHAPTER FOUR

HOW NEW DEFINITIONS AND UNDERSTANDING AFFECT KNOWLEDGE

ONCE MORE, THE ROUND

What's greater, Pebble or Pond?
What can be known? The unknown.
My true self runs toward a hill
More! O more! Visible.

Now I adore my life
With the bird, the abiding leaf,
With the fish, the questing snail,
And the eye altering all;
And I dance with William Blake
For love, for Love's sake;

And everything comes to One,
As we dance on, dance on, dance on.
                    —Theodore Roethke

WAYS OF KNOWING

HOW WE KNOW THINGS
The Limitations
of Lexical Knowledge

KOAN

Knowledge is another name for
ignorance.

This chapter is about knowledge, how we know things. The koan above is
your key. See how much mileage you can get out of it before reading my
commentary and introduction to this chapter on the next page. I hope you
are getting used to these outrageous koans by now. I think you know why
they are couched in such absolute terms. One reason is that it frees
everyone to speak out spontaneously. People don't feel respectful or self-
conscious when they explore such "far-out" ideas. Respect and pride put
stultifying limits on exploration. Another koan might well be, You can't be
respectable and think at the same time. At any rate, my students love
playing with ideas that seem fresh and new, bizarre or nutty. So do I. Kurt
Vonnegut says he has always been what people call sophomoric, always
thinking about ideas that can never be settled. Nevertheless, these are the
ideas that have proved seminal. My students call their critical thinking
class their think class. "What do you do in there?" "Oh, we just think."
"What about?" "Oh, anything. It doesn't matter."

Something else I have done in this book to make it less abstract is to
speak in my own voice, using the pronouns *I* and *me* and *my*. As you know,
most textbooks scrupulously weed out all personal references. Apparently, they do that in order to sound more authoritative, as if the ideas you
see there in print came straight from the gods. I have also used the pro-
noun *you*—another word carefully expunged from textbooks. I will leave it
to you to decide if my decisions have made this book more human and
accessible for you.

One thing is certain, and I say this authoritatively: Textbooks contain
some of the worst examples of prose style to be found in the United States.
As Neil Postman rightly points out in his speech to English teachers, *style* is
the message. The message of the majority of textbooks is that academic
thought is dry, pedantic, and bloodless, settled and complete. It harbors no
uncertainty and discourages independent thought. "Textbook language,"

176

you will recall Postman saying, "is apt to be the same from subject to subject and creates the impression that systematic knowledge is always expressed in a dull, uninspired monotone. I have seen recipes on the backs of cereal boxes written with more verve and personality than textbook descriptions of the causes of the Civil War." Some of the best writing I have seen anywhere comes from the journals of inspired students on the trail of an intriguing idea.

REFLECTION

Work up your ideas about the koan and do an entry in your learning log before you go on to my comments that follow.

COMMENTARY

Complete your own reflections before reading this
section.

Redefining Knowledge

If you have been following the themes of *Thinking about Thinking*, you can
bet that *knowing* and *knowledge* are about to be redefined—by me and by
you. For example, consider "Once More, the Round" at the beginning of
this chapter. If I guess rightly, you have immersed yourself in *Thinking
about Thinking* so much by now that the poem "computes" readily. Think
back to how you would have approached the poem just a few weeks ago.

> Take a little time out right now to make sure everyone groks the
> poem and sees how it fits into the general idea of *Thinking about
> Thinking.* Have someone read it out loud to the whole class. Work
> in small groups and clear up any confusion. Be sure everyone gets
> it. Then have someone read it out loud again. You will like this
> approach.

Back so soon? Roethke gets it all in, doesn't he? The eye altering all. Our
world existing *only* as we perceive it. The great enigma of BEING. *Enigma*,
great significance hidden in mysterious and challenging form. That's it,
that's us. The dance of life for Love's sake. Feeling, the senses, the tentative-
ness. My true self runs toward a hill, more, O more visible. Even the
rhythm and melody of it all. These themes are all woven into earlier chapters. Let's see what we have to show for it.

Well, hardly anything you can take home and put up on the refrigerator.
Knowledge isn't knowledge, that is, not as knowledge is popularly conceived. For it is not something solid and absolute and sure. If anything, it is
a kind of dance step, a rhythm, a melody with which the perceiver gets in
harmony with his or her extended self, the universe. I hope this far into
Thinking about Thinking that you will not take this to be an unconsidered
view.

Remember the split-brain experiments described by Julian Jaynes in
chapter 2 in which he shows how your brain can stitch over a hole so cun-
ningly that you cannot even know that it is there? Or *not* there might be a
better way to say it.

> But if you had your hemispheric connections cut, the matter would be very
> different. Starting at the middle of this line, all the print to your right would be
> seen as before and you would be able to read it off almost as usual. But all the

print and all the page to your left would be a blank. Not a blank really, but a nothing, an absolute nothing, far more nothing than any nothing you can imagine. So much nothing that you would not even be conscious that there was nothing there, strange as it seems. Just as in the phenomenon of the blind spot, the "nothing" is somehow "filled in," "stitched together," as if nothing were wrong with nothing.

In other words, this sort of not knowing is so unknowable that we cannot even imagine it. All the assumptions, axioms, premises on which "knowledge" rests may indeed be stitched together over an empty, empty nothingness.

But hang on. It's not so bad. Nothingness (no-thingness) can be perceived as the essential other half of the yin yang. Matter, energy, poof! Imagine it as the foundation of illumination or enlightenment—or if you prefer, clarity. You can see why it is so important in these discussions to use words in their full metaphoric sense with simultaneous multiple meanings. Thinking about thingness and no-thingness, creation and the void, spirit and matter, is like thinking about the box that slips back and forth as we look at it from one base to another:

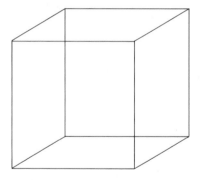

Which view is correct? Both together—and infinite others, too.

We have to be willing to flip-flop between the perceptions and hold all views of the box in our heads simultaneously. Ambiguity in this sense is not vagueness or fuzziness but a more accurate view. Ambiguity, multiple meaning, enigma, are the more precise version of that-which-is, just the opposite of what we are used to assuming.

All knowledge, the ivory citadel of human thought, rests on nonprovable "truths." We hold these truths to be self-evident? Oh, no. The axioms of mathematics, the laws of physics, the proofs of logic, have all been challenged successfully, leaving us with a great uncertainty—but paradoxically with greater clarity!

The traitors have come from within the sacred temples themselves. Kurt Gödel showed that the axiomatic system of proof in mathematics is incomplete—in other words, that math is not as foolproof as it appears. Noam Chomsky showed how far we are from a complete theory of the grammar of language. Werner Heisenberg showed that Newtonian certainty does not apply in subatomic physics. That is the Heisenberg uncertainty principle. Einstein felt that "God does not play dice with the universe." But Heisenberg found, and all subatomic physicists are finding, that He does. In several distinct disciplines it has been demonstrated that the mere act of observing can and does change the thing being observed. Sequence of behavior, once the bulwark of deductive reasoning, is now being replaced with simultaneity. If I spit on the street in Cleveland, they step in it in Hong Kong. If we are to live in the world being revealed by our present research we will have to replace heard melodies with those unheard—but sweeter. Monkeys who teach themselves to wash their sweet potatoes in one part of the world somehow are simultaneously teaching monkeys thousands of miles away to do the same thing without benefit of telephones. Nature is not as natural as it seems.

This chapter will focus on ways in which ambiguity, uncertainty, and even nothingness can be perceived as much more solid security than proof of certainty or IRAs. We start with another short passage from Colin Wilson's *The Mind Parasites*. What would happen if we dared to examine the deepest anchors of selfhood? What if memory were erased from your brain? It is done all the time. Who would you be then?

THE SENSE OF IDENTITY

Challenging Our Premises and Assumptions

Read the following passage as part of the dialogue developing in this chapter concerning knowledge and assurance. Connect Wilson's concept with "Once More, the Round" and with observations in the commentary that follows.

> **Reading Tip**
>
> Extract Wilson's metaphors.

From *THE MIND PARASITES*

Colin Wilson

KICKING AWAY THE CRUTCHES

I had reflected often enough that our human life is based completely on "premises" that we take for granted. A child takes its parents and its home for granted; later, it comes to take its country and its society for granted. We need these supports to begin with. A child without parents and a regular home grows up feeling insecure. A child that has had a good home may later learn to criticize its parents, or even reject them altogether (although this is unlikely); but it only does so when it is strong enough to stand alone.

All original thinkers develop by kicking away these "supports" one by one. They may continue to love their parents and their country, but they love from a position of strength—a strength that began in rejection.

In fact, though, human beings never really learn to stand alone. They are lazy, and prefer supports. A man may be a fearlessly original mathematician, and yet be slavishly dependent on his wife. He may be a powerful free thinker, yet derive a great deal more comfort than he would admit from the admiration of a few friends and disciples. In short, human beings never question *all* their supports; they question a few and continue to take the rest for granted.

Now I had been so absorbed in the adventure of entering new mental continents, rejecting my old personality and its assumptions, that I had been quite unaware that I was still leaning heavily on dozens of ordinary assumptions. For example, although I felt my identity had changed, I still had a strong feeling of identity. And our most fundamental sense of identity comes from an anchor that lies at the bottom of a very deep sea. I still looked upon myself as a member of the human race. I still looked upon myself as an inhabitant of the solar system and the universe in space and time. I took space and time for granted. I did not ask where I had been before my birth or after my death. I did not even recognize the problem of my own death; it was something I left "to be explored later."

What the parasites now did was to go to these deep moorings of my identity, and proceed to shake them. I cannot express it more clearly than this. They did not

181

actually, so to speak, pull up the anchors. That was beyond their powers. But they shook their chains, so that I suddenly became aware of an insecurity on a level I had taken completely for granted. I found myself asking: Who am I? In the deepest sense. Just as a bold thinker dismisses patriotism and religion, so I dismissed all the usual things that gave me an "identity": the accident of my time and place of birth, the accident of my being a human being rather than a dog or a fish, the accident of my powerful instinct to cling to life. Having thrown off all these accidental "trappings," I stood naked as pure consciousness confronting the universe. But here I became aware that this so-called "pure consciousness" was as arbitrary as my name. It could not confront the universe without sticking labels on it. How could it be "pure consciousness" when I saw that object as a book, that one as a table? It was still my tiny human identity looking out of my eyes. And if I tried to get beyond it, everything went blank.

I was not doing all this thinking for fun. I was trying to fight my way down to some solid bedrock on which I could take my stand against them. They had simply been cunning enough to show me that I was standing over an abyss. For my mind leapt on to recognize that we also take space and time for granted, although death takes us beyond them. *I saw* that what I call "existence" means existence in space and time, and that this universe of space and time is not absolute. Suddenly, *everything became absurd*. For the first time, a dreadful sense of insecurity and weakness gripped my stomach. I saw that everything I take for granted in this universe can be questioned—that they could all be a trick. As a thinker, I had got into the old romantic habit of feeling that the mind is beyond the accidents of the body, that it is somehow eternal and free, that the body may be trivial and particular, but the mind is universal and general. This attitude makes the mind an eternal spectator, beyond fear. But now I suddenly felt: "But if the universe itself is arbitrary, then my mind is as casual and destructible as my body." This is the point where one remembers the times of sickness and delirium, when the mind seems altogether less durable than the body, when one suspects that it is mainly the body's toughness that is preventing the mind from disintegrating.

COMMENTARY

**Don't read this section until you have completed
an entry in your learning log.**

Title: _____

> When you finish reading this section, give it a
> right-brained title, compare yours with other students',
> and reflect.

"Having thrown off all these accidental trappings," writes Wilson's narrator, "I stood naked in pure consciousness confronting the universe." Pure consciousness. Imagine that. What would that feel like? Beyond assumption, beyond space-time, who are you? If there is a bedrock of being or a security beyond temporal armor, what might that be? People who manage somehow to kick away the final supports glimpse an eternal, steadfast no-thingness.

Tennyson experienced this when he would sometimes sit and repeat his own name, Alfred, Alfred, Alfred, until the name became mere noise. It seemed, he wrote, that he was the eternal ground of being masquerading as Alfred, Lord Tennyson. Carl Sagan writes of an acquaintance who sensed another presence inside his mind. "Who are you?" he silently asked. "Who wants to know?" came the reply. Everyone has sensed at some time or other the limitless interconnectedness of the point called self with everything else there is and with what all that thingness comes out of, intimations of immortality, as William Wordsworth put it.

Would you agree that there is a thrust inside you the same as that described by Bertrand Russell?

> I *must*, before I die, find *some* way to say the essential thing that is in me, that I have never said yet—a thing that is not love or pity or scorn, but the very breath of life, fierce and coming from far away, bringing into human life the vastness and the fearful passionless force of non-human things.

You might want to read that over a couple of times to get the full implication of Russell's words: vast, passionless, non-human things. We have to go back that far, in fact, even farther.

Even the most left-brained thinker's reasoning must recognize that this flesh is connected, link by physical link, with the ancient beginning of all intelligence far down in the depth of the mind. When the narrator of *The*

Mind Parasites swims down toward these depths, he will encounter the dwellers of the caves of ice who speak in this poem by Eugene Guillevic:

> *in the cave of ice*
> *where light was fearful*
>
> *we have been dwelling*
> *these months,*
> *under the icicles.*
>
> *But this is only*
> *an image; need for an image;*
>
> *for where we crouched, hiding,*
> *was an amorphous place*
>
> *far down below language.*

As you will recall from earlier sections of *Thinking about Thinking*, subject matter, knowledge, is knowledge of language, and "things" are put into symbolic structures through language processes. *Amorphous* means "without form," that is, nonphysical. We have to go that far to reach the base of knowledge. This amorphous base is the foundation on which all knowledge is built. When we get beyond knowledge, where are we? "We're talking infinite here," said a student. The Marabar caves in *A Passage to India* for the English woman Mrs. Moore echoed the meaninglessness of a world so infinite that knowledge shrinks to zero and all thought is reduced to "ou-boum." What can we really know? In *The Myth of Sisyphus*, Nobel Prize winner Albert Camus could find no answer in science or art:

> I realize that if through science I can seize phenomena and enumerate them, I cannot, for all that, apprehend the world. Were I to trace its entire relief with my finger, I should not know any more. And you give me the choice between a description that is sure but that teaches me nothing and hypotheses that claim to teach me but that are not sure.

To will, says Camus, to act deliberately, to choose a life rather than accept one, is "to stir up paradoxes."

But then, as one student wrote, "Perhaps the power of knowledge is in knowing how much one does not really know about a thing." For knowledge ceases to be full of power the minute we take it as proved. The thinker is then most vulnerable, for at that moment thinking has ceased.

The point is that if there is to be a reason for living, like Theodore Spencer's "A Reason for Writing" at the end of chapter 3, it will lie elsewhere than in a safety deposit box. This is not to reject knowledge, which after all is the sum of all human creation and the physical structure of meaning, but to put it in its place. With knowledge alone we cannot see. But through it there is a possible glimpse of, what? a pebble of quartz, truth?

SOMETHING MORE OF THE DEPTHS

The Purpose of Inquiry

Next is a poem by Robert Frost, who did not like to jump to conclusions. It is a poem about searching, seeking, and finding only a glimpse—out of the corner of the eye.
   Work it over as you did "Once More, the Round." First have someone read it out loud. Clarify it in your small groups. Discuss its connection with "knowing," and then have someone read it out loud again.

FOR ONCE, THEN, SOMETHING

Robert Frost

Others taunt me with having knelt at well-curbs
Always wrong to the light, so never seeing
Deeper down in the well than where the water
Gives me back in a shining surface picture
Me myself in the summer heaven, godlike,
Looking out of a wreath of fern and cloud puffs.
Once, when trying with chin against a well-curb,
I discerned, as I thought, beyond the picture,
Through the picture, a something white, uncertain,
Something more of the depths—and then I lost it.
Water came to rebuke the too clear water.
One drop fell from a fern, and lo, a ripple
Shook whatever it was lay there at bottom,
Blurred it, blotted it out. What was that whiteness?
Truth? A pebble of quartz?
For once, then, something.

DIALOGUE AND REFLECTION

Clear up any confusion about this poem in your small groups (see that everyone gets it) and reflect on its concepts in your learning log. It should be easier to read a poem like this now than when you began thinking about thinking. Is it? Is a flash of an uncertain whiteness worth the trip?

COMMENTARY

Don't read this section until you and all your
classmates have grokked "For Once, Then,
Something."

The Search for . . . What?

You will recall that Frost wanted to get above pro and con. If you want a place to stand when looking at controversial issues, "choose something like a star." It is part of the message of his medium that he chooses language with painstaking care. To do this he has to resort to ambiguity, to multiple meanings, for words limited to only one meaning are inadequate and mislead us into inferring more or less than was intended. It is impossible to read "For Once, Then, Something" adequately without reading it several ways at once.

For example, Frost does not spell out what he was trying to do or see. To see himself? To see the bottom? Of himself, his self, life, or just the well? Was he trying to see the shining surface picture? Just that? Or by means of the picture to see through it, to see beyond? None of these answers alone would be sufficient, would it? Not if you want to see clearly. Isn't the best version, as we have observed before, a combination of all views?

If someone asks you what you are up to on this planet, what is your response? What are you trying for? What are you trying? If you say a job or happiness, those may be the shining surface picture, a metaphor for something more of the depths, something you are not quite sure of yourself—even though you wear yourself out trying every day. Maybe, as many thinkers have concluded, the surface picture is all there is.

So you stand before a mirror and see your visage. Looking fine, wreathed in cloud puffs like a god. With great effort and attention you discern something white, uncertain. But are you sure? Is it by means of thinking that you catch the glimpse? Is it something that swims into view while you are thinking? Or does "as I thought" mean "so it seemed"? Of course it means all of those possibilities, for only an Archie Bunker would be willing to declare any one of them the winner.

And what slows you down and keeps the sighting indefinite? The very stuff of the picture itself. The light gets too bright and blinds you or a drop of water blurs whatever it might be and blots it out.

We have only a hint to go on, but it is something, even if it happens only once. Is that enough for you? Will the memory of a glimpse sustain you through all the barren lands? Ultimately, there may well be no difference between truth and a pebble of quartz. They may be the same thing.

186

THE IQ MYTH
The Role of Intelligence in Thinking

KOAN

Define intelligence.

DIALOGUE AND REFLECTION

Like any other word in your vocabulary, *intelligence* has multiple meanings. In your dialogue see how many you and your group can identify. Then figure out one definition that is general enough to include all of them. Are trees intelligent? From what point of view is a pebble intelligent? Clay? (Did I go too far there?) To figure the intelligence quotient of a termite, should we treat a whole termite mound as an entity? Who is in charge of deciding these matters?

Continue your reflections on intelligence in your learning log.

COMMENTARY

Be sure to do your own reflecting before you read
this section

Kneeling at Well-Curbs

No two of us think the same way. You already know that. So how could
there be such a thing as IQ? The evidence is building that the idea that
there are higher and lower intelligences has no productive value. We are
finding something else, though. Something that may eventually get others
off our backs when we solve problems in our own sweet way. Maybe
society will learn to let people like Robert Frost look down wells any old
way they want. Finally, some researchers are developing the theory of different *kinds* of intelligence, different ways of structuring the perceived
world. Just as there is no such thing as a good reader, period, there is no
such thing as being more or less intelligent, period. Intelligent about
what? we will have to ask. We are not intelligent about everything or all the
time. We may use certain structures for thinking in certain situations and
have great results and not use them at all in other situations. There is no
such thing as absolute intelligence. It is always situational and always relative to environmental conditions.

People thought Frost was kneeling at well-curbs always "wrong to the
light." There is no such thing as "wrong to the light." (You may have noticed
you can take that phrase a couple of ways.) There is no right way to try
either, and no right way to think. If there were, we would indeed be
replaceable droplets in the intelligence pool. But every single person structures a picture of reality that is unique. No two mandalas are alike. IQs are
captured snowflakes, suffering.

When you think of the assumptions that IQ is based on, you see it is an
idea whose time has passed. Over eighty years ago in France one man,
Alfred Binet, thought up a way to predict which kids would fail in school.
Out of that has come a concept as entrenched in modern thinking as
witches were in seventeenth-century New England. Binet's test focused on
language skills (mainly vocabulary recognition) and on logical reasoning
(math is a form of logical reasoning).

Thus, if a person performed on Binet's test the way a typical (as defined
by Binet) ten-year-old did, he said the person had a mental age of ten and
would have trouble doing school work typical eleven-year-olds could do.

Don't doze off, just a few more figures: If a person with skills of Binet's
typical ten-year-old were actually twelve, Binet worked out a percentage:
10 divided by 12 is .83. The child had a quotient of 83. Binet called it the

child's *intelligence* quotient. If a child is ten and scores like a ten-year-old, that's 100. If the child is eight and scores like a ten-year-old, that's 125, and the parents will be proud.

Take a minute here to confer with another student and make sure you both do understand how your IQ is determined. When you're clear, get into your group of three or four and explore the following topic.

Fun with Witches and IQ

Use your amazing talents in analyzing advertising, propaganda, bias, prejudice, statistics, logical fallacies, definition tyranny, and question asking to find half a dozen flaws in Binet's IQ concept. Pool your ideas, reflect, and then go on reading.

IQ compares the dexterity of one human being with that of another in manipulating specific kinds of symbols and structures. To measure capacity to think with such a limited instrument reveals gross ignorance of how the human brain functions. Having read the first three chapters of *Thinking about Thinking,* you know how complex the process is. Implicit in the quotient is a definition of intelligence, Alfred Binet's definition. It would be more correctly labeled the Binet Quotient, BQ. For there is no attention to right-hemisphere thinking whatsoever, nor to your reptilian and limbic brains, nor to the role of the senses. There is no attention to how answers are arrived at, no awareness of social and economic biases built into the tests. How would a Hopi do? A Korean? There is no consideration of style of thinking or of pace. And there is no attention to whether the test measures what it claims to in the first place. All the above aside, the dehumanizing tendency among interpreters to treat the figures as reliable measures of permanent mental abilities has damaged the lives of millions.

If schools and parents persist in using the BQ, let them consider the score for what it is: a statistic that means absolutely nothing until it is given meaning in a specific instance. *A score of 80 for one person means something entirely different from the 80 of any other person on that test.* Without going over the test with the individual, item by item, and exploring how the person arrived at the response, we know nothing about the way that person structures reality. *A statistic has no meaning.*

Furthermore, the answer you get, as Neil Postman points out, depends on how the question is phrased. A test is a mandala for the test maker. We know more about how he or she thinks than about how the victim does.

MULTIPLE INTELLIGENCES
Structures for Knowing

KOAN

Is it better to think or to be
intelligent?

IQ puts whole human beings on a ladder: the closer to the top, the smarter the individual. There is nothing in nature that supports such an approach. In fact, psychologist Howard Gardner, in his book *Frames of Mind*, describes seven kinds of intelligence or, as he puts it, *cognitive potential*. We could call this the theory of multiple intelligences. When we look at nature, we can certainly see different ways of approaching and solving problems. Consider bees or ants, moths or trees—dare I include rocks? How about the way your dog processes data? How about the way we screen data and decide which data get chosen? Is this not ample evidence of many ways of processing information and recognizing patterns? The intelligence spectrum is more like a pie than a ladder, each creature with its own unique slice.

Multiple human intelligences? Look at your mandalas. Look at your mutual-aid picture. For starters Gardner has isolated seven kinds of intelligence. Which ones appeared on your college entrance tests?

Seven Frames of Mind

1. *Linguistic:* vocabulary, sentence structure
2. *Logical-mathematical:* deductive, inductive reasoning, quantification, shape, size, ratio
3. *Musical:* pitch patterns, rhythm patterns
4. *Fine motor* (kinesthetic): dancing, juggling, surgery
5. *Interpersonal:* understanding of others
6. *Spatial:* getting around in an environment, finding your way in a strange city.
7. *Intrapersonal:* understanding of self, self-concept

DIALOGUE AND REFLECTION

Take time here to work up Gardner's ideas in your small groups. Try them on for size. Find ways his frames of mind are used in your group. Explore differing configurations of mind and their contribution to understanding ideas you examine together. If any of his seven are not used in your group, would your thinking be more complete if someone were more experienced at using them?

While you are at it, think of the implications for the way schools are set up. Imagine schools based on a Gardner Quotient, GQ, instead of a Binet Quotient, BQ.

Also think up a few ways of knowing—frames of mind—Gardner hasn't listed. Hint: Look inside your own mind.

Now then, everyone make a right-brained definition of *intelligence*.

If you had to choose, would you rather be someone who thinks or someone who is intelligent?

In your large group pool your findings and later reflect on all this in your learning log.

COMMENTARY

Don't read this section until you have finished an entry in your learning log.

Models and Witnesses

The point is, isn't it, that each of us has a unique way of thinking, and that uniqueness is what makes us special. Rather than be molded to the one way of thinking dreamed up by educationists, we need to nourish and develop our minds, each in its own way. When students depart from a nourishing classroom, they will be less like each other than when they entered. The wattage in the eye will be higher.

On the other hand, working with others we can see ways of approaching life that hadn't occurred to us. Other people's minds represent models we can take from and incorporate into our own bag of tricks. Our dachshund puppy first thought of lifting his leg when he saw another dog do it. Oh, so *that's* how! All the frames of mind are available to us and exist in all of us to varying degrees. We can develop any that appear to have some usefulness.

An education that focuses on linguistic and logico-mathematical thinking is too confining for our spirits. We need to witness and experience a much larger frame of reference.

When my students are handed a box of Cray-Pas colors for their mandalas, most comment that they haven't been near any art materials for years, not since fourth or fifth grade. Years and years with blinders on and a rich, manifold world lying all about them.

Is it better to think than to be intelligent? It depends as usual on what is meant by "think" and "intelligent." If we can be intelligent just sitting there, phooey. That doesn't butter any parsnips. If we mean by thinking that we actually do something with what is available in the brain—and do it on purpose, not accidentally—then thinking wins hands down. Unused brilliance is window dressing. If there actually were these mythical brilliant and dull beings, I would choose the thinking "dull" person any day. How about you?

One way classrooms would have to change if we valued multiple intelligence would be in how much class time is devoted to students doing the talking. At present, teachers do almost all of the talking. But one can't get very good at wrapping language around ideas if he or she doesn't get a chance to practice. And there has to be lots of modeling of lots of different kinds of thinking. So class discussions are vital. In most classes there is only one model of thinking available, that of the teacher. Uniform time modules would have to go, too, because each human being thinks at his or her own pace and rhythm. If tests were still being used, the test would have to be different for each student. And of course our expectations would be drastically altered. Rather than sticking things into heads (in-structing), we would have to be drawing out (educating). We would nourish diversity and not uniformity. And so on. Do you think there is any chance of such a change taking place?

PATTERNS OF ORGANIC ENERGY
The Meaning of Knowledge in Subatomic Physics

What? Organic energy? Some poet messing around with language? No, a definition developed by major physicists who have been forced to such a view through a rigorous study of the guts of the atom.

In "Teaching into the Future," Neil Postman says each discipline has its own way of putting language around the part of nature it observes. History has its own definitions, linguistics its own, music its own. Each creates its own structure, its own medium. Economists have their own way of thinking about economics, their own frame of mind. And that is different from the way painters think, which is different from the way surgeons think. Of course, within a discipline no two frames of mind are identical. Picasso is different from Wyeth. And Andrew is different from Jamie. But it is quite true that at a middle distance the architecture of ballet certainly appears distinguishable from the architecture of physics.

Now along comes Gary Zukav with an idea that bridges the disciplines, that looks deeper and erases the distinctions among thinkers. As you read this abridged version of "Big Week at Big Sur," you will see the differences fade away. How can this be? How can we in one breath say each grain of sand is unique and then say every grain of sand is exactly the same as every other one, unique and universal at once? The answer will not fit into a syllogism.

Zukav argues that in the deepest sense all thinking may be alike. The writer and the surgeon may be brothers after all. The difference may not be among thinkers but between those who think—as defined by Zukav and Thinking about Thinking—and those who use their ideas, those who live for ideas and those who live off ideas. When you get into Zukav's article, take time especially to notice the distinction he makes between technicians and scientists.

In "Big Week at Big Sur" you will see a fresh view of scientific thinking and of what a scientist does. "They wonder what the universe is made of, how it works, what we are doing in it, and where it is going, if it is going anyplace at all." That's what we are all doing, isn't it? In Taiwan physics is called Wu Li. The closest English equivalent is patterns of organic energy. As with all metaphors, it has several other meanings as well. To understand modern physics, you have to keep all these meanings in mind, all at the same time. Come to think of it, you have to do that when you think of the words poet and poem, too. Zukav lists seven definitions of Wu Li, all fitting the science of physics perfectly.

Why do the Wu Li Masters "dance"? They tune in, get the rhythm of, the thing being observed and become one with it. They "dance" with it. The Master dances with the student, too, by finding the student's pace and getting in step. Shall we trade off our instructors for some Wu Li Masters?

Another intriguing idea in Zukav's article: Rather than discovering the nature of the atom, scientists, Wu Li Masters, may actually be creating that nature. "New" things may be simply new perspectives, acts of creation. That is how painters, writers and scientists may be brothers after all.

Use the BFAR method described in chapter 2 when you read "Big Week at Big Sur." You will emerge with a new description of what a scientist is and is not. I hope you will see some possibilities for your own ways of thinking and solving problems.

BIG WEEK AT BIG SUR

Abridged

Gary Zukav

When I tell my friends that I study physics, they move their heads from side to side, they shake their hands at the wrist, and they whistle, "Whew! That's difficult." This universal reaction to the word "physics" is a wall that stands between what physicists do and what most people think they do. There is usually a big difference between the two.

Physicists themselves are partly to blame for this sad situation. Their shop talk sounds like advanced Greek, unless you are Greek or a physicist. When they are not talking to other physicists, physicists speak English. Ask them what they do, however, and they sound like the natives of Corfu again.

On the other hand, part of the blame is ours. Generally speaking, we have given up trying to understand what physicists (and biologists, etc.) really do. In this we do ourselves a disservice. These people are engaged in extremely interesting adventures that are not that difficult to understand. True, *how* they do what they do sometimes entails a technical explanation which, if you are not an expert, can produce an involuntary deep sleep. *What* physicists do, however, is actually quite simple. They wonder what the universe is really made of, how it works, what we are doing in it, and where it is going, if it is going anyplace at all. In short, they do the same things that we do on starry nights when we look up at the vastness of the universe and feel overwhelmed by it and a part of it at the same time. That is what physicists really do, and the clever rascals get paid for doing it.

Unfortunately, when most people think of "physics," they think of chalkboards covered with undecipherable symbols of an unknown mathematics. The fact is that physics is not mathematics. Physics, in essence, is simple wonder at the way things are and a divine (some call it compulsive) interest in how that is so. Mathematics is the *tool* of physics. Stripped of mathematics, physics becomes pure enchantment. [*Wait. Slow-walk that. Simple wonder at* the way things are *and a divine interest in how that is so. Pure enchantment. How many people in your class ever thought of physics that way?*]

I had spoken often to Jack Sarfatti, who is the physicist director of the Physics/Consciousness Research Group, about the possibility of writing a book, unencumbered with technicalities and mathematics, to explain the exciting insights that motivate current physics. So when he invited me to a conference on physics that he and Michael Murphy were arranging at the Esalen Institute, I accepted with a purpose.

The Esalen Institute (it is named for an Indian tribe) is in Northern California. The northern California coast is an awesome combination of power and beauty, but nowhere so much as along the Pacific Coast Highway between the towns of Big Sur and San Luis Obispo. The Esalen facilities are located about a half hour south of Big Sur between the highway and the coastal mountains on the one side and rugged cliffs overlooking the Pacific Ocean on the other. A dancing stream divides the northern third of the grounds from the remainder. On that side is a big house (called the Big House) where guests stay and groups meet, along with a small home where Dick Price (co-founder of Esalen with Murphy) stays with his family. On the other side of the stream is a lodge where meals are served and meetings are held, accommodations for guests and staff, and hot sulfur baths.

Dinner at Esalen is a multi-dimensional experience. The elements are candle-light, organic food, and a contagious naturalness that is the essence of the Esalen experience. Sarfatti and I joined two men who already were eating. One was David Finkelstein, a physicist from Yeshiva University (in New York) who was attending the conference on physics. The other was Al Chung-liang Huang, a T'ai Chi Master who was leading a workshop at Esalen. We could not have chosen better companions.

The conversation soon turned to physics.

"When I studied physics in Taiwan," said Huang, "we called it Wu Li (pronounced 'Woo Lee'). It means 'Patterns of Organic Energy.'"

Everyone at the table was taken at once by this image. Mental lights flashed on, one by one, as the idea penetrated. "Wu Li" was more than poetic. It was the best definition of physics that the conference would produce. It caught that certain something, that living quality that we were seeking to express in a book, that thing without which physics becomes sterile.

"Let's write a book about Wu Li!" I heard myself exclaim. Immediately, ideas and energy began to flow, and in one stroke all of the prior planning that I had done went out the window. From that pooling of energy came the image of the Dancing Wu Li Masters. My remaining days at Esalen and those that followed were devoted to finding out what Wu Li Masters are, and why they dance. All of us sensed with excitement and certitude that we had discovered the channel through which the very things that we wanted to say about physics would flow.

[*Here Zukav gives you what reading theory calls an advanced organizer. He cues you in to look for a description of what a Wu Li Master is and why the Masters are said to dance.*]

The Chinese language does not use an alphabet like western languages. Each word in Chinese is depicted by a character, which is a line drawing. (Sometimes two or more characters are combined to form different meanings). This is why it is difficult to translate Chinese into English. Good translations require a translator who is both a poet and a linguist.

[*Below is Zukav's first approximation of Wu Li. He will gradually enrich the word as he develops his article. So, if you "dance" along with him, you will emerge with a good understanding without beating your head against the wall.*]

For example, "Wu" can mean either "matter" or "energy." "Li" is a richly poetic word. It means "universal order" or "universal law." It also means "organic patterns." The grain in a panel of wood is Li. The organic pattern on the surface of a leaf is also Li, and so is the texture of a rose petal. In short, Wu Li, the Chinese word for physics, means "patterns of organic energy" ("matter/energy" [Wu] + "universal order/organic patterns" [Li]). This is remarkable since it reflects a world view which the founders of western science (Galileo and Newton) simply did not comprehend, but toward which virtually every physical theory of import in the twentieth century is pointing! The question is not, "Do they know something that we don't?" The question is, "How do they know it?"

English words can be pronounced almost any way without changing their meanings. I was five years a college graduate before I learned to pronounce "consummate" as an adjective (con-SUM-ate). (It means "carried to the utmost extent or degree; perfect"). I live in anguish when I think of the times that I have spoken of *con*summate linguists, *con*summate scholars, etc. Someone always seemed to be holding back a smile, almost. I learned later that these were the people who read dictionaries. Nonetheless, my bad pronunciation never prevented me from being understood. That is because inflections do not change the denotation of an English word. "No" spoken with a rising inflection ("No?"), with a downward inflection ("No!"), and with no inflection ("No . . .") all mean (according to the dictionary) "a denial, a refusal, negative."

This is not so in Chinese. Most Chinese syllables can be pronounced several different ways. Each different pronunciation is a different word which is written differently and which has a meaning of its own. Therefore, the same syllable, pronounced with different inflections, which unaccustomed western listeners scarcely can distinguish, constitutes distinctly separate words, each with its own ideogram and meaning, to a Chinese listener. In English, which is an atonal language, these different ideograms are all written and pronounced the same way.

For example, there are over eighty different "Wu"s in Chinese, all of which are spelled and pronounced the same way in English. Al Huang has taken five of these "Wu"s, each of which, when combined with "Li," produces a different "Wu Li," each with the same English spelling, and each pronounced (in English) "Woo Lee."

The first Wu Li means "Patterns of Organic Energy." This is the Chinese way of saying "physics." (Wu means "matter" or "energy.")

The second Wu Li means "My Way." (Wu means "mine" or "self.")

The third Wu Li means "Nonsense." (Wu means "void" or "nonbeing.")

The fourth Wu Li means "I Clutch My Ideas." (Wu means "to make a fist" or "clutch with a closed hand.")

The fifth Wu Li means "Enlightenment." (Wu means "enlightenment" or "my heart/my mind.")

If we were to stand behind a master weaver as he begins to work his loom, we would see, at first, not cloth, but a multitude of brightly colored threads from which he picks and chooses with his expert eye, and feeds into the moving shuttle. As we continue to watch, the threads blend one into the other, a fabric appears, and on the fabric, behold! A pattern emerges.

In a similar manner, Al Huang has created a beautiful tapestry from his own epistemological loom:

PHYSICS = WU LI

Wu Li = Patterns of Organic Energy
Wu Li = My Way
Wu Li = Nonsense
Wu Li = I Clutch My Ideas
Wu Li = Enlightenment

Each of the physicists at the conference, to a person, reported a resonance with this rich metaphor. Here, at last, was the vehicle through which we could present the seminal elements of advanced physics. By the end of the week, everyone at Esalen was talking about Wu Li.

At the same time that this was happening, I was trying to find out what a "Master" is. The dictionary was no help. All of its definitions involved an element of control. This did not fit easily into our image of the Dancing Wu Li Masters. Since Al Huang is a T'ai Chi Master, I asked him.

"That is the word that other people use to describe me," he said. To Al Huang, Al Huang was just Al Huang.

Later in the week, I asked him the same question again, hoping to get a more tangible answer.

"A Master is someone who started before you did," was what I got that time.

My western education left me unable to accept a nondefinition for my definition of a "Master," so I began to read Huang's book, *Embrace Tiger, Return to Mountain*. There, in the foreword by Alan Watts, in a paragraph describing Al Huang, I found what I sought. Said Alan Watts of Al Huang:

> He begins from the center and not from the fringe. He imparts an understanding of the basic principles of the art before going on to the meticulous details, and he refuses to break down the t'ai chi movements into a one-two-three drill so as to make the student into a robot. The traditional way . . . is to teach by rote, and to give the impression that long periods of boredom are the most essential part of training. In that way a student may go on for years and years without ever getting the feel of what he is doing.

Here was just the definition of a Master that I sought. A master teaches essence. When the essence is perceived, he teaches what is necessary to expand the perception. [*A master teaches essence. Compare that approach with the way your own schooling has been conducted.*] The Wu Li Master does not speak of gravity until the student stands in wonder at the flower petal falling to the ground. He does not speak of laws until the student, of his own, says, "How strange! I drop two stones simultaneously, one heavy and one light, and *both* of them reach the earth at the same moment!" He does not speak of mathematics until the student says, "There must be a way to express this more simply."

In this way, the Wu Li Master dances with his student. The Wu Li Master does not teach, but the student learns. The Wu Li Master always begins at the center, at the heart of the matter. . . .

One of the greatest physicists of all, Albert Einstein, was perhaps a Wu Li Master. In 1938 he wrote:

> Physical concepts are free creations of the human mind, and are not, however it may seem, uniquely determined by the external world. In our endeavor to understand reality we are somewhat like a man trying to understand the mechanism of a closed watch. He sees the face and the moving hands, even hears its ticking, but he has no way of opening the case. If he is ingenious he may form some picture of a mechanism which could be responsible for all the things he observes, but he may never be quite sure his picture is the only one which could explain his observations. He will never be able to compare his picture with the real mechanism and he cannot even imagine the possibility of the meaning of such a comparison.

[*That is a seminal idea!* Physical concepts are free creations of the human mind. *Knowledge is an invention, a human fabrication. It is an idea* about *what may be there, not the thing itself—whatever that may be. Physics is an attempt by the thinker to get in step with nature, to dance with it.*] Most people believe that physicists are explaining the world. Some physicists even believe that, but the Wu Li Masters know that they are only dancing with it.

I asked Huang how he structures his classes.

"Every lesson is the first lesson," he told me. "Every time we dance, we do it for the first time."

"But surely you cannot be starting new each lesson," I said. "Lesson number two must be built on what you taught in lesson number one, and lesson three likewise must be built on lessons one and two, and so on."

"When I say that every lesson is the first lesson," he replied, "it does not mean that we forget what we already know. It means that what we are doing is always new, because we are always doing it for the first time."

This is another characteristic of a Master. Whatever he does, he does with the enthusiasm of doing it for the first time. This is the source of his unlimited energy. Every lesson that he teaches (or learns) is a first lesson. Every dance that he dances, he dances for the first time. It is always new, personal, and alive. . . .

Isidor I. Rabi, Nobel Prize winner in Physics and the former Chairman of the Physics Department at Columbia University wrote:

> We don't teach our students enough of the intellectual content of experiments—their novelty and their capacity for opening new fields. . . . My own view is that you take these things personally. You do an experiment because your own philosophy makes you want to

know the result. It's too hard, and life is too short, to spend your time doing something because someone else has said it's important. You must feel the thing yourself.

[*Wait. Get the feel of that.*]

Unfortunately, most physicists are not like Rabi. The majority of them, in fact, *do* spend their lives doing what other people have told them is important. That was the point Rabi was making.

[*Next is that description of a scientist versus a technician I mentioned earlier. Does it compute?*]

This brings us to a common misunderstanding. When most people say "scientist," they mean "technician." A technician is a highly trained person whose job is to apply known techniques and principles. He deals with the known. A scientist is a person who seeks to know the true nature of physical reality. He deals with the unknown.

In short, scientists discover and technicians apply. However, it is no longer evident whether scientists really discover new things or whether they *create* them. Many people believe that "discovery" is actually an act of creation. If this is so, then the distinction between scientists, poets, painters and writers is not clear. In fact, it is possible that scientists, poets, painters and writers are all members of the same family of people whose gift it is by nature to take those things which we call commonplace and to *re-present* them to us in such ways that our self-imposed limitations are expanded. Those people in whom this gift is especially pronounced, we call geniuses. [*A good definition of a thinker: someone who re-presents the commonplace so that it no longer appears "common." Remember how Sister Corita unclichéd the friendly skies?*]

The fact is that most "scientists" are technicians. They are not interested in the essentially new. Their field of vision is relatively narrow; their energies are directed toward applying what is already known. Because their noses often are buried in the bark of a particular tree it is difficult to speak meaningfully to them of forests! . . .

There are certain limitations which no book on physics can overcome. First, there is so much to present that not even twenty volumes could contain it all. There is that much *new* material published each year. Even physicists find it impossible to keep abreast of the whole field. It requires a steady diet of reading just to keep current in one area. . . . No matter how much you learn about physics, there always will be something that is new to you. Physicists have this problem, too.

Second, no complete appreciation of physics is possible without mathematics. Nonetheless, there is no mathematics in *The Dancing Wu Li Masters*. Mathematics is a highly structured way of thinking. Physicists view the world in this way. One point of view is that they impose this structure on what they see. Another point of view is that the world presents itself most completely through such structures. In any case, mathematics is the most concise expression of physics. The reason for writing *The Dancing Wu Li Masters,* however, is that most physicists are not able to explain physics very well without it. This makes them very concise but, unfortunately, unintelligible. The fact is that most of us use words to do our explaining.

199

However, it is important to remember that mathematics and English are both languages. Languages are useful tools for conveying information, but if we try to communicate experiences with them, they simply do not work. All a language can do is talk *about* an experience. Wu Li Masters know that a description of an experience is not the experience. It is only talk about it. . . . [*But keep in mind, too, that while you cannot get my experience directly through the words I use, I have created the experience in language. That is, my experience is linguistic and exists only in symbols.*] It cannot contain the experience itself. This does not mean that you will not have the experience of physics by reading [about] it; it only means that if you do, the experience is coming from you, and not from the book. Quantum mechanics, for example, shows us that we are not as separate from the rest of the world as we once thought. Particle physics shows us that the "rest of the world" does not sit idly "out there." It is a sparkling realm of continual creation, transformation, and annihilation. The ideas of the new physics, when wholly grasped, can produce extraordinary *experiences*. The study of relativity theory, for example, can produce the remarkable experience that space and time are only mental constructions! Each of these different experiences is capable of changing us in such ways that we never again are able to view the world as we did before.

There is no single "experience" of physics. The experience always is changing. Relativity and quantum mechanics, although generally unknown to nonphysicists, are more than a half century old. Today, the entire field of physics is quivering with anticipation. The air is charged with excitement. A feeling is shared among physicists that radical change is at hand. A consensus grows that the near future will see new theories exploding onto the scene, incorporating the older theories and giving us a much larger view of our universe and, consequently, of ourselves.

The Wu Li Masters move in the midst of all this, now dancing this way, now that, sometimes with a heavy beat, sometimes with a lightness and grace, ever flowing freely. Now they become the dance, now the dance becomes them. This is the message of the Wu Li Master: not to confuse the type of dance that they are doing with the fact that they are dancing.

DIALOGUE AND REFLECTION

Dancing might be a good metaphor for your dialogue in your discussion groups. When a conversation goes well, it feels musical. When it is left brained only, it feels mechanical and superficial. Wu Li is whole brained. Do you agree?

Work with three or four others and extract four or five ideas from the article that have some freshness for you and that have some connections to ideas in *Thinking about Thinking*. Pool your findings and do an entry in your learning log.

COMMENTARY

Don't read this section until you have completed
your reflections in your learning log.

Whole-Brained Physics:
The Music of the Spheres

Isn't the idea of Wu Li fascinating? To find hard-headed physicists actually defining their field as *organic* provides a wonderful symmetry for divergent ideas in *Thinking about Thinking*. All things are connected, says Chief Seattle, and quantum physics agrees. Energy is organic. So maybe the view that rocks "think" or are "intelligent" is not so farfetched.

One reason "Big Week at Big Sur" is included in this book is to help dispel the suspicion that whole-brained thinking is wishy-washy. The Wu Li Masters know that anything less is too limited. Zukav makes it clear, too, that "trying" is a divine, almost compulsive, interest in accuracy of thought, far more rigorous than attempts at left-brained or right-brained thinking alone. Whole-brained physics is no more rigorous than the choreography for *Swan Lake* or the score of a Bach fugue.

Wu Li integrates disciplines that have remained separate in Western thought far too long. The rich ambiguity of metaphor is precisely paralleled inside the atom. Idea and object, particle and wave, yin and yang, nonphysical and physical, merge. They are one thing.

These ideas are easier to understand than to define. As perhaps you have noticed, rather than providing dictionarylike definitions of *fact, truth, intelligence, thinking,* I have provided you with experiences of these words in various environments so that you become familiar with them and their multiple meanings. A satisfactory definition of any word must include the whole spectrum of thought and context in which it is embedded. As you no doubt realize, that is what discussion and reflection do for you.

Of course, the central idea of Zukav's article is that the physicist's interaction with his or her material is a dance, a musical activity. Thinking is musical. In his *Frames of Mind* Howard Gardner lists musical knowing as one of his seven kinds of intelligence. Infants "track" adult talk, practicing the rhythm and pace of speech, the music of it, long before they interject words. The understanding is basically melodic. A sentence, too, is a melody. So dancing is a good metaphor for thinking. Remove the dancer, the dance evaporates. "Is the tree the leaf, the blossom or the bole?" asks William Butler Yeats. "O body swayed to music, O brightening glance, How can we know the dancer from the dance?"

When we paraphrase Roethke or Frost, the message is diminished. It is not even the same message. The style, the structure, the choreography are inseparable from the message. The silver and the gold together hold and hook my heart. When we recite our "lessons" we must get the pitch, the key, the meter, right. The words *and* the melody. Indeed the universe itself may be melodic. The "music of the spheres" may emerge as a scientific description.

Detours are dancing lessons from God.
—Kurt Vonnegut

THE C-STUDENT MENTALITY
The Role of Goals in Thinking

In Franz Kafka's The Trial *a man has been placed on trial but cannot find out what crime he is accused of. At one point he visits the cathedral where he solicits help from a priest who tells him the following fable.*

Read the fable once or twice and let it steep awhile. In class have someone read it out loud and then discuss it in small groups. Discuss it from whatever angle you wish. My students usually have strong opinions about what the man from the country should have done. What do you think? Someone usually suggests that any other goal could easily be substituted for "the Law," say, medicine or ballet, and the "man from the country" could be replaced by any college student. Do you agree?

Also find a few connections with ideas in this chapter on ways of knowing.

IN THE CATHEDRAL
Franz Kafka

In the writings which preface the Law that particular delusion is described thus: before the Law stands a doorkeeper. To this doorkeeper there comes a man from the country who begs for admittance to the Law. But the doorkeeper says that he cannot admit the man at the moment. The man, on reflection, asks if he will be allowed, then, to enter later. "It is possible," answers the doorkeeper, "but not at this moment." Since the door leading into the Law stands open as usual and the door-keeper steps to one side, the man bends down to peer through the entrance. When the doorkeeper sees that, he laughs and says: "If you are so strongly tempted, try to get in without my permission. But note that I am powerful. And I am only the lowest doorkeeper. From hall to hall, keepers stand at every door, one more pow-erful than the other. And the sight of the third man is already more than even I can stand." These are difficulties which the man from the country has not expected to meet, the Law, he thinks, should be accessible to every man and at all times, but when he looks more closely at the doorkeeper in his furred robe, with his huge pointed nose and long thin Tartar beard, he decides that he had better wait until he gets permission to enter. The doorkeeper gives him a stool and lets him sit down at the side of the door. There he sits waiting for days and years. He makes many attempts to be allowed in and wearies the doorkeeper with his importunity. The doorkeeper often engages him in brief conversation, asking him about his home and about other matters, but the questions are put quite impersonally, as great men put questions, and always conclude with the statement that the man cannot be allowed to enter yet. The man, who has equipped himself with many things for his journey, parts with all he has, however valuable, in the hope of bribing the door-keeper. The doorkeeper accepts it all, saying, however, as he takes each gift: "I take this only to keep you from feeling that you have left something undone." During all these long years the man watches the doorkeeper almost incessantly. He forgets about the other doorkeepers, and this one seems to him the only barrier between himself and the Law. In the first years he curses his evil fate aloud; later, as he grows old, he only mutters to himself. He grows childish, and since in his prolonged study of the doorkeeper he has learned to know even the fleas in his fur collar, he begs the very fleas to help him and to persuade the doorkeeper to change his mind. Finally his eyes grow dim and he does not know whether the world is really darkening around him or whether his eyes are only deceiving him. But in the darkness he can now perceive a radiance that streams inextinguishably from the door of the Law. Now his life is drawing to a close. Before he dies, all that he has experienced during the whole time of his sojourn condenses in his mind into one question, which he has never yet put to the doorkeeper. He beckons the doorkeeper, since he can no longer raise his stiffening body. The doorkeeper has to bend far down to hear him, for the difference in size between them has increased very much to the man's disadvantage. "What do you want to know now?" asks the doorkeeper, "you are insatiable." "Everyone strives to attain the Law," answers the man, "how does it come about then, that in all these years no one has come seeking admittance but me?" The doorkeeper perceives that the man is nearing his end and his hearing is failing, so he bellows in his ear: "No one but you could gain admittance through this door, since this door was intended for you. I am now going to shut it."

DIALOGUE AND REFLECTION

In your large group pool your ideas, and later reflect in your learning log.

COMMENTARY

Don't read this section until you have completed
an entry in your learning log.

On the Knife-Edge

Most of my students are disgusted with the man from the country. A typical
C student, they say, a real wimp. Then we get a whole list of should-haves. He
should have bowled the doorkeeper over. He should have sneaked around.
He should have used force, cunning, trickery. He should have worked
harder. And so on.

The discussion is usually intense. Why? Probably because every college
student is standing before the door to "the Law," too, and has a personal
interest in how to get through that door. So I usually tell them, "You know,
don't you, that whatever approach you are arguing for is your own philosophy of how to approach life's hurdles? You are really talking about yourself when you say what the man from the country should do." Do you
agree? Take a minute to look back over your own views and see if they do
reveal how you think *you* should solve problems.

Sooner or later we make the fable more immediate. Let's say that the
"gate" is admission to grad school and the admissions officer says he or she
can't admit you at this time. Would you use the strategies you recommended for the man from the country? From this perspective some students begin to hedge. "Well, if you really want to be a doctor, you have to
play along. No, of course you wouldn't use force or cunning or trickery in
this 'real' situation." Would you sit there year after year—or what? If it
seems almost hopeless that you can ever get into law school or Julliard,
is your life ruined? If you want to be a surgeon and your right hand is
injured, should you hang yourself?

As you can see, the discussion leads to questioning goals and their per-
manence in our lives and the need for them. Who sets these goals, and
must we accept their authority? Should students jump out windows each
year because of low test scores? A few students argue that the man from
the country should never have entered into a game with rules set by
others. What happens outside yourself—whatever mountain blocks your
path, whatever the bureaucratic interference—has nothing to do with
actualizing yourself. It boils down, they say, not to what gates you stand
before but what you think you are on this planet for—aside from watching
TV. No one argues that sitting humbly beside the gate is reasonable
behavior.

A few students recommend a self-directed path. You cannot choose the
hand you are dealt, but you do control how you will play it. No one is dealt a

hand that forces us to feel one way or the other about it. A crummy hand does not require a miserable countenance. We have all sorts of options. Is it the M.D. degree you crave, or do you love doing what M.D.'s do? If you love doing, then you have lots of alternatives. If it is the label, then it is probably not a path with a heart. Some students say it doesn't matter what work you do; the secret is not to do what you love but to love what you do. Got that?

The fable involves risk taking. How much of a chance should the man from the country take? The doorkeeper looks fierce but may not be. If "the Law" is essential for the man to actualize himself, should he risk all, even his life, and try anything? Yes, some reply, he must take risks, but they must be within reason. No, say others. C students take "reasonable" risks, but if it is reasonable, it isn't a risk.

There is a knife-edge of risk on the path with a heart (self-actualization) which is between "just barely and not quite," to use Robert Frost's metaphor, and this is the path the pilgrim follows throughout his life. But why on earth would anyone live on such a thin edge moment by moment forever? Because, say Zorba the Greek and Albert Camus, Picasso, Einstein, Edison, and Shakespeare, we have no choice. That knife-edge is life. Anything else is not. Everyone knows that "not quite" feels like five hours of commercial TV. Those who went beyond "just barely" aren't talking.

Most of us don't live on the knife-edge all the time, some because they never thought of it, some because it is too scary. Some students argue that there is no knife-edge in accounting, teaching, economics, collecting garbage, directing traffic. Or being a student. How can you live on a knife-edge and keep appointments and turn in assignments? Look around at your classmates and you will see some who do. The truth is we can find people in any situation who make their work spacious enough to fit their spirits.

Other people's descriptions of your work is definition tyranny—if you accept their verdict. If you don't like the definition of "student" under which you now function, rewrite it. Write one that makes getting up in the morning a joy.

INTERLUDE

The Quest

> The gallant knight is the man from
> the country?

ELDORADO

Gaily bedight
A gallant knight
In sunshine and in shadow,
Had journeyed long,
Singing a song,
In search of Eldorado.

But he grew old—
This knight so bold—
And o'er his heart a shadow
Fell as he found
No spot of ground
That looked like Eldorado.

And, as his strength
Failed him at length,
He met a pilgrim shadow—
"Shadow," said he,
"Where can it be—
This land of Eldorado?"

"Over the Mountains
Of the Moon,
Down the Valley of the Shadow,
Ride, boldly ride,"
The shade replied,—
"If you search for Eldorado."
               —Edgar Allan Poe

KNOWING AND KNOWING ABOUT

TO KNOW IS TO BE

The man who "knows" cannot learn. If you want a new idea, invention, solution to a problem, don't go to the person who "knows." Knowledge is an impenetrable sphere. When you "know" something, what does that mean? Something is settled, concluded, completed, closed off. But the person who is consciously aware of what he or she does not know has a chance to find out. The great thinkers spend their time not on what they know but on what they don't know. In the future, experts will be replaced by computers. As yet no one has conceived of a computer that can explore the unknown. When one is born, it will be human.

All this research, questing, seeking, turns up all sorts of things, piles and piles, librariesful. But we still do not really "know." We "know about." That is, through symbol systems, language, we classify, organize, interconnect, a vast network. We cast this net of ideas over the perceived world. When we speak of what we know, we are looking at the net. People who consider themselves experts, when they speak of "knowing," look smugly at the net.

Thinkers define "knowing" in another way entirely. It is what happens when you are working with "things" (ideas, facts, rocks, dorsal fins) and suddenly get beyond "concept," become transformed yourself. You see with your whole being and not just with your intellect. You enter into and become one with the world you are observing. You are the atom; you are the tree, the leaf, the cell.

Artists, scientists, all thinkers, fiddle with the material world until these glimpses occur. They "know" dancing when dancer and dance and observer are indistinguishable.

In this sense of knowing, you cannot claim to know algebra simply because you can apply formulas. When you can ride algebra like a bicycle, when you don't even have to think about it, you are getting closer. When you catch a glimpse of yourself at one with algebra, that is closer yet. To know in this sense is to be totally alive and to be conscious of it.

The point is that if we settle for "knowing about"—which is what commonly passes for knowledge—we shortchange ourselves. We don't get the chance to experience that-which-is.

"Knowing about" is watching. "Knowing" is being.

"The rest of the world does not sit idly 'out there,'" writes Gary Zukav. "It is a sparkling realm of continual creation, transformation, and annihilation. The ideas of the new physics when wholly [note the word

208

wholly] grasped, can produce extraordinary *experiences.*" Knowing is experiencing.

If you think of knowledge the way experts do, you find homework boring. If you see it as your opportunity to *experience,* to get beyond the picture, by means of the picture, a chance to dance, you find it exhilarating. It is all in the definition.

You can be a Wu Li Master or a Ditto Master, wrote a student, Harjit Dhillon. You can absorb reality or just get a copy of it.

> *He who knows others has knowledge.*
> *He who knows himself is illuminated.*

WAYS OF KNOWING
Hemispheric Crossover

In your discussion group find several ways to connect the ways of knowing that follow. Then find connections with other ideas in *Thinking about Thinking.*

Ways of Knowing I

"I know of two ways to do research," said Eric Hoffer, the longshoreman philosopher. "One is to go to a library. The other is to stand on a street corner in San Francisco."

Ways of Knowing II

The knowledge gained in following Déscarte's thinking through *The Critique of Pure Reason* lies not in the conclusion that is reached but in the journey itself.

Ways of Knowing III

Impossible is a synonym for *won't try.* If you know it can't be done, you may not have the guts to go ahead and do it. Do you agree? The article on the next page about liberal-arts majors in business has some clues.

INTERLUDE

Liberal-Arts Majors in Business

I have owned a scrap-metal business for 35 years. A year ago, I hired a new manager with unusual qualifications. He has an educational background of history and English; he holds a master's degree in foreign languages and speaks French and German fluently.

He knew nothing about the scrap-metal business. I gave him one week of instruction, and told him to make mistakes and then use intelligence, imagination, and logic. He has turned this into one of the most efficiently run metal industries in the Middle West.

My company took a contract to extract beryllium from a mine in Arizona. I called in several consulting engineers and asked, "Can you furnish a chemical or electrolytic process that can be used at the mine site to refine directly from the ore?" Back came a report saying that I was asking for the impossible—a search of the computer tapes had indicated that no such process existed.

I paid the engineers for their report. Then I hired a student from Stanford University who was home for the summer. He was majoring in Latin American history with a minor in philosophy.

I gave him an airplane ticket and a credit card and told him, "Go to Denver and research the Bureau of Mines archives and locate a chemical process for the recovery of beryllium." He left on Monday. I forgot to tell him that I was sending him for the impossible.

He came back on Friday. He handed me a pack of notes and booklets and said, "Here is the process. It was developed 33 years ago at a government research station in Rolla, Mo." He then continued, "And here also are other processes for the recovery of mica, strontium, columbium, and yttrium, which also exist as residual ores that contain beryllium." After one week of research, he was making sounds like a metallurgical expert.

He is now back in school, but I am keeping track of him. When other companies are interviewing the engineering and the business-administration mechanics, I'll be there looking for that history-and-philosophy major.

During this past year, I, like every other businessman, was looking for new sources of financing because of the credit crunch created by the interest market. I located my new sources. I simply hired a journalism student and gave him an assignment to write a report titled, "The Availability of Money and Credit in the United States."

These few examples represent simple solutions to business problems—solutions that require nothing more than the use of free, unrestrained intelligence and imagination.

It is unfortunate that our business world has become so structured that it demands specialization to such a degree that young people feel the need to learn only specific trades. By getting that type of education they hope to be able to find their way into one of those corporate niches.

If we continue with the present trend of specialized education, we are going to be successful in keeping a steady supply of drones moving to a huge beehive. Our country was not built by a bunch of drones. It was built by people.

Have we lost sight of the fact that people are the most important commodity we have? They are not a collection of drones. They are individuals— each with intelligence, imagination, curiosity, impulses, emotions, and ingenuity.

In my business I want people who have those intangible qualities. Anyone can meet them. They are marching across the pages of books— poetry, history, and novels.

—Sam Bittner, Omaha businessman

SUPERLUMINAL: FASTER THAN LIGHT
More Ways of Knowing

Illogical Physics: Everything Is *Now*

Does one thing lead to another? It certainly would seem so. It is a basic assumption of Western logic. It is a commonsense idea beyond which even Einstein could not go. A fundamental assumption. Ironically, with two other scientists, Boris Podolsky and Nathan Rosen, Einstein was responsible for an experiment that violated that assumption. Brilliant as he was, Einstein could not accept the results of his own experiment.

Here is the situation. If I do or say something in Boston, it is going to take some time for news of it to get to San Francisco. For example, sound travels about 700 miles an hour. If I could send out a powerful enough shout in Boston, it would take an hour to reach Pittsburgh. What is the fastest way to get around? On a beam of light. At least that was the conclusion of science until the 1930s. Even today most scientists and schooled laypersons will tell you that. That is 957,000 times as fast as a sound wave can go, 186,000 miles a second.

If you televise an event from Boston to San Francisco, it will seem to be in both places at the same time, but we know better. We know it takes an infinitesimal amount of time to travel the 3000 miles. No place on earth being more than 12,000 miles away, we don't notice the time lapse, but we all know it is there. If you send that same TV show out to the moon, for example, it will definitely take a few seconds to bounce off the moon and get back home again. At any speed, travel takes time. You can't be in two places at once.

Oh yeah? In the 1930s Einstein, Podolsky, and Rosen carried out an experiment with amazing, inexplicable results. A particle of matter in one place knew, *without any time delay whatsoever,* what a particle in another location was doing!

Critical Mass. Even when there is a spacelike separation between two areas and no time to get from the one to the other, they found that the condition of a particle in the one area changes with what the observer in the other place decides to observe. It is as if the particles were not separate but were in the same place, in fact, were *the same event.* Time itself seems to be an illusion.

That is the situation in subatomic physics that scientists have been wrestling with since the 1930s. In 1964 J. S. Bell in Switzerland published a theory that extends these findings to the larger perceived world as well. And in 1972 two Berkeley scientists, John Clauser and Stuart Freedman, conducted an experiment that shows Bell's theorem to be correct.

If you have conditioned yourself to think within one frame of reference, such ideas are impossible, unthinkable—no matter what evidence is supplied. But after the initial shock, scientists began to think up other explanations. For example, we assumed messages had to be sent on some sort of carrier, such as sound, radio, or light waves. But there is nothing to prevent the idea that a thought structure in my head can get into your head *without signals. It is already there.* It is not *me* thinking; it is you-me thinking and changing together.*

Washing Sweet Potatoes: The Critical-Mass Phenomenon

Next, consider the story of the Japanese monkey, *Macaca fuscata.* As you read this, are your thoughts influencing me, the writer? Perhaps they are. You may be far more powerful than you have been led to believe. What you say and do and think may have tremendous importance to what happens on this planet, even the universe.

WORKING TOGETHER
Ken Keyes, Jr.

In 1952, scientists on the island of Koshima were providing monkeys with sweet potatoes dropped in the sand. The monkeys liked the taste of the raw sweet potatoes, but they found the dirt unpleasant. An 18-month-old female named Imo found she could solve the problem by washing the potatoes in a nearby stream. She taught this trick to her mother. Her playmates also learned this new way and they taught their mothers, too. This cultural innovation was gradually picked up by various monkeys before the eyes of the scientists.

Between 1952 and 1958, all the young monkeys learned to wash the sandy sweet potatoes to make them more palatable. Only the adults who imitated their children learned this social improvement. Other adults kept eating the dirty sweet potatoes.

Then something startling took place. In the autumn of 1958, a certain number of Koshima monkeys were washing sweet potatoes—the exact number is not known. Let us suppose that when the sun rose one morning there were ninety-nine monkeys on Koshima Island who had learned to wash their sweet potatoes. Let's further suppose that later that morning the hundredth monkey learned to wash potatoes.

---

*For a more detailed, nontechnical explanation, see the final chapter of Gary Zukav's *The Dancing Wu Li Masters.*

Then it happened.

By that evening almost everyone in the tribe was washing sweet potatoes before eating them. The added energy of this hundredth monkey somehow created an ideological breakthrough.

[*But here is where the story gets interesting.*]

The scientists found that the habit of washing sweet potatoes jumped spontaneously over the sea. Colonies of monkeys on other islands and the mainland troop of monkeys at Tasasakiyama began washing their sweet potatoes.

Rebuking the Too-Clear Water

The British mathematician and philosopher Bertrand Russell once observed that *pure mathematics is the subject in which we do not know what we are talking about, or whether what we are saying is true.* You now know that statement can be taken several ways. In the middle level, it can mean that mathematical systems don't have meaning. One reason symbols like 3, 6, y, V, ⊃, ∃, ~, =, are used is to make sure no one will be tempted to hang a bunch of external meaning onto them and the structures built on them. Much like logic—indeed, math is a branch of logic—math has been made mindless and meaningless on purpose. That doesn't mean minds don't work on math.

Furthermore, whether math statements are "true" is an irrelevant issue. As with a computer program or chess, once the rules are established, you can develop any variation the rules allow—but no other ones. Math systems are *closed* systems. (Actually, all systems are closed. "Closed" is part of the definition of a system.) Chess isn't true or not true. Likewise with math.

[*Talk over these ideas with another student before going on.*]

A second meaning of Russell's statement—not excluded by the first—is the broader idea that no matter how brilliant our calculation, no matter how closely we look, we really can't destroy the barrier between what we think is there and what is.

A third meaning, one Russell may not have intended, is that there are flaws in mathematical reasoning, possible contradictions within the system itself, inconsistencies: a set of rules that doesn't cover all the bases.

That is exactly what the Viennese mathematician Kurt Gödel demonstrated in a paper published in 1931.* It shook the foundations of all math-

---

NOTE: *This excerpt is from Keyes' book* The Hundredth Monkey *(Coos Bay, Ore.: Vision Books, 1982). Keyes cites as his source for this story* Lifetide *by Lyall Watson (New York: Bantam Books, 1980).*

*A nontechnical explanation of Gödel's proof is available in the lucid book by Ernest Nagel and James R. Newman, *Gödel's Proof* (New York: New York University Press, 1958).

ematical systems. As in logic, math is built on assumptions. Once these assumptions or axioms are locked into place, are conclusions drawn from them *necessary logical consequences?* If another possibility exists, the system is flawed. Gödel showed that logically incompatible statements can exist within a mathematical structure. In other words, the basis for mathematical logic has built-in limitations, and even the rules of ordinary arithmetic cannot be completely proved. While most mathematicians were thinking it was only a matter of time until a complete set of axioms could be developed for every branch of mathematics, Gödel demonstrated there was almost no likelihood of a complete systematization, at least not by means of the method presently employed. There simply are too many problems that fall outside elementary number theory for the present methods ever to be capable of solving. The axiomatic method is inconsistent and incomplete.

The foundations of mathematics are uncertain.

Does this mean no proof of any kind is possible? There are always alternative ways of thinking. We may have to redefine *proof.* If "proof" cannot be established in purely physical or in purely linguistic structures, a glance back over *Thinking about Thinking* reminds us that mind is infinitely more inclusive than its linguistic structures. No created structure is as complete as the mind that conceived it. That ought to make everyone feel much better.

As Einstein himself observed, mathematical structures are inventions or creations of human beings. These inventions are organs for seeing that which cannot be seen directly. However clever or ingenious, they always must be recognized as guesses as to what "really" is inside the black box. If systematic logic is incomplete, that does not mean the human mind is, too. We are back to the idea of Chapter 1: We have always had to work with incomplete data, with flawed information. We have no choice but to work with hints, with bits and pieces, pebbles of quartz.

The complete mind may use incomplete structures as flawed mirrors to get a peek at itself. But it may be perfectly capable of smoothing out the flaws and arriving at an accurate reflection. In the words of Alfred Noyes,

> *This infinite circle hath no line to bound it.*
> *Behold its strange, deep center everywhere.*

THE UNCERTAINTY PRINCIPLE
Whole-Brained Science

In 1927 Werner Heisenberg revealed that down in the atom there is an "ambiguity barrier," to use Gary Zukav's phrase. Beyond this point we cannot be certain which face nature will show. Thus, we cannot measure accurately at the same time both the momentum of a particle and its position. If you could set up an electron microscope powerful enough to illuminate a speeding electron, Heisenberg showed that the beam of, say, gamma rays you would use as your light source would have to have more energy than the electron and would knock it off its course in an unpredictable direction.

If you used a beam gentle enough not to disturb the electron's flight, you might be able to trace its path, but you could not see the electron. It would be invisible. That is, the "eye" we use to see with is of necessity so constituted that it interferes with what it is trying to see, gets right in there and changes things around—and we can't say what the new situation will be. Heisenberg showed that there can be no separation at this level between the viewer and what he or she is looking at. The two alter together.

We are only now beginning to see that the observer alters experiments in other disciplines, too—history, art, learning theory, testing, biology. If an evaluator sits in a class, you know that you and your teacher behave differently. Set up any experiment and the structure you create determines what you will see. Also, the act of setting up and carrying out the experiment causes the experimenter to change. It is a broader version of the praying-while-smoking anecdote. The structure of your question determines what kind of answer you will get. The structure of your experiment always controls what you will be able to see.

So the objectivity of any experiment is beginning to appear highly doubtful. The act of observing affects the experiment. The punch line here is that the "scientific method" is in for an overhaul. Holistic methods are sprouting everywhere. What we are "trying to do" is coming up for review, too. Instead of a search for "truth," maybe a better look at the pebble of quartz. Robert Frost would have been right there at the wellcurb, trying. Trying.

DIALOGUE AND REFLECTION

Take some class time to work in your small group on a new, whole-brained scientific method. A new science, a new kind of scientist. Create some goals for this new science consistent with themes developed in *Thinking about Thinking*. Will your new scientists need dance lessons?

> *The universe does not send us a telegram saying, "Do this, take that job; that's your soul mate." The universe is more subtle than that. Simply notice what comes your way. If something comes up and it strikes a chord, put it in your back pocket and just let it be. Should it come up a second time, take it out and examine it, then set the idea someplace within easy reach, but still don't do anything about it. When it comes up a third time, LISTEN. The universe is talking to you.*
>
> —Deborah Nuckols, Student

AN AMERICAN WU LI MASTER

Wait to read this page and the following article until
after your learning-log entry is completed.

*Rather than my own commentary on what the new science and scientists might be like,
I am providing you this time with an example instead. Nobel Prize winner Richard
Feynman seems like a good model of a whole-brained thinker. Following is a word-for-
word transcription of a TV interview with Feynman aired in January 1983 for "Nova"
on PBS.* See if his approach to discovering the nature of nature fits the criteria you
and your group thought up.*

*A good approach to this transcript would be to do some passes through it using
BFAR (chapter 2). But then cull out the attitudes and strategies that seem to you essential to whole-brained thinking in general. You will find symbols like this ■ throughout
the transcript. They appear after some of Feynman's ideas worth stopping to ponder.
You will see that they are connected with themes in* Thinking about Thinking.

*There are a few paragraphs about quarks, hadrons, gluons that may get a little
sticky for some readers. But the key ideas are easy enough to grasp if you glide over
these terms the first couple of times you browse those sections. At first just go for the
general ideas. Save mastery for when and if you need it. Your right brain will do a lot of
work for you if you relax and give it a chance.*

Photograph © WGBH Educational Foundation 1983; used with permission of NOVA.

---

*This transcript will give you a rare opportunity to see what speech looks like in print when it
is recorded exactly as it was spoken. I saw the "Nova" program when it was aired and was
surprised to see the difference between my experience and the literal record. The mind
smooths over the rough edges, apparently screening out noise of any kind that doesn't
contribute to the concept. I heard an articulate, organized discussion, a lucid, rich interview.
Apparently I wasn't hearing words and sentences at all. I was hearing ideas, thoughts,
concepts. The mind stitches over the physical carrier and retains only the fine mental
tapestry. Watch. After your first reading, your mind will probably get in tune with the
transcript and you will not even notice speech characteristics that are carried over into print.
Mind is fantastic.

THE PLEASURE OF FINDING THINGS OUT:
AN INTERVIEW WITH RICHARD FEYNMAN

RICHARD FEYNMAN: I have a friend who's an artist and he's sometimes taken a view which I don't agree with very well. He'll hold up a flower and say, "look how beautiful this is," and I'll agree, I think. And he says, "you see, I as an artist can see how beautiful this is, but you as a scientist, oh, take this all apart and it becomes a dull thing." And I think that he's kind of nutty. First of all, the beauty that he sees is available to other people and to me, too, I believe, although I might not be quite as refined aesthetically as he is. But I can appreciate the beauty of a flower. At the same time, I see much more about the flower than he sees. I could imagine the cells in there, the complicated actions inside which also have a beauty. I mean, it's not just beauty at this dimension of one centimeter: there is also beauty at a smaller dimension, the inner structure . . . also the processes. The fact that the colors in the flower are evolved in order to attract insects to pollinate it is interesting—it means that insects can see the color. It adds a question—does this aesthetic sense also exist in the lower forms that are . . . why is it aesthetic, all kinds of interesting questions which a science knowledge only adds to the excitement and mystery and the awe of a flower. ■ It only adds. I don't understand how it subtracts.

I've always been rather, very one-sided about the science, and when I was younger I concentrated almost all my effort on it. I didn't have time to learn and I didn't have much patience with what's called the humanities. Even though in the university there were humanities that you had to take, I tried my best to avoid somehow to learn anything and to work at it. It's only afterwards, when I've gotten older, that I got more relaxed, that I've spread out a little bit. I've learned to draw and I read a little bit, but I'm really still a very one-sided person and I don't know a great deal. ■ I have a limited intelligence and I used it in a particular direction.

NARRATOR: Richard Phillips Feynman was born and brought up in New York. His father was intensely interested in science and the natural world. He had a profound and enduring influence on his son.

RICHARD FEYNMAN: It's true my father, even before I was born, told my mother if it was a boy he was going to be a scientist. And he made an effort in a way to influence that so, no doubt, that had a lot to do with it. I think it does. When I was just a little kid, very small in a high chair, he had brought home a lot of tiles, little bathroom tiles—seconds, of different colors, that he'd brought home. We played with them, setting them out like dominoes, I mean vertically, on my high chair—so they tell me this anyway—and when we'd got them all set up I would push one end so that they would all go down. Then after a while I'd help to set them up and pretty soon we were setting them up in a more complicated way—two white tiles and a blue tile, two white tiles and a blue tile, and so on—and when my mother said that . . . she complained, "Leave the poor child alone, if he wants to put a blue tile let him put a blue tile." He said, "No, I want to show him what patterns are like and how interesting they are as it's a kind of elementary mathematics." ■ So he started very early to tell me about the world and how interesting it was.

We had the Encyclopaedia Britannica at home and even when I was a small boy he used to sit me on his lap and read to me from the Encyclopaedia Britannica. We would read, say, about dinosaurs and maybe it would be talking about the *Brontosaurus* or something, and it would say something like—or the *Tyrannosaurus Rex*—and it would say something like "this thing is twenty-five feet high and the head is six feet across," you see. So he'd stop all this and say, "let's see what that means. That would mean that if he stood in our front yard he would be high enough to put his head through the window but not quite because the head is a little bit too wide and it would break the window as it came by." Everything we'd read would be translated as best we could into some reality and so that I learned to do that, everything that I read I try to figure out what it really means, what it's really saying by translating. ■ So I used to get read the encyclopaedia when I was a boy but with translation, you see, so it was very exciting and interesting to think there were animals of such magnitude. I wasn't frightened that there would be one coming in my window as a consequence of this, I don't think, but I thought that it was very, very interesting, and that they all died out and that at that time nobody knew why.

We used to go to the Catskill mountains. We lived in New York and the Catskill mountains is the place where people went in the summer. There was a big group of people there but the fathers would all go back to New York to work during the week and only come back over in the weekend. On the weekends, when my father came, he would take me for walks in the woods and would tell me various things about, interesting things that were going on in the woods—which I'll explain in a minute. But the other mothers see this, of course, thought this was wonderful and that the other fathers should take their sons for walks. They tried to work on them but they didn't get anywhere at first. And they wanted my father to take all the kids, but he didn't want to because he had a special relationship to me—we had a personal thing together. So it ended up that the other fathers had to take their children for walks the next weekend. The next Monday when they were all back to work we were, all the kids were playing in the field and one kid said to me "see that bird, what kind of a bird is that?" And I said, "I haven't the slightest idea what kind of a bird it is." He says, "It's a brown-throated thrush," or something, "Your father doesn't tell you anything." But it was the opposite, my father had taught me, looking at a bird, he , says, "Do you know what that bird is? It's a brown-throated thrush—but in Portuguese it's a ———, in Italian, a ———." He says, "In Chinese it's a ———, in Japanese, a ———, etcetera. Now," he says, "You know all the languages, you want to know what the name of that bird is and when you've finished with all that," he says, "you'll know absolutely nothing whatever about the bird. ■ You only know about humans in different places and what they call the bird. Now," he says, "let's look at the bird and what it's doing." ■

Once we were again walking somewhere and he picked a leaf off of a tree or something. This leaf had a flaw—a thing we never look at much—but a little brown line that started in the middle of the leaf and like a C-shape. You've seen, they're sort of deteriorated, a leaf's got brown from something. This little brown line was like the shape of a C, starting somewhere in the middle of the leaf and in a curl and came to the edge. And he said, "You look at this and you see it's narrow at the beginning and it's wider as it goes to the edge. Now what this is," he said, "is that a fly has come, a blue fly with yellow eyes and green wings comes and lays an egg on this leaf. Then, when the egg hatches into a small caterpillar like the maggot-like thing, which has its whole life eating this leaf, that's where it gets its food. That's why the egg is left there, and as it eats along, it leaves behind this trail of eaten leaf which is brown. As the maggot grows, you see, the trail grows wider until he's grown to full length at the end of the leaf, where he turns into a fly—a blue fly with yellow eyes and green wings—who flies away and lays an egg on another leaf." Now I knew that he didn't know that it was a blue fly with green wings and yellow eyes, but the idea (or even if it was really precisely correct), it might have even been a beetle and had not . . . but the idea that he was trying to tell me was the amusing part of life that the whole thing was just reproduction. No matter how complicated the business is, the main point is to do it again, to have it come out again. ■

He had taught me to notice things. ■ One day when I was playing with what we call an "express wagon," which is a little wagon which has a railing around it for children to play with that they can pull around—it had a ball in it, I remember this, it had a ball in it—and I pulled the wagon and I noticed something about the way the ball moved. So I went to my father and I said, "Say, Pop, I noticed something. When I pull the wagon, the ball rolls to the back of the wagon; it rushes to the back of the wagon. And when I'm pulling it along and I suddenly stop, the ball rolls to the front of the wagon," and I say, "Why is that?" And he said that, he says nobody knows. He said, "The general principle is that things that are moving try to keep on moving and things that are standing still tend to stand still unless you push on them hard." And he says this tendency is called *inertia,* but nobody knows why it's true. Now that's a deep understanding. He doesn't give me a name. He knew the difference between knowing the name of something and knowing something, which I learned very early. He went on to say, "If you look close, you'll find the ball does not rush to the back of the wagon, but it's the back of the wagon that you're pulling against the ball . . . that the ball stands still, or as a matter of fact, from the friction starts to move forward really and doesn't move back. So I ran back to the little wagon and set the ball up again and pulled the wagon from under it and looking sideways and seeing indeed he was right. The ball never moved backwards in the wagon when I pulled the wagon forward. It moved backward relative to the wagon, but relative to the sidewalk, it was moved forward a little bit.

So that's the way I was educated by my father, with those kind of examples and discussions; no pressure, just lovely interesting discussions. ■

My cousin at that time, who was three years older, was in high school and was having considerable difficulty with his algebra and had a tutor come. And I was allowed to sit in a corner while the tutor would try to teach my cousin algebra. And so problems like $2x$ plus. . . . I said to my cousin then, "What are you trying to do?" You know, I hear him talking about x. He said, "What do you know? $2x + 7$ is equal to 15," he said, "and you're trying to find out what x is." I say, "You mean 4." He says, "Yeah, but you did it with arithmetic. You have to do it by algebra." And that's why my cousin was never able to do algebra, because he didn't understand how he was supposed to do it.

There was no way. I learned algebra fortunately by not going to school and knowing the whole idea was to find out what x was and it didn't make any difference how you did it. ■ There's no such thing as, you know, you do it by arithmetic, you do it by algebra. That was a false thing that they had invented in school so that the children who have to study algebra can all pass it. ■ They had invented a set of rules which, if you followed them without thinking, could produce the answer. Subtract 7 from both sides; if you have a multiplier, divide both sides by the multiplier and so on—a series of steps by which you could get the answer if you didn't understand what you were trying to do.

There was a series of math books which starts *Arithmetic for the Practical Man,* and then *Algebra for the Practical Man,* and then *Trigonometry for the Practical Man,* and I learned trigonometry for the practical man from that. I soon forgot it again because I didn't understand it very well. But they were going to get . . . and the series was coming out and the library was going to get *Calculus for the Practical Man.* And I knew by this time by reading the encyclopaedia that calculus was an important subject and it was an interesting one and I ought to learn it.

This was—I was older now, perhaps thirteen—and then the calculus book finally came out and I was so excited. And I went to the librarian to take it out and she looks at me and she says, "Oh, you're just a child. What are you taking this book out for? This book is a . . . " So this was one of the few times in my life I was uncomfortable and I lied and I said it was for my father, he selected it. So I took it home and I learned calculus from it and I tried to explain it to my father. And he'd start to read the beginning of it and he found it confusing, and that really bothered me a little bit. I didn't know that he was so limited, you know, that he didn't understand. And I thought it was relatively simple and straightforward and he didn't understand it. So that was the first time I knew I had learned more in some sense than he.

One of the things that my father taught me besides physics—whether it's correct or not—was a disrespect for respectable ■ . . . for certain kinds of things. For example when I was a little boy, in a rotogravure—that's printed pictures in newspapers—first came out in the *New York Times,* he used to sit me again on his knee and he'd open a picture. And there was a picture of the Pope and everybody bowing in front of him. And he'd say, "Now look at these humans. Here is one human standing here, and all these others are bowing in front of him. Now what is the difference? This one is the Pope," (he hated the Pope anyway) and he'd say, "the difference is epaulettes." Of course, not in the case of the Pope, but if he was a general—it was always the uniform, the position, but this man has the same human problems, he eats dinner like anybody else, he goes to the bathroom, he has the same kind of problems as everybody. He's a human being. Why are they all bowing to him? Only because of the name and his position, because of his uniform, not because of something special he did, or his honor, or something like that. He, by the way, was in the uniform business. So he knew what the difference was with the man with the uniform off and the uniform on; it's the same man for him.

He was happy with me, I believe. Once, though, when I came back from MIT, (I'd been there a few years) he said to me, "Now you've become educated about these things and there's one question I've always had that I've never understood very well and I'd like to ask you now that you've studied this to explain it to me." And I asked him what it was. And he said that he understood when an atom made a transition from one state to another, it emits a particle of light called a *photon.* I said that's right. And he says, "Well now, is the photon in the atom ahead of time that it comes out, or is there no photon in it to start with?" I say, "There's no photon in, it's just that when the electron makes a transition it comes . . ." And he says, "Well, where does it come from then, how does it come out?" So I said . . . of course I couldn't answer him . . . "The view is that photon numbers aren't conserved, they're just created by the motion of the electron." I couldn't try to explain it to him, something like that, the sound that I'm making now wasn't in me. It's not like my little boy who said when he was just little one day, starting to talk, suddenly said that he could no longer say a certain word (the word was "cat") because his word bag has run out of the word "cat." So there's no word bag that you have inside that you use up the words as they come out. You just make them as they go along. And in the same sense, there was no photon bag in an atom and when the photons come out they didn't come from somewhere; but I couldn't do much better. He was not satisfied with me in that respect that I was never able to explain any of the things that he didn't understand. So he was unsuccessful. He sent me through all these universities in order to find out these things and he never did find out.

NARRATOR: While researching his Ph.D. thesis at Princeton on the principle of least action in quantum mechanics, young Feynman was asked to join the project to develop the atomic bomb.

RICHARD FEYNMAN: It was a completely different kind of thing. It would mean that I would have to stop the research in what I was doing (which is my life's desire to take time off to) to do this which I felt I should do in order to protect civilization, if you want. Okay? So that was what I had to debate with myself. My first reaction: well, I didn't want to get interrupted in my normal work to do this odd job. There was also the problem, of course, of any moral thing involving war. I wouldn't have much to do with that, but it kinda scared me when I realized what the weapon would be, which I realized . . . and that since it might be possible, it must be possible, there was nothing that I knew that indicated that if we could do it, they couldn't do it. And therefore it was very important to try to cooperate.

NARRATOR: So, in early 1943, Richard Feynman joined Robert Oppenheimer's team of scientists at Los Alamos, New Mexico.

RICHARD FEYNMAN: With regard to moral questions, I do have something I would like to say about it . . . because the original reason to start the project which was that the Germans were a danger, started me off on a process of action which was to try to develop this first system at Princeton and then at Los Alamos, to try to make the bomb work . . . all kinds of attempts to redesign to make it a worse bomb or whatever and so on and all working all this time to see if we could make it go. And so it was a project on which we all worked very, very hard, all cooperating together. And with any project like that, you continue to work trying to get success, having decided to do it. But what I did immorally I would say was not remember the reason that I said I was doing it. ■ So that when the reason changed (which was that

Germany was defeated) not the singlest thought came to my mind at all about that . . . that meant now that I have to reconsider why I am continuing to do this, I simply didn't think, okay?

The only reaction that I remember (perhaps I was blinded by my own reaction) was a very considerable elation and excitement. And there was kind of parties and people got drunk and it would make a tremendously interesting contrast of what was going on in Los Alamos at the same time as what was going on in Hiroshima. I was involved with this happy thing and also drinking and drunk and playing drums sitting on the hood of the bonnet of a Jeep and playing drums and excitement running all over Los Alamos at the same time as the people were dying and struggling in Hiroshima.

I had a very strong reaction after the war of a peculiar nature. It may be from just the bomb itself and it may be for some other psychological reasons—I'd just lost my wife or something. But I remember being in New York with my mother in a restaurant immediately after, and thinking about New York and I knew how big the bomb in Hiroshima was, how big an area it covered and so on. And I realized from where we were—I don't know, 59th Street—to drop one on 34th Street, it would spread all the way out here and all these people would be killed and all the things would be killed and that wasn't only one bomb available, but it was easy to continue to make them. And therefore that things were sort of doomed, because already it appeared to me (very early, earlier than to others who were more optimistic) that international relations and the way people were behaving, was no different than it had ever been before and that it was just going to go out the same way as any other thing. And I was sure that it was going therefore to be used very soon. So I felt very uncomfortable and thought, really believed, that it was silly—I would see people building a bridge and I would say, "They don't understand." I really believed that it was senseless to make anything because it would all be destroyed very soon anyway, but they didn't understand that. And I had this very strange view of any construction that I would see, I always thought how foolish they are to try to make something. So I was really in a kind of depressive condition.

NARRATOR: Feynman decided to accept an appointment at Cornell University's Department of Theoretical Physics, where he would work with Hans Bethe. He had turned down a prestigious position offered by Princeton's Institute for Advanced Study, much to their surprise and consternation.

RICHARD FEYNMAN: They expected me to be wonderful, to offer me a job like this, and I wasn't wonderful. And therefore I realized a new principle was I'm not responsible for what other people think I am able to do. I don't have to be good because they think I'm going to be good. And somehow or other I could relax about this and I thought to myself, "I haven't done anything important, and I'm never going to do anything important, but I used to enjoy physics and mathematical things. And because I used to play with it, it was never very important, but I used to do things for the fun of it." So I decided I'm going to do things only for the fun of it. ∎

And only that afternoon while I was eating lunch, some kid threw up a plate in the cafeteria which has a blue medallion on the plate—the Cornell sign in the cafeteria. And as he threw up the plate and it came down it wobbled and the blue thing went around like this. And I wondered—it seemed to me the blue thing went around faster than the wobble and I wondered what the relation was between the two. You see, I was just playing—no importance at all. So I played around with the equations of motion of rotating things and I found out that if the wobble is small, the blue thing goes around twice as fast as the wobble goes round. And then I tried to figure out if I could see why that was directly from Newton's laws instead of through the complicated equations. And I worked that out for the fun of it.

And then I went to Hans Bethe and I said, "Hey, by the way, I'll show you something amusing here," and I explained this to him and he said to me, "Yes, it's very amusing and interesting, but what is the use of it?" I said, "That doesn't make any difference. It hasn't any use; I'm just doing it for the fun of it." And then Bob Wilson, who was the head of the nuclear lab there, has some kind of instinct or something. Because it was the same day or other that he called me in and he told me that when they hire a professor at the university, it's their responsibility what the professor does and it's their risk. And if he doesn't do anything or he doesn't accomplish anything, it's not his thing to worry about that. And they had taken the risk to put him in the environment and I should do whatever I want, amuse myself or whatever I want. So with that double combination I could relax. Somehow I was getting out from some psychological problem and I relaxed and started to play, played as I said with this rotation. ■ And this rotation led me to a problem—a similar problem of the rotation of the spin of an electron, according to Dirac's equation. And that just led me back into quantum electrodynamics, which is the problem I'd been working on. And I kept continuing now to play with it in the relaxed fashion I had originally done. And everything—it was just like taking the cork out of a bottle—everything just poured out. ■ I, by the way, in very short order worked the things out for which I later won the Nobel Prize.

NARRATOR: Feynman was awarded a Nobel Prize for his work in quantum electrodynamics.

RICHARD FEYNMAN: What I essentially did (and also it was done independently by two other people—Tomanaga in Japan and Schwinger) was to figure out how to analyze and discuss the original quantum theory of electricity and magnetism that had been written in 1928 . . . how to interpret it so as to avoid the infinities to make calculations on which there were sensible results . . . which have since turned out to be in exact agreement with every experiment which has been done so far. So that in quantum electrodynamics, we have a theory which fits experiment in every detail where it's applicable, not involving nuclear forces, for instance. And it was the work that I did in 1947—to figure out how to do that—for which I won the Nobel Prize.

NARRATOR: And what does the Nobel Prize mean to Feynman?

RICHARD FEYNMAN: I don't know anything about the Nobel Prize. I don't understand what it's all about or what's worth what. And if the people in the Swedish Academy decide that x, y or z wins the Nobel Prize, then so be it. I won't have anything to do with the Nobel Prize. It's a pain in the . . . I don't like honors. I appreciate it for the work that I did and for the people who appreciate it and I know there's a lot of physicists use my work. I don't need anything else. ■ I don't think there's any sense to anything else. ■ I don't see that it makes any point that someone in the Swedish Academy decides that his work is noble enough to receive a prize. I've already got the prize. The prize is the pleasure of finding the thing out, the kick in the discovery, the observation of other people using it. ■ Those are the real things; the honors are unreal to me. I don't believe in honors. It bothers me, honors bother, honors are epaulettes, honors are uniforms. My Papa brought me up this way. I can't stand it. It hurts me.

When I was in high school, one of the first honors I got was to be a member of the Arista, which is a group of kids which got good grades. And everybody wanted to be a member of the Arista. And when I got into the Arista, I discovered that what they did in their meetings was to sit around to discuss who else was worthy to join this wonderful group that we are, okay? So we sat around trying to decide who it was who would get to be allowed into this Arista. This kind of thing bothers me psychologically for one or another reason, I don't understand myself—honors—and from that day, this always bothered me.

I had trouble with . . . when I became a member of the National Academy of Science and I had ultimately to resign. Because there was another organization most of whose time was spent in choosing who was illustrious enough to be allowed to join us in our organization . . . including such questions as we physicists have to stick together because they've a very good chemist that they're trying to get in and we haven't got enough room for so-and-so. What's the matter with chemists? The whole thing was rotten because its purpose was mostly to decide who could have this honor, okay? I don't like honors. ■

NARRATOR: Since 1950, Feynman has been Professor of Theoretical Physics at the California Institute of Technology, where he lectures and does his physics, trying to figure out more about the world and how it works.

RICHARD FEYNMAN: One way that's kind of a fun analogy in trying to get some idea of what we're doing in trying to understand nature is to imagine that the gods are playing some great game and you don't know the rules of the game, but you're allowed to look at the board, at least from time to time. And in a little corner perhaps and from these observations, you try to figure out what the rules are of the game, what the rules of the pieces moving. You might discover after a bit, for example, that when there's only one bishop around on the board that the bishop maintains its color.

Later on you might discover the law for the bishop as it moves on the diagonal which would explain the law that you understood before that it maintained its color, and that would be analogous till we discover one law and then later find a deeper understanding of it. Then things can happen. Everything's going good, you've got all the laws, it looks very good and then all of a sudden some strange phenomenon occurs in some corner. So you begin to investigate that, to look for it. It's a castling, something you didn't expect. ■

We're always, by the way, in fundamental physics, always trying to investigate those things in which we don't understand the conclusions. We're not trying to check all the time our conclusions. After we've checked them enough, we're okay. ■ The thing that doesn't fit is the thing that's the most interesting, the part that doesn't go according to what you expected. ■ Also, we could have revolutions in physics after you've noticed that the bishops maintain their color and they go along the diagonal and so on for such a long time and everybody knows that that's true, then you suddenly discover one day in some chess game that the bishop doesn't maintain its color; it changes its color. Only later do you discover a new possibility: that a bishop is captured and that a pawn went all the way down to the queen's end to produce a new bishop. That can happen but you didn't know it, and so it's very analogous to the way our laws are. They sometimes look positive, they keep on working and all of a sudden, some little gimmick shows that they're wrong. And then we have to investigate the conditions under which this bishop change of color happened and so forth, and gradually learn the new rule that explains it more deeply.

Unlike the chess game, though (in the case of the chess game, the rules become more complicated as you go along) but in the physics, when you discover new things, it looks more simple. ■ It appears on the whole to be more complicated because we learn about a greater experience. That is, we learn about more particles and new things. And so the laws look complicated again. But if you realize all the time what's kind of wonderful—that is, if we expand our experience into wilder and wilder regions of experience, every once in a while we have these integrations in which everything's pulled together into a unification which turns out to be simpler than it looked before. ■

If you are interested in the ultimate character of the physical world or the real or the complete world (and at the present time, our only way to understand that is through a mathematical type of reasoning) then I don't think a person can fully appreciate, or in fact can appreciate much of these particular aspects of the world—the great depth of character of the universality of the laws, the relationships of things—without an understanding of mathematics. I think it's just, I don't know any other way to do it. We don't know any other way to describe it accurately and well or to see the interrelationships without it. So I don't think a person who hasn't developed some mathematical sense is capable of fully appreciating this aspect of the world. Don't misunderstand me. There are many, many aspects of the world that mathematics is unnecessary for, such as love, and which are very delightful and wonderful to appreciate and to feel awed and mysterious about. And I don't mean to say that the only thing in the world is physics, but you were talking about physics and if that's what you're talking about, then to not know mathematics is a severe limitation in understanding the world.

Well, what I'm working on in physics right now is a special problem which we've come up against and I'll describe what it is. You know that everything's made out of atoms. We've got that far already and most people know that already, and that the

227

atom has a nucleus with electrons going around. The behavior of the electrons on the outside is now complete; the laws for it are well understood as far as we can tell in this quantum electrodynamics that I told you about. And after that was evolved, then the problem was how does the nucleus work? How do the particles interact? How do they hold together?

One of the by-products was to discover fission and to make the bomb. But in investigating the forces that hold the nuclear particles together, it was a long task. At first, it was thought that it was an exchange of some sort of particles inside which were invented by Yukawa called *pions*. And it would be predicted that if you hit the protons against (the proton is one of the particles of the nucleus) against the nucleus, it would knock out such pions . . . and sure enough, such particles came out.

Not only pions came out, but other particles, and we began to run out of names—*kaons* and *sigmas* and *lamdas* and so on. They're all called *hadrons* now. And as we increased the energy of the reaction and got more and more different kinds until there were hundreds of different kinds of particles, then the problem was, of course, doing all this—(this period is 1950 up to the present) was to find the pattern behind it. ■ And there seemed to be many, many interesting relations among the particles, patterns among the particles until a theory was evolved to explain these patterns; that all of these particles were really made of something else, that they were made of a thing called *quarks*. And that it—three quarks, for example—would form a proton. The proton is one of the particles of the nucleus; another one is a neutron.

The quarks came in a number of varieties. In fact, at first only three were needed to explain all the hundreds of particles and the different kinds of quarks. They're called a *u-type, d-type, s-type*. Two *u*'s and a *d* made a proton; two *d*'s and a *u* made a neutron. If they were moving in a different way inside, they were some other particle, and so on.

Then the problem came: what is the behavior? What exactly is the behavior of the quarks and what holds them together? And a theory was thought of which is a very close analogy to quantum electrodynamics (not exactly the same but very close) in which the quarks are like the electron and the photons which go between the electrons, which makes them attract each other electrically, were called *gluons*. The mathematics was very similar, but there's a few terms slightly different. The difference in the form of the equations that were guessed at were guessed by principles by such beauty and simplicity that it isn't arbitrary; it's very, very determined. ■ What is arbitrary is how many different kinds of quarks there are but not the character of the force between them.

Now, unlike electrodynamics, there's a thing in electro. . . . Two electrons can be pulled apart as far as you want. As a fact, when they are very far away, the force is weakened. If this were true and these were made out of quarks, you would have expected that when you hit things together hard enough, the quarks would come out. But instead of that, when you're doing an experiment with enough energy that quarks come out, instead of that, you found a *big jet*—that is, all particles going about in the same direction of the old hadrons . . . no quarks. And the theory . . . it was clear that what was required was that when the quark comes out, it kind of makes these new pairs of quarks and they come in little groups and make hadrons.

The question is: why is it so different in electrodynamics? How do these small terms differ—these little terms that are different effects, entirely different effects? In fact, it was very surprising to most people that this would really come out . . . that first you would think that the theory was wrong. But the more it's studied, the more clear it became that it's very possible that these extra terms would produce these effects.

Now we were in a position that's different in history than any other time in physics, that's always different. We have a theory—a complete and definite theory—of all of these hadrons and we have an enormous number of experiments and lots and lots of details. So why can't we test the theory right away to find out whether it's right or wrong? Because what we have to do is calculate consequences of the theory—if this theory is right, what should happen, and has that happened? Well, this time, the difficulty is in the first step. If the theory is right, what should happen is very hard to figure out. The mathematics needed to figure what the consequences of this theory are have turned out to be at the present time insuperably difficult . . . at the present time, all right?

And therefore that my problem is to try to develop a way of getting numbers out of this theory to test it really carefully, not just qualitatively to look like it might give the right result. I spent a few years trying to invent mathematical things that would permit me to solve the equations, but I didn't get anywhere. And then I decided that in order to do that, I must first understand more or less how the answer probably looks. It's hard to explain this very well, but I had to get a qualitative idea of how the phenomenon works rather before I can get a good quantitative idea. ■ In other words, people didn't even understand roughly how it worked, and so I have been working most recently in the last year or two on understanding roughly how it works (not quantitatively yet) . . . with the hope that in the future that rough understanding can be refined into a precise mathematical way, too, or an algorithm, to get from the theory to the particles. You see, we're in a funny position. It's not that we're looking for the theory; we've got the theory—a good, good candidate. But we're in the step in science that we need to compare it, we're stuck in seeing what the consequences are. ■ And checking it, we're stuck in seeing what the consequences are. And it's my aim . . . it's my desire to see if I can work out a way to work out what the consequences of this theory are. It's a kind of a crazy position to be in, to have a theory that you can't work out the consequences of. I can't stand it. I have to figure it out. Some day maybe.

NARRATOR: And when he *has* figured it out, what difference will it make? What is the use of this obsession with physics?

RICHARD FEYNMAN: Let's take an example which is easier to understand, an example of astronomy, to find out about. . . . Of course, in the very beginning of astronomy, it was the interest in the planets because of their magic, a godlike character perhaps . . . whatever. After the planets were worked out and the locations of a few stars, there is no more applications of astronomy. There were for time and navigation, but that's over. What we're finding out about the sizes of the stars, the distances of the stars, the enormity of the galaxies, the history of the universe—all this stuff is marvelous things out there. With the big telescopes and all this effort, it has absolutely no application, none. There's nowhere that I know anywhere (except perhaps that you can put the name "Galaxy Crisps" on a package of crisps or something). But aside from that, I don't know that there are any applications of all this knowledge about astronomy.

There's never been any question, however, of supporting telescopes and trying to get more information about the universe. There is, somehow, deep inside of humans a motivation to understand their universe. ■ I've given you an example of astronomy. It's the same in mathematics. It's the same in physics. And this motivation, this difference between thinking everything has to be useful—has to have something to do with what I'm eating and it has something to do with what I'm thinking, and I like to know more, is a thing which I think has its own motivation. ■

Now at the present time, it may be possible—and it probably is—that in physics of high energy where there are again (as far as I can see) no applications, the highest energy physics trying to find the fundamental laws of the tiniest dimension, a very expensive apparatus and I don't see any applications. Of course all history, there is . . . you can always look back at these foolish scientists who say what we are finding out now has no application. So in order to make the people of the future just as happy as we've been, looking back, I'm going to make a prediction: there's no application whatsoever of what we are finding out about high energy physics. So you can find me wrong in the future. But I don't think there is any application really for a long, long time, if ever.

To do the kind of high, real good physics work, you do need absolute solid lengths of time. ■ So that when you're putting ideas together which are vague and hard to remember, it's much that, I get this feeling, very much like building those houses of cards when you're putting together and each of the cards is shaky, and if you forget one of them, the whole thing collapses again. ■ You don't know how you got there and you had to build them up again; and if you're interrupted and kind of forget half the idea of how the cards went together (your cards being different type parts of the ideas, ideas of different kinds that have to go together to build up the idea), the main point . . . you put the stuff together, it's quite a tower and it's easy to slip, it needs a lot of concentration—that is, solid time to think—and if you've got a job in administrating anything like that, then you don't have the solid time. ■

So I have invented another myth for myself: that I'm irresponsible. I'm actively irresponsible. ■ I tell everybody I don't do anything. If anybody asks me to be on a committee to take care of admissions, "No, I'm irresponsible. I don't give a damn about the students." Of course I give a damn about the students, but I know that somebody else'll do it. And I take the view, "Let George do it,"—a view which you're not supposed to take, okay, because that's not right to do. But I do that because I like to do physics and I want to see if I can still do it. And so I'm selfish, okay, I want to do my physics. ■

All those students are in the class. Now you ask me how should I best teach them. Should I teach them from the point of view of the history of science? From the applications? My theory is that the best way to teach is to have no philosophy; is to be chaotic and confuse it in the sense that you use every possible way of doing it. ■ That's the only way I can see to answer it, so as to catch this guy or that guy on different hooks as you go along. That during the time when the fellow who's interested in history's being bored by the abstract mathematics, on the other hand, the fellow who likes the abstractions is being bored another time by the history. If you can do it so you don't bore them all, all the time, perhaps you're better off. I really don't know how to do it. I don't know how to answer this question of different kinds of minds with different kinds of interests—what hooks them on, what makes them interested. ■ How do you direct them to become interested? One way is by a kind of force: you have to pass this course; you have to take this examination. It's a very effective way. Many people go through schools that way and it may be a more effective way. I'm sorry. After many, many years of trying to teach and trying all different kinds of methods, I really don't know how to do it. ■

I got a kick, when I was a boy, of my father telling me things. So I tried to tell my son things that were interesting about the world. When he was very small, we used to rock him to bed, you know, and tell him stories. I'd make up a story about little people that were about so high would walk along and they would go on picnics and so on and they lived in the ventilator. And they'd go through these woods which had great big long tall blue things like trees, but without leaves and only one stalk. And they were on all . . . they had to walk between them and so on. And he'd gradually catch on that that was the rug, the nap of the blue rug, and he loved this game because I would describe all these things from an odd point of view. ■

And he liked to hear the stories and we got all kinds of wonderful things. He even went to a moist cave where the wind kept going in and out; it was coming in cool and went out warm and so on. It was inside the dog's nose that they went. And then, of course, I could tell him all about physiology by this way and so on. He loved that and so I told him lots of stuff. And I enjoyed it because I was telling him stuff that I liked. ■ And we had fun when he would guess what it was and so on.

And then I have a daughter and I tried the same thing. Well, my daughter's personality was different. She didn't want to hear this story. She wanted the story that was in the book repeated again and re-read to her. She wanted me to read to her, not to make up stories, and it's a different personality. And so if I were to say a very good method for teaching children about science is to make up these stories of the little people, it doesn't work at all on my daughter. ■ It happened to work on my son. Okay?

Because of the success of science, there is a kind of, I think a kind of pseudoscience that. . . . Social science is an example of a science which is not a science. They don't do scientific . . . they follow the forms . . . or you gather data, you do so-and-so and so forth, but they don't get any laws, they haven't found out anything. ■ They haven't got anywhere yet. Maybe someday they will, but it's not very well developed.

But what happens is on an even more mundane level. We get experts on everything that sound like they're sort of scientific experts. They're not scientific. They sit at a typewriter and they make up something like, oh, food grown with fertilizer that's organic is better for you than food grown with fertilizer that's inorganic. May be true; may not be true, but it hasn't been demonstrated one way or the other. ■ But they'll

231

sit there on the typewriter and make up all this stuff as if it's science and then become an expert on foods, organic foods and so on. There's all kinds of myths and pseudo-science all over the place.

I may be quite wrong; maybe they do know all these things. But I don't think I'm wrong. You see, I have the advantage of having found out how hard it is to get to really know something—how careful you have to be about checking the experiments, how easy it is to make mistakes and fool yourself. ■ I know what it means to know something. ■ And therefore I can't . . . I see how they get their information, and I can't believe that they know it. They haven't done the work necessary, haven't done the checks necessary, haven't done the care necessary. I have a great suspicion that they don't know, that this stuff is . . . and they're intimidating people by . . . I think so. I don't know the world very well, but that's what I think.

If you expected science to give all the answers to the wonderful questions about what we are, where we're going, what the meaning of the universe is and so on, then I think you could easily become disillusioned and then look for some mystic answer to these problems. How a scientist can take a mystic answer I don't know, because the whole spirit is to understand ■ . . . Well, never mind that. Anyhow, I don't understand that.

But anyhow, if you think of it, the way I think of what we're doing is we're exploring. ■ We're trying to find out as much as we can about the world. People say to me, "Are you looking for the ultimate laws of physics?" ■ No, I'm not. ■ I'm just looking to find out more about the world. ■ And if it turns out there is a simple ultimate law which explains everything, so be it. That would be very nice to discover.

If it turns out it's like an onion with millions of layers and we're just sick and tired of looking at the layers, then that's the way it is. But whatever way it comes out, its nature is there and she's going to come out the way she is. And therefore, when we go to investigate it, we shouldn't pre-decide what it is we're trying to do, except to try to find out more about it. ■ If you say your problem is, why do you find out more about it? If you thought you were trying to find out more about it because you're going to get an answer to some deep philosophical question, you may be wrong. It may be that you can't get an answer to that particular question of finding out more about the character of nature. But I don't look at it. My interest in science is to simply find out about the world; and the more I find out, the better it is to find out. ■

There are very remarkable mysteries about the facts that we're able to do so many more things than apparently animals can do, and other questions like that. But those are mysteries I want to investigate without knowing the answer to them. And so altogether, I can't believe these special stories that have been made up about our relationship to the universe at large because they seem to be too simple, too connected, too local, too provincial. The earth, he came to the earth, one of the aspects of God came to the earth, mind you . . . and look at what's out there. How can He . . . it isn't in proportion. Anyway, it's no use arguing. I can't argue it. I'm just trying to tell you why the scientific views that I have do have some effect on my belief.

And also, another thing has to do with the question of how you find out if something's true. And if you have all these theories of the different relations, have all the different theories about the thing, then you begin to wonder. Once you start doubting—just like you're supposed to doubt—you asked me if the science is true. ■ You say, "No, no, we don't know what's true. We're trying to find out and everything is possibly wrong." ■ Start out understanding religion by saying everything is possibly wrong. Let us see. ■ As soon as you do that, you start sliding down an edge which is hard to recover from and so on, with the scientific view (or my father's view) that we should look to see what's true and what may not be true. Once you start doubting . . . which I think to me is a very fundamental part of my soul is to doubt and to ask . . . and when you doubt and ask, it gets a little harder to believe. ■

You see, one thing is, I can live with doubt and uncertainty and not knowing. ■ I think it's much more interesting to live not knowing than to have answers which might be wrong. ■ I have approximate answers and possible beliefs and different degrees of certainty about different things. ■ But I'm not absolutely sure of anything and there are many things I don't know anything about, such as whether it means anything to ask why we're here, and what the question might mean. I might think about it a little bit and if I can't figure it out, then I go on to something else. But I don't have to know an answer. ■ I don't feel frightened by not knowing things, by being lost in a mysterious universe without having any purpose, which is the way it really is, so far as I can tell possibly. ■ It doesn't frighten me.

> *"I wonder when Richard Feynman will retire."*
> *"He can't retire. He never started to work."*

DIALOGUE AND REFLECTION
Traits of a Whole-Brained Thinker

There are no rules for whole-brained thinking.

In your discussion groups work back and forth between the interview with Richard Feynman and the above statement.

Find some points of view from which there can be no rules for thinking.

Then contradict yourselves and find half a dozen of Feynman's traits that might come in handy in doing your school work or fixing your car.

Reflect in your learning log.

COMMENTARY

Don't read this section until you are finished with
the dialogue and reflection about whole-brained
thinking.

Getting Your Balance

People have tried to distill lists of good thinking habits, just as they have
tried to teach reading by the rule, or algebra or writing. Some think the
rules of logic are the way to think and have banished metaphor and emotion. Others wait to be inspired. Some apprentice themselves to great masters and try to clone themselves on their model. But it won't wash. Nature
allows you to get "the" answer any way you can, in fact, insists that you
figure it all out yourself. Maybe *that's* the rule: Take the gloves off and get
the answer any way you can. Of course, there may not even be any answer
and seeking one may be altogether the wrong path. Maybe the rule is this:
Do whatever you are doing, whatever that may be, anyway you can. After
all, intelligence is structured uniquely in each creature that houses it.

Thinking is more a condition, a state of mind, than a sequence of rules,
isn't it? It is a knack, like skiing. Once you have caught yourself at it and
realize you can do it on purpose, you can begin refining your art. There is
a distinct line between trying to stay up on skis and then suddenly doing it.
You can't even list all the minute components working together to keep you
balanced. But once over that barrier, you can let yourself get more and
more skillful. And you will never go back to the nonskier condition.

That is an exact parallel to how people can take over their own minds.
The process is that they catch themselves at it from time to time until they
see what it is that they have been doing so well all along out-of-awareness.
That is one reason *Thinking about Thinking* is structured as it is: It's to provide you experiences and to get you to catch yourself at it, doing it and
seeing yourself doing it enough that you catch on, get your balance.

You notice how your senses are contributing; you experience them
doing it. You see your emotions contributing and your reptilian brain
helping. You get the feel of metaphor, of multiple meaning, of thought
structured by sentence patterns, and so on. You notice more and more
until you feel an "aha!" and find yourself on skis and deliberately kick off
down the slopes. At some precise point you crack the code and from then
on choose exactly how far you will go with it, a Fred Astaire of the mind.

But there are no rules and no step-by-step sequence. It is an all-at-once
sort of thing. Have you noticed that? The difference is that while we all are

234

thinkers, most of us haven't realized we can do it on purpose. We act as if it is out of our control, as if we are computer users but not programmers.

So we could not make a rule book out of Richard Feynman's way of thinking and end up thinking better. What we can do, as with anything we observe, is get the feel of what he does and allow our right brain to process whatever it wants in whatever way it chooses. That is what happens anyway, but if we trust it, we will be in harmony with our nature instead of fighting it.

Consider Feynman's statement that he doesn't know anything. You can't make a rule out of that: "I don't know anything." Unless you understand it in the same way that Feynman does, the idea is useless to you. But in this chapter we have spent some time on "knowing" and "knowing about" and perhaps you have the feel of it now. In that case you are already using the idea. It is part of your balance. That is, "knowing" means something different to you now. So when you seek to "know," quite naturally you go about it in a different way.

And so it goes. When you have the feel of words and symbols and have experienced their multiplicity, you can't go back to using them narrowly. When you see your mind functioning as a whole, and see that that works, you can relax and allow it to organize data for you. When you realize that *you* give meaning to the structures you form, you are more likely to take charge.

So when you read that Feynman felt confined by the "importance" of his work and by his own and other people's expectations of him, the issue is, have you experienced that, too? When you read that he decided to do things only for the fun of it and allowed himself to treat what he does as play, have you experienced what that feels like? If these have been part of your experience, too, and the Feynman interview suddenly makes you conscious of it, you can begin allowing fun and play to be part of your thinking process.

What about being irresponsible and disrespectful? Again, it is a matter of redefining. If you are dutifully responsible and respectful, behaving that way because it is expected of you, by others and by yourself, these traits will be like an ill-fitting garment and will hamper your skiing. When Feynman pursues his own interests and allows himself to become absorbed, his thinking accelerates and the results nourish his self-actualization. Although he might not say so, he is tremendously responsible to the organism labeled Richard Feynman and by extension to you and me. While he is indifferent to titles and honors, including his own, he is deeply respectful of that-which-is and whatever-may-be.

Ego interferes with thinking. If you have experienced its interference, then you will gradually begin to think without leaning on it. You will find yourself getting a kick out of algebra and being less and less enslaved by grades. More than likely you will change what it is you are up to. You will begin to enjoy ambiguity, that-which-is, and will find premature answers unpalatable.

Because you will prefer solid blocks of time for thinking, you will join fewer clubs and need fewer diversions. You will find that-which-is-not-known more fascinating than that-which-is-known.

No one would get very far imitating Feynman. You would be enslaved by another man's system. But if you allow yourself to notice things Feynman does that you didn't realize were possible, if you play with those strange traits until you get the feel of them, they become accessible to your way of thinking, too. They extend your possibilities.

There are no rules, but there is a knack.

THE INFLUENCE OF WOLF JUICE
ON SCIENTIFIC INQUIRY

Ways of knowing. Let's see. I could gather statistics, make up tables, gather samples and create standard deviations, discover trends. But I would know absolutely nothing about the unique individual. Or I could do a case study of an individual and know nothing of trends. Obviously neither is satisfying alone. If I am trying to "see" or to "dance" with life, if I have redefined what it means to "know," a new science is needed, one similar to Richard Feynman's. Of course, this kind of science is really what the great thinkers, the poets and scientists, have been doing all along.

When he went out to the Barren Lands to study the arctic wolves, the young biologist Farley Mowat found he had to throw out everything he "knew" and start from scratch. By the time he was done, he had developed a new integration of his childhood joy in nature and his training as a biologist—with a touch of the laser thrown in.

The "facts" were that wolves were vicious, deadly, wanton killers and the sole cause of the destruction of the vast herds of caribou that had ranged in the arctic Barrens. Mowat was sent out alone to "do something about the wolf," to study it and find a way to destroy it. By the time he had read the "scientific" literature, listened to hair-raising yarns in a bar on Hudson Bay, and been deposited by a bush pilot with all his scientific gear and twelve rolls of toilet paper on the desolate frozen Barren Lands, he was thoroughly convinced.

Here is his account of his contact with the wolves and the events that caused him to become a new kind of scientist.

From *NEVER CRY WOLF*

Farley Mowat

HAVING TO LEARN SOMETHING NEW

The den was located in a small wadi in the esker, and was so well concealed that I was on the point of walking past without seeing it, when a series of small squeaks attracted my attention. I stopped and turned to look, and there, not fifteen feet below me, were four small, gray beasties engaged in a free-for-all wrestling match.

At first I did not recognize them for what they were. The fat, fox faces with pinprick ears; the butterball bodies, as round as pumpkins; the short, bowed legs and the tiny upthrust sprigs of tails were so far from my conception of a wolf that my brain refused to make the logical connection.

Suddenly one of the pups caught my scent. He stopped in the midst of attempting to bite off a brother's tail and turned smoky blue eyes up toward me. What he saw evidently intrigued him. Lurching free of the scrimmage, he padded toward me with a rolling, wobbly gait; but a flea bit him unexpectedly before he had gone far, and he had to sit down to scratch it.

At this instant an adult wolf let loose a full-throated howl vibrant with alarm and warning, not more than fifty yards from me.

237

The idyllic scene exploded into frenzied action.

The pups became gray streaks which vanished into the gaping darkness of the den mouth. I spun around to face the adult wolf, lost my footing, and started to skid down the loose slope toward the den. In trying to regain my balance I thrust the muzzle of the rifle deep into the sand, where it stuck fast until the carrying-strap dragged it free as I slid rapidly away from it. I fumbled wildly at my revolver, but so cluttered was I with cameras and equipment straps that I did not succeed in getting the weapon clear as, accompanied by a growing avalanche of sand, I shot past the den mouth, over the lip of the main ridge and down the full length of the esker slope. Miraculously, I kept my feet; but only by dint of superhuman contortions during which I was alternately bent forward like a skier going over a jump, or leaning backward at such an acute angle I thought my backbone was going to snap.

It must have been quite a show. When I got myself straightened out and glanced back up the esker, it was to see *three* adult wolves ranged side by side like spectators in the Royal Box, all peering down at me with expressions of incredulous delight.

I lost my temper. This is something a scientist seldom does, but I lost mine. My dignity had been too heavily eroded during the past several days and my scientific detachment was no longer equal to the strain. With a snarl of exasperation I raised the rifle but, fortunately, the thing was so clogged with sand that when I pressed the trigger nothing happened.

The wolves did not appear alarmed until they saw me begin to dance up and down in helpless fury, waving the useless rifle and hurling imprecations at their cocked ears; whereupon they exchanged quizzical looks and silently withdrew out of my sight.

I too withdrew, for I was in no fit mental state to carry on with my exacting scientific duties. To tell the truth, I was in no fit mental state to do anything except hurry home to Mike's and seek solace for my tattered nerves and frayed vanity in the bottom of a jar of wolf-juice.

I had a long and salutary session with the stuff that night, and as my spiritual bruises became less painful under its healing influence I reviewed the incidents of the past few days. Inescapably, the realization was being borne in upon my pre-conditioned mind that the centuries-old and universally accepted human concept of wolf character was a palpable lie. On three separate occasions in less than a week I had been completely at the mercy of these "savage killers"; but far from attempting to tear me limb from limb, they had displayed a restraint verging on contempt, even when I invaded their home and appeared to be posing a direct threat to the young pups.

This much was obvious, yet I was still strangely reluctant to let the myth go down the drain. Part of this reluctance was no doubt due to the thought that, by discarding the accepted concepts of wolf nature, I would be committing scientific treason; part of it to the knowledge that recognition of the truth would deprive my mission of its fine aura of danger and high adventure; and not the least part of that reluctance was probably due to my unwillingness to accept the fact that I had been made to look like a blithering idiot—not by my fellow man, but by mere brute beasts.

Nevertheless I persevered.

When I emerged from my session with the wolf-juice the following morning I was somewhat the worse for wear in a physical sense; but I was cleansed and purified spiritually. I had wrestled with my devils and I had won. I had made my decision that, from this hour onward, I would go open-minded into the lupine world and learn to see and know the wolves, not for what they were supposed to be, but for what they actually were.

DIALOGUE AND REFLECTION

In your small group discuss the "new kind of scientist" Mowat probably had to become. That is, if he really wanted to know the wolves, what would he do? He would have to get his three brains in gear, of course, and his senses, and so on. You know what all. So imagine the daily activities. If anyone in your class has read *Never Cry Wolf*, let him or her recount what Mowat did indeed do, but only after you have a go at it on your own.

Then complete the process of pooling your observations and reflecting on methods of inquiry in your learning log.

COMMENTARY

Complete your own reflections before reading this section on scientific methods.

A Poetic and Scientific Way of Knowing

The "new" science or method of inquiry grows out of a change in purpose. This purpose could be associated with what Frost was trying as he looked down that well in "For Once, Then, Something" (included earlier in this chapter). This new approach to inquiry is not so interested in answers as in seeing. It is as if the observer is being fitted for glasses. When the right lenses are fitted and everything becomes clear, the quest is completed. That is, science becomes a *way* of knowing. It is not something that happens "out there" in test tubes and graphs. It is a change inside oneself, inside you, inside me.

As this process of internal change progresses, the scientist is likely to report that change to the rest of us. But even if he or she didn't speak of these changes, we would witness a different behavior, and consequently our own reality structures would alter. Mowat's wolf book alters its readers; the altered readers affect everyone they come in contact with, even in such subtle acts as pausing longer to observe a bird's behavior or a teacher's or a student's. We are all in this together: the hundredth-monkey phenomenon. Mowat changed; his approach to the world around him altered; and his environment, including readers of *Thinking about Thinking*, alters as well. This situation is exactly what subatomic physicists found: The observer influences the experiment. Objectivity is impossible.

After his night with wolf-juice, Mowat went back to the way he had "studied" nature as a child. His wasted time in the fields around his grandmother's house had resulted in a full-fledged love affair with nature.

> *Rule One of the New Science:* You have to fall in love with whatever it is you are looking at.
>
> *Rule Two:* There are no other rules.

If this sounds sloppy, find anyone in love with anything and you will find a thoroughgoing, sensitive, investigative approach. The lover will be able to give you minute details and broad interrelated patterns. The thinker as lover is perfectly happy wading through dry statistics, spending hour on hour with the tiniest cells, rigging ingenious contraptions to move huge piles of rubble—whatever it takes to cozy up to the object of his or her affection. Why? Because it feels wonderful, because the lover himself or herself is vibrantly alive. The word is *joy*.

Mowat returned to this joy that had inspired his childhood days, this joy with the touch of the laser, but not as an unwitting child. He brought a conscious, deliberate adult mind along with it. He brought skills with microscope and test tubes, statistics and logic, too. He combined the simplicity and joy of the child with the conscious awareness of the adult to direct that joy on purpose. But ultimately the thinker is in it for the joy, the pleasure of finding things out.

You can see how this principle works in school subjects. Those you are not in love with are boring or difficult to compute. But you can spend all night on a love affair and feel refreshed at dawn. An utterly simple but all-encompassing approach. Is there any other?

A SYNTHESIS

Watching the Water Clear

As a way of reviewing chapter 4, "Ways of Knowing," browse through the chapter and review your learning entries.

In class try this method of pulling everything together:

Think up a good right-brained title for your experience of this chapter. Have someone list everyone's, including the teacher's, on the chalkboard. Take a slow walk over each one, but don't discuss these yet.

Next create a seventeen-syllable explanation of your title. To give everyone the same handicap, follow these rigid game rules:

> Set up your statement in three lines.
> The first must have exactly five syllables.
> The second line contains seven syllables.
> The third contains five.
> So, that is five, seven, and five syllables.

Go the whole way with this review. Bring in a typewriter, some three-by-five cards, and some colored paper cut large enough to make a border for each card. Then set up an assembly line.

One person checks each title and statement for spelling, sentence structure, and punctuation. One types the title, statement, and creator's name onto a card. Then each author mounts his or her card onto a piece of colored paper. Use loops of scotch tape on the backs of the cards or some rubber cement.

These mounted cards are then displayed on a classroom wall, and everyone wanders around the gallery grokking each one, making sure not to miss any.

Afterward, talk about the effects of your review.

Thus:

```
            Science of Cold Plums

        The less I'm sure of,
        The more I look around this
        Brilliant light display.


                --Roger Piper
```

Finally, create a synthesis of your experience of "Ways of Knowing" in your learning log. A synthesis can easily be an expansion of your haiku. By the time you read this, someone will have pointed out that the three-line statement is in the Japanese poetic form of that name.

Start with your haiku and reflect on what you meant by your poem. Review the avenues of thought to which this chapter has led you. Get it all down on paper, taking forty-five minutes to an hour or so for your rough draft. Avoid editing at this stage. Then go through cutting out anything that interferes with the clarity of your thoughts.

Rearrange, compress, expand, cut and paste till you are happy with the results. Put the emphasis on pleasing you yourself. That is what makes your work good.

Then check spelling, punctuation, and so on. If you are not good at that, get a second opinion. It is always smart to have a friend who is a good editor standing by.

Then type your final draft or write it legibly in ink and double-check for typos.

Your synthesis will make good reading.

While Eeyore frets...

...and Piglet hesitates

...and Rabbit calculates

...and Owl pontificates

...Pooh just *is*.

CHAPTER FIVE

APPLICATIONS OF THINKING ABOUT THINKING

I TELL THEM I'M A LIBERAL-ARTS MAJOR
(Abridged)

And then, of course, they say:
how quaint, and what are you going to do with that?
As though these four phenomenal years
were an object I could cart away from college—
a Bachelor's Degree across my back like an ermine jacket,
or my education hung from a ceiling on a string.
What am I going to do with it?
Well, I thought perhaps I'd put it in a cage
to see if it multiplies or does tricks or something
so I could enter it in a circus and realize a sound
dollar-for-dollar return on my investment. . . .
I might have it shipped and drive it through Italy.
Or sand it down and sail it.
What am I going to do with it?
I'll tell you one thing:
I'm probably never going to plant sod around it.
You see, I'm making it a definitive work
repapering parts of my soul
that can never be toured by my friends. . . .
You don't understand—
I'm using every breath to tred water
in all-night swimming competitions
with Hegel, Marx and Wittgenstein;
I'm a reckless diver
fondling the bottom of civilization
for ropes of pearls;
I'm whispering late into the night
on a river bank with Zola. . . .
What am I going to do with it?

I'm going to sneak it away from my family
gathered at my commencement
and roam the high desert.
making love to it.

—Carol Jin Evans

WAYS OF BECOMING

THE BASIC TRUST
THAT ONE CAN LEARN

> ### KOAN
>
> Define learning.

DIALOGUE AND REFLECTION

What does it mean to learn? Do some lateral thinking in your discussion group and find several possibilities for the koan. Start with "I Tell Them I'm a Liberal-Arts Major" at the beginning of this chapter.

In your large group find a way to integrate your ideas and make them all compatible.

This process of course will lead you to reflections in your learning log. By now you will have explored four chapters in *Thinking about Thinking*. Remember the chapter titles: Ways of Being, Ways of Meaning, Ways of Thinking, Ways of Knowing? What are you going to *do* with all that?

COMMENTARY

Don't read this section until you have completed
your own reflections on learning.

From Sackcloth to Cloth-of-Gold

What are you going to do with it? In Louis Pauwels and Jacques Bergier's *The Morning of the Magicians*, Pauwels concludes, "Today there is nothing about which I am absolutely certain." But "a man's life is only justified by his efforts, however feeble, towards better understanding. And to understand better is to become more attached. The more I understand, the more I love. For everything that is understood is good." The evidence is that clearer vision does not bring certainty, but it does bring wonder and oneness. The trade-off is worth the loss.

What are these explorers up to, these Mozarts, these Feynmans, these Shakespeares, you, me? What is the point of all this curiosity, this sniffing, this reflecting? A change inside oneself, a change in one's relationship with the extended self. What was the point of those hundreds of thousands of experiments of the medieval alchemists? It is said that the alchemists wanted to transform ordinary metals into gold. But what if we take these words metaphorically? In their research, Pauwels and Bergier found that the essential thing in alchemy was not the transmutation of metals but the transformation of the experimenter himself. The experiment, as we have seen in modern science, acts on the observer himself and puts him in a privileged position, and he thereby gains access to a view of the universe ordinarily hidden from us by time-space-matter-energy. A pure, unadulterated interaction. Gold.

Lawrence Durrell made a similar discovery about his work as a writer, his work with "mind and heart." He was able to rework and reorder ordinary experience and reveal its significant pattern. "Our common actions," it turns out, "are simply the sackcloth covering which hides the cloth-of-gold, the meaning of the pattern." Learning is something that takes place inside, something that happens to you, in the mind, in the spirit, on the nerve endings.

We peer into microscopes, tease words into new connections, empty the garbage, stare out the window, look in the mirror. We are all doing the same thing, all prospectors trying for a glimpse of the extraordinary: one's own awakened self. This awakened state is a pleasure, as Einstein said, that cannot be induced by coercion and a sense of duty. The enjoyment of seeing and searching cannot be promoted by such means.

This is TEGWAR, The Exciting Game Without Any Rules, but there are some strategies. There are many ways of transforming ourselves. But first we must understand that that is what the real game is and that it is indeed possible to do so on purpose. This chapter includes a number of ways of becoming.

ALTERNATIVE
FRAMES OF REFERENCE

> **STRATEGY ONE**
> Reframe.

In their introduction to *Reframing*, neurolinguists Richard Bandler and John Grinder recount the story of a farmer in a poor Chinese village. This man was considered well-off because he had a horse for plowing and for transportation. One day the horse ran away, and all the neighbors considered it a terrible misfortune. But the farmer simply said, "Maybe."

A few days later the horse returned bringing with it two other horses that had apparently been wandering the fields. What a stroke of fortune, exclaimed the villagers. "Maybe," the farmer replied.

The next day the farmer's son attempted to ride one of the wild horses, was thrown off, and broke his leg. A disaster, said the neighbors. "Maybe," said the farmer.

Then government officials showed up in the village, taking all able-bodied young men to fight in the emperor's army. The convalescing son was exempted. Everyone said that that was indeed wonderful luck. But the farmer simply replied, "Maybe."

This story may remind you of the idea developed in *Thinking about Thinking* that there is no meaning in things or events. Meaning takes place in the mind. What's more, there is absolutely nothing in events that forces us to derive one particular meaning. By now most readers will have an excellent understanding of this idea. If so, you also know that you are free to *redefine* any circumstance of your life and work. Another word for redefining is *reframing*.

Having considered how your mind processes information, having got the feel of how thinking actually takes place, you will have no trouble seeing how powerful the idea of reframing can be as a problem-solving strategy.

You can reframe *internally* by seeing the situation from a different angle or from several angles. You can explore definitions until you find one that allows you productive, positive action. This is always possible, even while hanging by your fingertips off high cliffs. But you must have had enough experience at reframing that it becomes a habit, a reflex. That means practice.

You can also reframe by changing the physical structure of the situation. Inventors are always doing this. Weightlessness in outer space, for instance, necessitated the reframing of toilet design. A book is reframed speech. TV is reframed smoke signals. Electricity is reframed sunlight. If these examples don't compute, talk them over with a classmate. Come to think of it, you are reframed sunlight, too.

So now we can offer a practical application of *Thinking about Thinking*. To take charge of your world,

> Change your point of view. Redefine.
> And / or
> Change the physical structure.

DIALOGUE AND REFLECTION

Work in your small group. Pick out a crummy school situation and use reframing to eliminate the problem, whatever it may be. Such problems might include a personality conflict with a teacher, test anxiety, boring textbooks, tedious assignments, not enough money.

Everyone work together on one problem and come up with several attractive definitions and several attractive new structures.

After your whole class pools its results, discuss some of the valuable aspects of reframing, and later reflect on the strategy in your log. Find some positive implications of reframing for you. Find areas of your own life where you can use it.

COMMENTARY

Don't read this section until you have finished your
reflections in your log.

Frogs into Princes

Frogs into Princes is another of Bandler and Grinder's books on neurolin-
guistic programming. Essentially, the idea of both their books is that if
you have a behavior pattern that isn't getting you the results your self-
actualizing calls for, you can reprogram yourself almost instantly. Almost
as fast as the fairy-story frog was transformed into a prince by one kiss.
Thus, if you have a habit of panicking during a test situation, you can probably think of quite similar situations in which you not only did not panic
but actually enjoyed yourself. So imagine yourself in a hideous test situation. Then summon up your situation in which you were brave. Deliberately take hold of your right earlobe at the same time. Next time you start
to panic in a test, take hold of your right earlobe. See what happens. What
you have done is overlay an alternate behavior on your old habit. You have
frustrated your old idea that a test and panic are inevitably connected. You
can see that behavior is a choice, not a necessity.

Possibilities such as these should be easy for you to understand after
your reflections on how your mind works. If you had been given a left-
brained account of reframing without the background, it would have been
intellectual and difficult to apply. With a feel for whole-brained thought,
you can move directly to practical application. It should be effortless. You
have been reframing all your life anyway. Now you can do it intentionally.

There are examples of reframing all over the place. St. Exupérey's little
prince reframes his rose several times. First he is blinded by her beauty.
Then he sees her flaws. Later he sees her as just one of millions of roses.
Finally he sees her, with the fox's help, as a unique being. "It is the time you
have spent on your rose that makes her unique in all the world." It is the
time you have spent on your rose.

Most readers will recognize themselves in the little prince and the constant reframing of a parent, a friend, a pet. Reframing can take the pain
out of relationships or situations and free us to enjoy them. There is no
inevitable necessity. We are not stuck. Knowing there are alternatives
makes TEGWAR a pleasure.

REFRAMING A HOUSE

*Near the end of chapter 4 you read Farley Mowat's description of having to learn some-
thing new about wolves. His transformation is a story about reframing, reframing not
only of the concept of wolves but also of scientific inquiry and of the observer himself.*

In the excerpt from The People of the Deer *that follows, Mowat reframes his concept of what a house is. Notice that reframing is something that happens in the
observer, not in what is "out there."*

*The ultimate purpose of scientific inquiry is the transformation of the alchemist
himself.*

From *THE PEOPLE OF THE DEER*

Farley Mowat

A Housing Project: Surprise and Wild Connections

The location of the Ihalmiut homes had roused my curiosity, but it became even
more acute as I examined the houses the Ihalmiut built for themselves. As I grew to
know the People, so my respect for their intelligence and ingenuity increased. Yet it
was a long time before I could reconcile my feelings of respect with the poor,
shoddy dwelling places that they constructed. As with most Eskimos, the winter
homes of the Ihalmiut are snow-built domes we call igloos. (Igloo in Eskimo means
simply "house" and thus an igloo can be built of wood or stone, as well as of snow.)
But unlike most other Innuit, the Ihalmiut make snow houses which are cramped,
miserable shelters. I think the People acquired the art of igloo construction quite
recently in their history and from the coast Eskimos. Certainly they have no love for
their igloos, and prefer the skin tents. This preference is related to the problem of
fuel.

Any home in the arctic, in winter, requires some fuel if only for cooking. The coast
peoples make use of fat lamps, for they have an abundance of fat from the sea
mammals they kill, and so they are able to cook in the igloo, and to heat it as well.
But the Ihalmiut can ill afford to squander the precious fat of the deer, and they dare
to burn only one tiny lamp for light. Willow must serve as fuel, and while willow
burns well enough in a tent open at the peak to allow the smoke to escape, when
it is burned in a snow igloo, the choking smoke leaves no place for human
occupants.

So snow houses replace the skin tents of the Ihalmiut only when winter has
already grown old and the cold has reached the seemingly unbearable extremes
of sixty or even seventy degrees below zero. Then the tents are grudgingly abandoned and snow huts built. From that time until spring no fires may burn inside the
homes of the People, and such cooking as is attempted must be done outside, in
the face of the blizzards and gales.

Yet though tents are preferred to igloos, it is still rather hard to understand why. I
have mentioned the great, gaping slits which outline each hide on the frame of a

tent. Such a home offers hardly more shelter than a thicket of trees, for on the unbroken sweep of the plains the winds blow with such violence that they drive the hard snow through the tents as if the skin walls did not really exist. But the People spend many days and dark nights in these feeble excuses for houses, while the wind rises like a demon of hatred and the cold comes as if it meant to destroy all life in the land.

In these tents there may be a fire; but consider this fire, this smoldering handful of green twigs, dug with infinite labor from under the drifts. It gives heat only for a few inches out from its sullen coals so that it barely suffices to boil a pot of water in an hour or two. The eternal winds pour into the tent and dissipate what little heat the fire can spare from the cook-pots. The fire gives comfort to the Ihalmiut only through its appeal to the eyes.

However, the tent with its wan little fire is a more desirable place than the snow house with no fire at all. At least the man in the tent can have a hot bowl of soup once in a while, but after life in the igloos begins, almost all food must be eaten while it is frozen to the hardness of rocks. Men sometimes take skin bags full of ice into the beds so that they have water to drink, melted by the heat of their bodies. It is true that some of the People build cook shelters outside the igloos but these snow hearths burn very badly, and then only when it is calm. For the most part the winds prevent any outside cooking at all, and anyway by late winter the willow supply is so deeply buried under the drifts, it is almost impossible for men to procure it.

So you see that the homes of the Ihalmiut in winter are hardly models of comfort. Even when spring comes to the land the improvement in housing conditions is not great. After the tents go up in the spring, the rains begin. During daylight it rains with gray fury and the tents soak up the chill water until the hides hang slackly on their poles while rivulets pour through the tent to drench everything inside. At night, very likely, there will be frost and by dawn everything not under the robes with the sleepers will be frozen stiff.

With the end of the spring rains, the hot sun dries and shrinks the hides until they are drum-taut, but the ordeal is not yet over. Out of the steaming muskegs come the hordes of bloodsucking and flesh-eating flies and these find that the Ihalmiut tents offer no barrier to their invasion. The tents belong equally to the People and to the flies, until midsummer brings an end to the plague, and the hordes vanish.

My high opinion of the People was often clouded when I looked at their homes. I sometimes wondered if the Ihalmiut were as clever and as resourceful as I thought them to be. I had been too long conditioned to think of home as four walls and a roof, and so the obvious solution of the Ihalmiut housing problem escaped me for nearly a year. It took me that long to realize that the People not only have good homes, but that they have devised the one perfect house.

The tent and the igloo are really only auxiliary shelters. The real home of the Ihalmio is much like that of the turtle, for it is what he carries about on his back. In truth it is the only house than can enable men to survive on the merciless plains of the Barrens. It has central heating from the fat furnace of the body, its walls are insulated to a degree of perfection that we white men have not been able to surpass, or even emulate. It is complete, light in weight, easy to make and easy to keep in repair.

It costs nothing, for it is a gift of the land, through the deer. When I consider that house, my opinion of the astuteness of the Ihalmiut is no longer clouded.

Primarily the house consists of two suits of fur, worn one over the other, and each carefully tailored to the owner's dimensions. The inner suit is worn with the hair of the hides facing inward and touching the skin while the outer suit has its hair turned out to the weather. Each suit consists of a pullover parka with a hood, a pair of fur trousers, fur gloves and fur boots. The double motif is extended to the tips of the fingers, to the top of the head, and to the soles of the feet where soft slippers of hare-hide are worn next to the skin.

The high winter boots may be tied just above the knee so that they leave no entry for the cold blasts of the wind. But full ventilation is provided by the design of the parka. Both inner and outer parkas hang slackly to at least the knees of the wearer, and they are not belted in winter. Cold air does not rise, so that no drafts can move up under the parkas to reach the bare flesh, but the heavy, moisture-laden air from close to the body sinks through the gap between parka and trousers and is carried away. Even in times of great physical exertion, when the Ihalmio sweats freely, he is never in any danger of soaking his clothing and so inviting quick death from frost afterwards. The hides are not in contact with the body at all but are held away from the flesh by the soft resiliency of the deer hairs that line them, and in the space between the tips of the hair and the hide of the parka there is a constantly moving layer of warm air which absorbs all the sweat and carries it off.

Dressed for a day in the winter, the Ihalmio has this protection over all parts of his body, except for a narrow oval in front of his face—and even this is well protected by a long silken fringe of wolverine fur, the one fur to which the moisture of breathing will not adhere and freeze.

In the summer rain, the hide may grow wet, but the layer of air between deerhide and skin does not conduct the water, and so it runs off and is lost while the body stays dry. Then there is the question of weight. Most white men trying to live in the winter arctic load their bodies with at least twenty-five pounds of clothing, while the complete deerskin home of the Innuit weighs about seven pounds. This, of course, makes a great difference in the mobility of the wearers. A man wearing tightfitting and too bulky clothes is almost as helpless as a man in a diver's suit. But besides their light weight, the Ihalmiut clothes are tailored so that they are slack wherever muscles must work freely beneath them. There is ample space in this house for the occupant to move and to breathe, for there are no partitions and walls to limit his motions, and the man is almost as free in his movements as if he were naked. If he must sleep out, without shelter, and it is fifty below, he has but to draw his arms into his parka, and he sleeps nearly as well as he would in a double-weight eiderdown bag.

This is in winter, but what about summer? I have explained how the porous hide nevertheless acts as a raincoat. Well, it does much more than that. In summer the outer suit is discarded and all clothing pared down to one layer. The house then offers effective insulation against heat entry. It remains surprisingly cool, for it is efficiently ventilated. Also, and not least of its many advantages, it offers the nearest thing to perfect protection against the flies. The hood is pulled up so that it covers the neck and the ears, and the flies find it nearly impossible to get at the skin underneath. But of course the Ihalmiut have long since learned to live with the flies, and they feel none of the hysterical and frustrating rage against them so common with us.

In the case of women's clothing, home has two rooms. The back of the parka has an enlargement, as if it were made to fit a hunchback, and in this space, called the *amaut,* lives the unweaned child of the family. A bundle of remarkably absorbent sphagnum moss goes under his backside and the child sits stark naked, in unrestricted delight, where he can look out on the world and very early in life become familiar with the sights and the moods of his land. He needs no clothing of his own, and as for the moss—in that land there is an unlimited supply of soft sphagnum and it can be replaced in an instant.

When the child is at length forced to vacate this pleasant apartment, probably by the arrival of competition, he is equipped with a one-piece suit of hides which looks not unlike the snow suits our children wear in the winter. Only it is much lighter, more efficient, and much less restricting. This first home of his own is a fine home for the Ihalmio child, and one that his white relatives would envy if they could appreciate its real worth.

This then is the home of the People.

SUPRALOGICAL THINKING

> **STRATEGY TWO**
> Make love

Ordinarily we get along with conscious, superficial thinking: "To get to the bus station, go to the third traffic light, turn left, and go one-half block. It's on the left." When we need to satisfy several variables in a housing problem or in a complex mathematics problem, such thinking can become extremely taxing. Even the most complicated problem involving only known formulas, though it requires much energy and effort, requires the same *kind* of thinking. But another kind is uniquely distinctive of human beings. Although as far as we know it is exclusively our own, it is generally neglected and ignored. This thinking is what makes us human, but few are aware of it. The mixture of spirit and flesh we find embodied in a metaphor, once understood, is a model for this supralogical (supra-logical) thinking, coupling the reservoir of unconscious, irrational knowledge with the conscious, logical left brain. It does not make "sense" to see one thing in terms of another, yet this process is the basis of all culture: the bridging of distinctions, the developing of a single concept for the entire universe.

By examining each instance of the universe in a systematic, step-by-step manner, we could never comprehend anything so infinitely variable; we would soon break down under the weight. (Most schools seem designed to do just that, however, and continue dishing up basket after basket of plastic-coated facts, never mixing chemistry and poetry, algebra and German.) We become human only by jumping to the conclusion of *language*. The benchmark for membership is the capacity to make this leap. Any who fail must be cared for by the others.

As those who study language soon realize, such a complex system could never be mastered by step-by-step analysis alone. Indeed, no mature mind has yet been able to explain all the complexities of language which even young children can handle with absolute assurance. It is only through symbolic thinking, metaphoric thinking, that we can grapple with such complexities. But remember Keats's comment that we may, like a spider, spin a beautiful circuiting out of our own selves. We will never have complete and absolutely correct information. A few points will be enough "to tip with the fine Web of his [Man's] Soul, and weave a tapestry empyrean."

In ordinary analogical thinking, images and words are stripped of their ambiguity and are used to compare one thing with another in detail-for-detail parallels. In symbolic analogy, however, there is an instantaneous blurt of association, compressing awareness of the totality of a situation in one immediate flash of insight. We kick into another gear entirely. The mind leaps over all the intervening steps and details and arrives at a solution all at once. Point-for-point identification takes a long time for all the nuances to be seen, but symbolic thinking travels at electronic speed, establishing thousands of connections in a flash. Becoming consciously aware of this process and mastering its use is the work of the maturing mind. Those who stop at logical thinking might as well retire at forty, but symbolic thinkers travel a thrilling road on into the years of light.

Setting the Stage for Supralogical Thinking. In the language of *Thinking about Thinking* supralogical thinking is whole-brained thinking, but it involves more than just the brain. It is whole bodied, too, the two together: body-mind. In this kind of thinking, one does not attack an idea; one makes love to it. The only way to crash through computerlike two-dimensional thinking into laserlike mental holography is to open the gates of the corpus callosum, that network of nerve fibers between your two hemispheres, so that your two ways of knowing can freely share their worlds.

Veterans of foreign wars claim the best place to learn a foreign language is in bed. That is, when the conditions of love exist, the conditions of learning are at their best. The mind and body feel secure, the surroundings are warm and supportive. You don't have to be there; you want to be there. You love the object of your affection (whatever you are trying to grok). You can't get enough of it. You are infinitely interested, quite literally absorbed. You are harmoniously tuned in to your "subject matter." And so on. Under these conditions, learning is not like arithmetic but like calculus—or even beyond that. You become your subject; you are one with it. Frogs into princes.

The next time you decide to master tennis, typing, chemistry, try Strategy Two:

> Make love to it.

DIALOGUE AND REFLECTION

In your discussion group, explore the love-making metaphor for insights into reading a boring textbook. Work out the love-making techniques that will reframe the book into a love object.

In your large group, pool your findings, and later in your learning log get as much mileage as you can from this metaphor.

EFFORTLESS EFFORT

> **STRATEGY THREE**
> Abandon hope.

Years ago when my daughter came home from second grade with her essay on flowers, I noticed along with all the red corrections, "Try harder, Kathy." This advice to a creature who with no sweat at all had mastered English syntax before she was five. Trying harder is a good way to shut the gates of the corpus callosum with a bang. If teachers cannot resist offering unsolicited advice, then let it be, "Try easier."

Here is how it works. The more squinty-eyed we get, the more we try to force an idea into our heads, the harder it is to get the cooperation of our two hemispheres, and of our spirits and bodies, too. They require a congenial atmosphere, one much more playful than serious. Our right brains are not only indifferent to well-meaning, serious, and proper behavior, they are literally turned off by it. They will refuse to come out and play. In fact, they will even play tricks on our sober-sided left brains and will cause slips of the tongue and stumbling and bumbling until we come to our senses.

Tim Gallwey, who has written a number of books on effortless effort, sees two selves inside there: the one who actually does learn the complex skills and solves the complicated problems for us and is so good at it—our

257

synthesizing right brain—and the self who does our housekeeping and linguistic programming for us but also acts as a puritanical critic every chance it gets—our analytical, sequential left brain.

If we are to gain full use of our minds, we have to find ways to shut this critic up so that the two hemispheres can reinforce each other. This noisy censor is all too happy to point out our shortcomings, tell us how lazy we are, tell us to try harder, fill us with doubts and fears and clumsiness. *Now look what you've done. You can't do anything right. How dumb can you get? You could never be that good. Ha, that's exactly where you screwed up yesterday.* Most of us have a tape recorder going in our heads all day making sure that we know our place and mind our manners.

But what if you could turn off that recording? What would that feel like? Gallwey found he could perform at peak efficiency. And it was amazingly easy. Effortless. He could run without tiring. He could work for hours without fatigue. Everyone, of course, has experienced learning in a non-critical atmosphere. It is called childhood. We all learned to walk and talk that way. We wanted to; we loved to. Can you imagine being *taught* these skills? Being watched for errors, being judged and tested day by day? We would have fifteen-year-olds in remedial walking classes.

Gallwey suggests a few simple ways to turn off the censor. You will see that they are all connected with ideas we have already explored in *Thinking about Thinking*. Your background will make it easy for you to begin using Gallwey's ideas right away.

1. *Keep your eye on the ball.* That does not mean you must *force* yourself to watch the ball. It means you must *allow* yourself to become fascinated. Fall in love with it. That is an extension of Strategy Two, isn't it? *What a wonderful, interesting spherical white object, what a splendid arc it is making, what rich texture, what fine craftsmanship, how intriguing!*

You have seen dogs catch frisbees that way. If the frisbee comes anywhere near where it should, they never miss. You can bet there is no critic in there gumming up the performance. Watch the dog's eye track the frisbee and see a whole body-mind rise to meet it as one coordinated frisbee catcher.

Humans sometimes have trouble figuring out what the ball is. Dogs never do. In the school game, for instance, what is the ball? The subject matter, the test, the teacher? It's the teacher. You can figure out why. If you allow yourself to become fascinated, absorbed in the teacher, good grades are almost guaranteed.

What about tests? Tests cause more anxiety than anything else in American schools. When you are taking a test, what is the ball? Your own performance, the subject matter, or the test structure itself? In this case, it is the test itself. *Look at how that question is phrased! Look at all those clever answers the teacher dreamed up! Look at all those clues scattered all over! What a delightful crossword puzzle!* To achieve peak performance on a test, fall in love with it.

2. *Let it happen.* Keep your pride out of it. Don't anticipate. When you worry about how well you are doing, you are bound to tighten up. When you are totally absorbed in your love object, it doesn't occur to you to wonder how you are performing.

Instead of judging each attempt, try kitten watching. Simply observe what *is* happening—as a matter of curiosity, not pride. Gallwey, for example, advises his students to imagine the ball hitting the target and then just let the conscious mind notice where it does land. As they continue hitting balls, the right brain takes over and adjusts the delivery without conscious intervention. The ball, seemingly on its own, comes closer and closer to the target. The left brain is so busy watching what does happen it forgets to judge. But you must always give the left brain something to do or it will start carping. Keep it busy.

The more we allow the right brain to take over our complex thinking, the more we silence the judgmental left brain, the more success we have. We begin to see how easily the right brain can get the hang of things, and we begin to trust in our natural, effortless capacity to master anything. Information organizes itself; the mind provides the setting.

3. *Focus on the present.* The only place we can ever be is in the present moment. We cannot dwell in the future or in the past. Any energy put into anxiety is unavailable for the task at hand. When we stop looking ahead and allow ourselves to look around, to be fully in the present, we find our game improving. The left brain will want to judge events, but it must be told that events are neither good nor bad. They are simply information.

I can remember working on what I considered a steep roof and being so concerned about falling that I was very tense. *Steep* was equated in my left brain with *dangerous*, a judgment. The *information* is that the roof had a certain degree of pitch that called for a certain positioning of the body—a physics problem. That being solved, as soon as I allowed myself to focus on what I was actually doing—nailing on the new roof—and stopped thinking about what I might be doing—falling off and killing myself—I could feel the tension seeping out of my muscles and nerves. As I became absorbed in the nailing process, my performance and comfort increased dramatically. Balance, after all, is a matter of trust and centeredness.

There is no future or past of success or failure. There is only now. Instead of dwelling on some imagined disaster or victory or on how rotten the performance was yesterday, the left brain is much better occupied with the task of noticing the characteristics of the present surroundings.

That is what is meant by abandoning hope. Once we give up all the concern about what *will* happen, we can relax and give ourselves fully to what we are doing. Looking at the clock or the finish line will actually hinder our performance. Our three brains are not in harmony.

But when we are centered, when we are absorbed in the present moment, fascinated, abandoned, we kick over into that other gear, the flow of peak performance, the trying without trying of the Buddhists, or the effortless effort of Tim Gallwey.

Strategy Three

Abandon hope.

1. Keep your eye on the ball.
2. Let it happen.
3. Focus on the present.

PATTERNING

KOAN

Define creative thinking.

DIALOGUE AND REFLECTION

Having explored and extended ideas about thinking, what would you now consider a good word or phrase that captures the essence of creative thinking? Gather four or five in each small group, pool and explore your results, and reflect in your learning log.

COMMENTARY

Don't read this section until you have finished your reflections in your learning log.

Breaking through Boundaries

Let's see. Creative thinking? In terms of *Thinking about Thinking*, how about Body-mind manifesting? Self-actualizing? Whole-brained thinking? Restructuring? Sackcloth into cloth-of-gold? I would love to see your list.

The usual left-brained terms are rather drab, not much mileage in them. Obviously, good thinking doesn't dwell on being right, at least not during the trip. You have to get fun in there—and wild connections. Well, really, all the things you have been asked to think about in *Thinking about Thinking* are involved. A left-brain list of all the titles would still leave out the spirit of the thing. As you now know, it is a knack, a different way of approaching one's environment. I designed *Thinking about Thinking* so that you would have to use whole-brained thinking. If you look back over the structure, you will see the whole book is set up that way. I hope it has worked for you.

To *create* means to make something, something that hasn't been made already. If you create a painting of a sad-eyed child and then another and then another, you may end up as rigid as any other bigot. Many people who started out breaking through imposed boundaries end up imprisoned in channels of their own devising. Thus, *creative* doesn't mean simply *different.* Like the lessons taught by the Dancing Wu Li Masters, the idea never comes out the same way twice. The artist does not mass-produce one idea. Each attempt with brush and canvas is a fresh try at seeing, eternal mind's eternal recreation. The results are always infinitely various, as is life itself. But variety is not the purpose, it is a by-product. Seeing is the purpose. Changing is.

Edward de Bono, who has studied creativity for many years, calls the kind of thinking we have been emphasizing *lateral thinking,* a way of "breaking out of the concept prison of old ideas."

Linear Thinking   Lateral Thinking

Left-brained thinking is sequential and channeled. But lateral thinking deliberately breaks through channels to arrive at fresh insight, "to create new patterns and escape the dominance of old ones." A purpose of thinking, says de Bono, is *to make the best possible use of information, to restructure old patterns and generate new ones.* Obviously, *Thinking about Thinking* shares these views.

BASE TEN VERSUS BASE TWELVE
Problem-Solving Workshop

Work in small groups to solve the following puzzles. Find out what problem-solving attitude their solutions have in common.

1. Arrange six matches so that they form four equilateral triangles.

2. Add a line to the number IX to make a six.

3. Arrange the flat surfaces of four blocks so that each block touches three others.

4. Arrange ten dots so that they can be connected by five straight lines without lifting the pencil off the page.

5. Here is an extra puzzle. If you haven't seen it in some bar already, you can take it home and figure it out on your own. I'm not going to give you any of the solutions.

   Connect these nine dots using four straight lines without lifting the pencil off the paper. •   •   •

   •   •   •

   •   •   •

(solutions on page 272)

263

CONVENTIONS OF THOUGHT
More Problem-Solving

One of my students once lost a Ping-Pong ball down a hole in his grand-mother's patio. When he told me how he and his brother got it out, it reminded me of an almost identical problem in *Conceptual Blockbusting* by James L. Adams.* Let's set limits similar to those in the Adams problem and see if your group can help my student get his ball back. It has survived three generations in his family and has considerable sentimental value.

The ball has fallen to the bottom of a pipe set four inches into the concrete to hold a sun umbrella.

The hole is six hundredths of an inch wider than the ball.

Let's allow my student and his brother only a few items to work with. They cannot leave the area, and nothing else is available. They must not damage the pipe, the ball, or the floor.

Items

- Their clothes: T-shirts, belts, sneakers, shorts, underwear
- A bag of potato chips
- A fingernail file
- The Ping-pong net and its metal braces
- The paddles
- A brick
- A light bulb

There are two parts to this activity. First, see how many solutions your small group can generate in ten minutes. In your large group list all solutions on the chalkboard, and discuss how any unusual ones were arrived at. Then read the Commentary and instructions for the next step.

---

*Stanford, Calif.: Stanford Alumni Association, 1974.

COMMENTARY

Don't read this section until you have finished the
first part of the Ping-pong ball problem.

Disreputable Thinking

James Adams's *Conceptual Blockbusting* identifies a number of habits of
thought that interfere with possible unique solutions to problems: responsible adult behavior, linear thinking, reliance on traditional patterns of
thought, self-censorship, respectability, and so on.

The first part of our Ping-Pong problem calls for quantity—fluency. But
when my students list solutions, there will usually be one or two that are
intriguing. Maybe someone thought up a use of the potato chips. (Smash
them up, mix with saliva into a paste, apply to paddle handle, and use as
sticky probe to pull up the ball.)

Rarely does anyone suggest using urine to float the ball to the surface. In
the original case my student and his brother did have access to a garden
hose and did think of using it. Urinating is the same principle, but it's not
respectable. The message: *Respectability hampers thought.*
Aha, say my students, give us another chance. Their
second round emphasizes *divergent* thinking, surprise and
wild connections. *Flexibility,* category crossovers. More
chattering, more humor, more enthusiasm.

DIALOGUE AND REFLECTION

Now repeat the steps you took in part one. Afterward, reflect on this experience in your learning log.

COMMENTARY

Wait to read this section until you have finished
your entry in your learning log.

Get On With It

This chapter reframes ideas of earlier chapters. One definition of thinking
is that it is the rearranging or restructuring of what we already know. If
we want to grow and change, we must enlarge or rearrange old patterns
or piece together new ones from them. We keep reworking the same raw
materials. One purpose of this chapter is to make these natural thinking
strategies accessible.

By the time most of us are nine or ten, we have settled into habits that
virtually exclude innovation. According to a study reported by V. J.
Popenek (*Solving Problems Creatively*), 90 percent of five-year-olds are
highly innovative. By age eight only about 10 percent are, and after that
only about 2 percent!

Imagine yourself at about age five at play and with all the elements
of productive thinking: playfulness, absorption, sensory awareness,
fantasy—you can complete the list.

What is an adult sandbox like? Pretty much like a child's. In his study of
the largest businesses in this country, Thomas J. Peters found that not a
single major product had come from the formal planning process.* They
were all developed by mavericks who weren't supposed to be messing with
them and didn't know that what they were trying to do was impossible, or
by illegitimate, unsanctioned, or barely tolerated teams of enthusiastic,
even fanatical, grown-up children working with bootlegged or scrounged
materials in garages or sheds on their own time. These highly successful
operations violate virtually every respectable standard planning-and-
development process.

If it's worth doing, it's worth doing right, goes the conventional wisdom.
These skunkworks teams, as they are sometimes called, seem to think, *If
it's worth doing, get on with it.* Their slogan: DO IT. Their procedures are
sloppy. There may be overlapping or duplication by independent teams,
sometimes in open competition with each other. They want to get something in hand, however clumsily slapped together, as quickly as possible—
within ninety days and often much sooner. "I like to see an idea as soon as

---

*Peters is the author of *In Search of Excellence: Lessons from America's Best Run Companies.*
Harper and Row; New York, 1982; Warner Books; New York, 1984. The bootleg operations
described here are derived from his "The Mythology of Innovation, or A Skunkworks Tale,"
The Stanford Magazine, Summer 1983.

possible," says one experimenter. "I want to hold it and touch it." (You can see the implications for your own projects here.) Most researched projects in contrast are one to two years in planning stages and don't work right on the first or second go-round, even so.

The skunkworks interlopers, Peters found, are *quicker* and *dirtier.* They don't care how they get their product working. It is not usually pretty, but they find out fast what the bugs are and have the product on the market before the careful planners are halfway through the first phase of paperwork.

As for scientists, if you imagine their world to be systematic, orderly, and well thought-out, look again. You will find almost all major discoveries to have come from messy, sloppy, self-centered, and irrational activities. Even the famous Manhattan Project, which produced the atomic bomb, had lots of skunkworks activities going on offstage.

The optimal size of these groups ranges from about six to twenty and rarely gets beyond fifty. There is a team spirit in these groups, somewhat like the atmosphere in which your class created the mutual-aid composite picture. And like your group, each person feels completely committed to the large picture, even has a sense of ownership. Your four- or five-person discussion groups are structured on the skunkworks model. I would bet your best results emerged from sessions that mirrored skunkworks conditions: "Touch. Feel. Do. Try. Fix."

You can see the implications for doing schoolwork, solving personal problems, taking classes. The most joyous and productive students conduct their lives as a continuous skunkworks operation.

TOUCH. FEEL. DO. TRY. FIX.

THE JOY OF REJECTION
The Role of Pride in Problem Solving

People who fear rejection make lousy problem solvers. It has been said that people prefer the familiar to the comfortable. Billions of great ideas die because of pride: fear of failure, fear of rejection. Does anyone like rejection? I never met a student who did. It's not too late, I tell them. If you hurry, you can get yourself rejected several times before midnight.

At first, seeking rejection seems like a crazy idea, but like any other word *rejection* can be reframed and redefined, and the mind can be reprogrammed for a more productive interpretation. There is nothing in rejection itself that means we have to crawl in a hole. *No, stop, yield, flunk, yes, go, pass* are merely information. We choose the feelings we associate with them.

But rejection really does hurt, doesn't it? Maybe, the Chinese farmer would say. A professional seducer cheerfully observed, "I get slapped eleven out of twelve times an evening."

Successful problem solvers get rejected all along the way. For every "right" answer there are a thousand wrong ones. It is simply the nature of the process. When Edison failed more than 1500 times trying to find a durable filament for the incandescent light bulb, people thought he wasn't getting anywhere. Surely he must have felt terrible. On the contrary, Edison told them, he was making great progress. His team was zeroing in. They had already eliminated 1500 useless materials. Reframing. Edison's interpretation was every bit as valid as that of his critics.

In an article in *California Living* Magazine,* "The Art of Accepting Rejection," Robert Kerwin wrote that you have to face rejection head on, even become a Professional Rejection-Taker. If you don't put a hook in the water, send a letter, knock on a door, it is impossible to get *accepted*. Acceptance, of course, is what we all want. But it can't come if we are not out there getting rejected, and not just once, but every day, many times a day.

Check the history of any successful person and you will find rejection after rejection after rejection. Kerwin cites Lily Tomlin bombing nightly for eight years, F. Scott Fitzgerald getting trunkfuls of rejections. Saul Bellow, Einstein, Mozart, Lincoln. Once you start getting rejected it never stops. In fact, it *can't* stop. The person who goes all day without being rejected simply isn't trying. The person who gets accepted first thing in the morning need not feel defeated; there are limitless opportunities to get rejected the rest of the day. One simply keeps on trying. The day is young.

Kerwin's view is that rejection is a natural part of the process of trying. We can define it as information. We have to get used to it, expect it, train for it. We have to seek it. Try once today, a couple of times tomorrow. Ten rejections is a good day. Twenty is a great day. One acceptance—ecstasy.

Once we see how it works, how *necessary* it is in the process of problem solving, it will have less and less power to immobilize us. There is no way around it; seeking acceptance means seeking rejection.

Worry is left brained.
—Steve Chambers, Student

---
*December 3, 1978.

INTERLUDE

If I Had My Life to Live Over

If I had my life to live over again, I'd try to make more mistakes next time. I would relax. I would limber up. I would be sillier than I have been this trip. I know of a very few things I would take seriously. I would take more trips. I would climb more mountains, swim more rivers, and watch more sunsets. I would do more walking and looking. I would eat more ice cream and fewer beans. I would have more actual troubles and fewer imaginary ones. You see, I am one of those people who lives prophylactically and sensibly and sanely hour after hour, day after day. Oh, I've had my moments; and if I had it to do over again, I'd have more of them. In fact, I'd try to have nothing else. Just moments, one after another, instead of living so many years ahead each day. I have been one of those people who never go anywhere without a thermometer, a hot water bottle, a gargle, a raincoat, aspirin, and a parachute. If I had it to do over again, I would go places, do things, and travel lighter than I have.

If I had my life to live over, I would ride on more merry-go-rounds . . . pick more daisies.

—Nadine Stair, 85 years old, Louisville, Ky.

PERFORMING MAGIC
A Problem-Solving System

There ought to be a systematic approach to whole-brained thinking, and sure enough there is. In fact there are a number. The one that comes closest to gathering up all the elements explored in *Thinking about Thinking* is the Synectics method developed by W. J. J. Gordon, Arthur D. Little, and George M. Prince. Their procedure is demonstrated in a 1981 film, *Problem-Solving Strategies: The Synectics Approach.* Prince's book *The Practice of Creativity** contains a more detailed account. Notice how well the steps they have identified fit the concepts of *Thinking about Thinking.*

1. *Statement of the Problem:* Remember Neil Postman's idea that how you pose your question will determine the answer you get? One of my students, who had committed himself to becoming an electrical engineer, had become so obsessed with his goal that he couldn't enjoy his schooling. Finally someone asked, "Tony, is it the pleasure of doing the kinds of things electrical engineers do that you really want, or is it the E.E. degree itself?" He pointed out that Tony wouldn't even have to have a degree to enjoy

---

*New York: Macmillan, Collier Books, 1972.

269

electrical engineering. On the other hand, if it was the degree he wanted, he would be much more efficient if he saw that as a school game and went after it directly.

So stating what the problem really is is a major step in solving it. Once that is clear, Tony should write it down so that he has a good grasp of what he is after.

2. *Goal Wishing:* Synectics work is usually done in skunkworks-size groups of six or seven people. No one wants to look ridiculous in front of others. If we are to achieve effortless effort, Tim Gallwey found that we have to silence that self-censor. And censorship by one's peers can be murderous to tender new ideas.

George Prince and his associates found they could eliminate the risk of looking foolish if this step is seen as pure fantasy, no commitment. It is socially unacceptable for grown-ups to present far-out ideas seriously, but it is fine to label them wishes or fantasies. What if you could violate all the laws of physics, the constraints of society—what do you *wish* would happen? "I wish, I wish . . . " Even if you do your problem solving alone, this step frees you to break through those rigid assumptions and sealed-off patterns that hamper our discovery of new patterns. You are free to daydream of any wonderful magic you would like. This gives your right brain a chance to contribute safely and playfully—right up its alley. Write down these wishes. Your left brain will like having something practical to do.

3. *Excursion:* The wish list will contain at least a couple of attractive ideas. Maybe what you want for your new "product" is that it be *indestructible* or *cheap.* Maybe Tony wants to have some *fun* getting his E.E. If he keeps on thinking about boring classes and teachers and homework drudgery, he will keep going round and round with the same old unsuccessful solutions. His thinking will be boxed in. He needs "surprise and wild connections, untried circuitry."

So now Tony sets the E.E. problem aside temporarily—as much as possible—and goes on a trip. He can go to any "country" he wants so long as it isn't the country of conventional schooling. Maybe he chooses the world of the stand-up comic, maybe the world of gambling or of gardening or of skunkworks mavericks or of motorcycling.

Fun on a motorcycle. What makes it fun? What are the ingredients? Tony would play with this awhile. "It's something *I* choose; I'm in charge. I fix it so there is just the right amount of danger. There has to be a thrill, intense feeling. I love the feel of it." And so on.

4. *Force Fit:* After he has played with "fun" in the world of motorcycle riding, Tony deliberately carries these elements of fun back to fun getting

270

an E.E. "Now what would I have to do getting an E.E. if I were to approach it like a motorcycle ride?" You can see that this crossover activity is quite like Bandler and Grinder's reframing or reprogramming: deliberately putting a new pattern on top of an old one. This opens the mind to alternatives, breaking through rigid limits and assumptions. Tony assumed school has to be a grind. It could be designed—by Tony—as a motorcycle ride. As has been seen in *Thinking about Thinking,* there are innumerable points of view from which to observe *any* situation, and no experience has to be seen as absolutely good or absolutely bad. Change our assumption and we can change our response.

5. *Itemized Response:* At this stage Tony should have a possible solution. But his new baby is delicate and fragile and must be given tender attention or it will die. The worst thing Tony could do would be to start in listing all the things *wrong* with his new idea of how to take classes. He would kill it in a flash. He has to love this baby.

A much more supportive approach is to see all the things he *likes* about it. *What a beautiful baby!* His left brain can make a list of the good things, and his mammalian brain will feel much better.

6. *Concerns:* Once the baby is secure and strong, Tony's left brain can list its concerns. We have to take care of this infant. What things might hurt its development? Tony's left brain has concerns, and his right brain will want to make him feel better. Even at this stage there is no criticism and no fault-finding. All of Tony's selves are working together to see that the baby gets a chance to grow.

So Tony finds ways to overcome the concerns. Once this is done he has a solution he will be eager to try out. Any snags he encounters in actual practice can be run through the Synectics procedure and eliminated.

7. *DO IT:* Tony should start right in with his motorcycle approach to school. His left brain will say, *Play it safe; don't take chances; wait a few months; do some more research.* That is the respectable planning-and-development process that has almost never produced any interesting product. If Tony now engages in a skunkworks operation of TOUCH, FEEL, DO, TRY, FIX, he will have a workable model within ninety days. Guaranteed.

You can see that this process uses every idea developed in this chapter. Go back over the headings and see if it leaves anything out.

DIALOGUE AND REFLECTION

The best way to evaluate the Synectics procedure is to try it right away in your discussion group. But remember *not* to start with concerns. Save these for last. You might start with Tony's problem: How can I make going after an academic degree a joy? Let each discussion group do its own goal wishing, select its own world for the excursion, and so on, and then compare results with those of the other groups. Again, avoid criticism. Work first with all that is positive about the procedure and then eliminate the concerns. Finish off with reflection in your learning log.

Of course, if your discussion group really wants to know if its solution works, it will have to go right into skunkworks testing and get the model on line as soon as possible, quick and dirty. TOUCH, FEEL, DO, TRY, FIX.

THE TYRANNY OF ASSUMPTIONS
Solutions

You may have found other solutions than those shown. The more the better.

1.  Make a pyramid. They don't have to be on one surface.

2.  A *letter* can be a line.

3.  One can lie under the other three.

4.

What difficulty any of these solutions may present lies in self-imposed boundaries we place around our thinking. Unquestioned assumptions, as we have seen, are the hardest barriers to smash through. Practice helps.

KOAN

What is the purpose of
Thinking about Thinking?

Do some hip shots on this koan. No more than two sentences. A single phrase is fine. List these on the chalkboard. Choose a winner. Award a prize.

COMMENTARY

Here are some student views on what
Thinking about Thinking is all about. Don't read
them until your class finishes its own list.

Just Thinking

- To analyze those ideas and concepts that seem to be the most defined. Well-defined ideas are often full of fallacies and misconceptions.
- Its purpose for me is to let me see that I can understand only what I want to understand and only what I *need* to understand.
- Let's put it this way: Toto, I don't think we're in Kansas anymore.
- To be deliberately spontaneous.
- To connect up again with the original primordial "meaning."
- To think about what we are thinking about.
- To rewrite the dictionary.
- To help me get a clear sense of myself.
- To examine and redefine a variety of "normal" ideas.
- To make my mind user-friendly.
- To change me from a pure scientific person into an artistic, poetic, intuitive scientific person.

A GLOSSARY FOR
THINKING ABOUT THINKING

We must all redefine the bedrock ideas of our thinking and beliefs or be enslaved by someone else's. So as a final activity for your thinking about thinking, find key words from your work with this book and redefine them. But give them right-brained or metaphoric definitions. Have each small group come up with ten.

Put the words from all groups on the chalkboard and reduce the list to twenty-five.

Back in small groups create your right-brained definitions. You should end up with five or six definitions for each word on the chalkboard.

See how well your group has overcome definition tyranny.

A FINAL SYNTHESIS

But What Are You Going to Do With It?

A good reader of any book ends up being its coauthor. It is time now to write your version of the ending of *Thinking about Thinking.*

A Trivia Review

To review for your final synthesis, try this trivia game. Without any notes, everyone, including the teacher, must contribute a bit of information remembered with no notes of any kind from any part of the course throughout the term.

No one is allowed to repeat an item already listed. Do as many rounds as you can in forty to forty-five minutes and try for the maximum number of items.

Two students should record items on the chalkboard, one doing the odd-numbered items, the other doing the even ones. They should write fast and abbreviate.

As you will see, the game brings the experiences of the course back into conscious awareness. Each item is like a hologram; it is not just a place marker but a multidimensional experience charged with feeling and rich associations. This session is guaranteed to make everyone feel great. You will be impressed with the amount and quality of your work together.

Title

To complete this session, think up right-brained words or phrases that capture the whole experience represented by all those items on the board. These become the titles for your syntheses.

Syntheses

The synthesis is the meaning each student gives to the experience of the course. It is written like any other learning-log entry but is longer. The first draft represents an hour and a half to two hours of writing-thinking. This draft is then edited, proofread, cleaned up—whatever it takes to get it ready for the final typewritten version.

See to it that you enjoy writing this synthesis. If it starts to seem like a chore, stop everything and reframe.

Follow-up Session

Wrap sessions usually involve small groups reading and discussing abstracts from each other's syntheses. Have the large group do an itemized response on the assignment itself—and of course eliminate any negatives so that you end up with a wholly positive session.

Final Test

If there could be a final test of thinking about thinking, what would it be?

From "El Viaje Definitivo"

And I will leave. But the birds
will stay, singing; and my garden
will stay, with its green tree,
with its water well.
—Juan Ramon Jimenez

GLOSSARY

> DEFINITION TYRANNY: *The process of accepting without reflection someone else's definition of a word, a problem, or a situation.*
>
> —Neil Postman

ARGUMENT: A reason or reasons for or against something. In law or logic, an argument is supposed to be emotionless. Since we think with our whole minds and not with our left brains only, that is impossible. To understand a line of reasoning, get the feeling of it as well as its surface features.

ASSUMPTION: Anything taken for granted. Almost any field of study is built on a few ideas everyone is willing to accept. However, no assumption is sacred. All assumptions must be reexamined continuously. The best way to treat an assumption is to consider it tentative.

BIAS: An inclination. All ideas and thoughts have a bias, a leaning in one direction or another. All things are biased for themselves and their own existence, a tree for sunlight, a rock for its own continuance. In thinking, we have to recognize and accept bias as fundamental to our relationship with the rest of our environment—our own bias and that of every other thing.

COHERENT: Sticking together, making sense according to the conventional thinking of a like-minded group. To get a new idea across to others, put it in a frame of reference they are used to. The game inside oneself is to get all the pieces of the reality puzzle to fit together, stick together, with no leftover pieces and no forcing.

CONCEPT: An idea. We "conceive" an idea in the same way as a baby is conceived. A concept is something we make up by taking two or more things and making one out of them. Thenceforth the concept takes on a life of its own.

CRITICAL THINKING: Clear, human, organic, whole-brained, and deliberate thought. It means using everything we have as well as possible. How would *you* define it?

DEDUCTION: Drawing a conclusion from information assumed to be correct, figuring out something from what we think is already known. However, since all assumptions are tentative, conclusions must also be.

DEFINITION: What a thing is or what it means. There is never one meaning for any word. There can be *a* definition but not *the* definition. In any conversation find out what meaning is being given to important words being used—whole-brained meaning.

EVIDENCE: Grounds for belief. What constitutes evidence depends on the bias of the observer. There is no such thing as hard evidence. It is always soft and always dependent on the situation.

FACT: Something that is. From a whole-brained view, there is no such thing. A *fact* is a collection of commonly agreed-upon observations so deeply ingrained in a group's thinking that it is no longer thought about. A more productive view is that a fact is a temporary placeholder.

GROK: To understand an idea or thing to the depth that you "become" that idea or thing. The word was invented by Robert Heinlein because he felt we had come to take the word *understand* too lightly. *Grok* means to become one with the thing being observed.

HOLISTIC: Whole. It could be spelled *wholistic.* This book takes a holistic view of the thinking process: everything all at once.

INDUCTION: Drawing a general view from a number of particular observations. In other words, making a good guess.

IRRELEVANCE: Not having a bearing on the situation at hand. At any instant the mind sifts out much, much more than it lets in for consideration. The decision of relevance is best left to the right brain. Our linguistic left brain is far too ignorant.

KOAN: A puzzle designed to get the thinker to see or realize. Its answer is not important. The change in the thinker is.

LASER THINKING: Whole-brained thinking. It is so much more powerful than conventional thinking that it has been compared with laser light as contrasted with ordinary light.

LATERAL THINKING: Getting out of the rut of one-track thinking. Edward de Bono invented the term to distinguish it from conventional channeled thought.

LINEAR THINKING: Thinking like a computer, sequentially and from known cause to predictable effect. A way of processing information according to predetermined rules for limited and specific results. Linear thinking is considered by most people to be the only way human beings think, but it is only part of a much larger thinking process.

LOGIC: A theory of valid inference. A system for reasoning from accepted statements to verifiably correct conclusions. The basis for computer programming and for mathematics.

MANDALA: A drawing with a center and a design radiating from it. Metaphorically speaking, it is a fingerprint of one's self or spirit. Jung called it "eternal mind's eternal recreation."

METAPHOR: An implied comparison. In the broadest sense, anything "seen" is a comparison for what it stands for. That is, what we "see" stands for what is actually "out there." This idea of metaphor works both biologically and linguistically. A DEAD METAPHOR is a forgotten metaphor. *Daisy* is based on a comparison with the "day's eye," the sun. All language is an implied comparison, and almost all of it is, and has to be, dead.

MIND: That which thinks.

PERCEPT: A message from the senses. Although associated with sense impressions, a perception is every bit as much an *idea* as a conception is. It is something the mind does to data received from the nerve endings. No two minds perceive the same thing or in the same way.

PERSONA: A mask one's self wears. A personality is the physical outer cloak of the inner being, an implied comparison.

PREJUDICE: Prejudgment. A judgment made before the facts are known or in disregard of the facts. Since the facts can never be known with absolute certainty, any judgment is a prejudgment or prejudiced. We make judgments all day long, every second, and they are all prejudiced.

PROOF: Conclusive evidence. There is no such thing. Use everything you have to see as well as you can, and mark the results "tentative."

PROPAGANDA: Something extended or transmitted through space. An attempt to persuade one's surroundings to take on the characteristics of one's self. Anything that wants to continue to exist will do what it can to perpetuate itself and is a propaganda machine for its own continuation.

OBJECTIVE: Without bias, impersonal, not involving thoughts or feelings. Since ideas, perceptions, conceptions are all products of thinking, objective thinking is impossible. Clarity requires heart and mind.

REALITY: An implied comparison (metaphor) for that-which-is. A blueprint or wetware program. There are infinite variations, no two alike.

REASON: To think logically. Reason is commonly considered a left-brained process, but sound reasoning requires the whole mental process. The left brain can be used to store one's reasoning in language structures.

RHETORIC: The use of words to influence or persuade.

SCIENTIFIC METHOD: A passionate attempt to find things out any way one can.

SEMANTICS: The study of meaning, especially of how words mean.

SENSORIUM: Sensory apparatus: sight, hearing, taste, touch, smell, and any other sense like humor, shame, decency, wonder, the ridiculous. The system of nerve endings designed to filter out information from the environment suitable for integration into an organism's wetware program.

SUBJECTIVE: Emphasizing thoughts and feelings. All thinking is subjective and needs to be so.

SUPRA INTELLIGENCE: Enlightenment. Thinking with effortless effort. A fully awake organism.

SYLLOGISM: A pair of statements and the conclusion it is possible or not possible to draw from them, used in formal logic as a method of determining validity.

TRUTH: The judgment that one's perception of reality is accurate.

YIN YANG: The interconnectedness of universal forces:

INDEX

Thinking about Thinking is the product of Clark McKowen's nearly thirty years of teaching. He is also the author of *Get Your A Out of College,* a book on college skills; *It's Only a Movie,* a film-appreciation text; *Image: Reflections on Language,* a freshman English text; and coauthor of the groundbreaking *Montage: Investigations in Language.*

The author has conducted seminars on the educational process at various colleges throughout the United States. His articles on teaching have appeared in numerous professional journals. He teaches English at Diablo Valley College in Pleasant Hill, California, where he has also served as division head.

Mr. McKowen is a graduate of Indiana State University in Indiana, Pennsylvania, and of Bucknell University in Lewisberg, Pennsylvania.

He spends his summers in Montana at Flathead Lake near Glacier National Park at a little motel called the Northernaire that he and his wife, Ruth, have owned and run since 1976.